Sunny Days, Balmy Nights

Entertaining Miami Style

Sunny Days, Balmy Nights

Entertaining Miami Style

The Young Patronesses
of the Opera, Inc.

Mission Statement

The Young Patronesses of the Opera (YPO) is a nonprofit, tax-exempt organization of volunteers who have been advocating on behalf of opera education in the Miami community since 1956. YPO's mission is to cultivate, promote, sponsor, and develop the understanding and love of opera; to promote the education in the community of opera; and to assist the Florida Grand Opera, Inc., in such education of the general public. YPO has been recognized by the Florida Grand Opera for contributing over $2 million and countless volunteer hours to opera education in South Florida.

Sunny Days, Balmy Nights
Entertaining Miami Style

The Young Patronesses of the Opera, Inc.

Published by The Young Patronesses of the Opera, Inc.

Copyright © 2008 by The Young Patronesses of the Opera, Inc.
P. O. Box 347616
Coral Gables, Florida 33234
305-665-3470

Photography © Dan Forer
Kevin P. Scott, AIFD, Design Stylist
Patty Forrestel, Food Stylist

This cookbook is a collection of favorite recipes,
which are not necessarily original recipes.

Library of Congress Control Number: 2007937594
ISBN: 978-0-9795725-0-0

Edited, Designed, and Manufactured by
Favorite Recipes® Press
An imprint of

FRP

P. O. Box 305142
Nashville, Tennessee 37230
800-358-0560

Art Director and Book Design: Steve Newman
Project Editor: Linda A. Jones

Manufactured in the United States of America
First Printing: 2008
7,500 copies

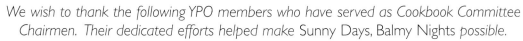

Contents

South Beach Soirée
Soups and Drinks

Reunion Tropicál
Appetizers

Romantic Interlude in the Tropics
Breads and Brunch

Yachting on Biscayne Bay
Vegetables and Side Dishes

South Beach is famous for its sizzling nightlife, filled with A-list East Coast partiers and European jet-setters. Filming for TV and movies, photo shoots, celebrity parties, and rocking nightclubs are all part of the scene. South Beach is a high-energy feast for the senses.

After beachside lounging, our partiers are starting with cocktails and appetizers in the early evening hours before they move on to dinner and clubbing. Our host and hostess decided to set this party in Lummus Park, directly across from a famous Art Deco skyline. Guests are enjoying a view of the beach to the east and to the west, the glowing neon framed by coconut palms.

Our hostess has mixed drinks and nearly all the food is made ahead of time. Only a few tables are needed for this large party, since no one is interested in sitting this early in the evening. Each chic, shiny chrome and glass bar table is decorated with a simple arrangement of calla lilies. A large offset umbrella serves as a gathering place to start the evening.

Many of the guests are enjoying Mango Margaritas and Caribbean Cosmopolitans. After a day relaxing in the sun, everyone is ready to nibble on Fresh Salmon Tartare, Tasty Crostini, and West Indian Empanadas. The warm ocean breezes and the guests' glamorous and sexy attire contribute to the sultry atmosphere of the party.

Anticipating a fantastic evening of dinner and dancing, our host and hostess leave the breakdown of the party to a well-selected staff. The night's revelries are just beginning!

As the sun sets, the neon lights up our South Beach Soirée. The Mango Margarita (page 27), Kwitini (page 28), Strawberry Mojito (page 26), and Blue Shark (page 23) all look irresistible.

Soups and Drinks

South Beach Soirée

Menu

*Relaxing in a chaise lounge and sipping a
cocktail on South Beach—what a wonderful
life! Chaise lounges courtesy of Patio & Things.*

Creamy Baby Green Pea Soup, Fresh Salmon Tatare,
West Indian Empanadas, and Tasty Crostini
are our South Beach starters.

Work Plan

SEVERAL DAYS AHEAD

All of the cocktails featured here can be
  made ahead and kept in the freezer
  until ready to serve.
West Indian Empanadas can be made up
  to three days ahead and frozen. Thaw
  before frying or baking.

THE MORNING OF THE PARTY

Prepare Creamy Baby Green Pea Soup.
Prepare Fresh Salmon Tartare and
  keep refrigerated.

Make the bread for Tasty Crostini and
  wrap tightly until final assembly.
Empanadas can be made 6 hours ahead
  and refrigerated until cooked.
Cut fruit for garnishes for drinks.

JUST BEFORE SERVING

Assemble Crostini.
Bake or fry Empanadas.

Carrot, Leek and Ginger Soup

This combination of carrots and ginger is light and refreshing. This recipe allows you to choose how much ginger you prefer. This recipe tastes best when made the day before and served at room temperature.

6 garlic cloves, minced
1 tablespoon butter
2^1/2 pounds carrots, peeled and sliced (16 carrots)
5 potatoes, chopped
2 leeks, cleaned and sliced
2 ribs celery without leaves, chopped
2 (49-ounce) cans chicken broth
2^1/2 teaspoons grated ginger, or to taste
Salt and freshly ground pepper to taste
Juice of 3 oranges
^{1}/8 teaspoon nutmeg
2 tablespoons chopped chives for garnish

Sauté the garlic in the butter in a skillet for 30 seconds. Remove from the heat. Bring the sautéed garlic, carrots, potatoes, leeks, celery and one can of the broth to a boil in a large stockpot over medium heat. Reduce the heat and simmer for 45 minutes or until the vegetables are tender. Process in batches in a food processor until the mixture is creamy and smooth. Return to the stockpot and stir in the remaining can of broth. Cook until heated through. Add the ginger ^{1}/4 teaspoon at a time, stirring well and tasting after each addition until the soup has reached your preferred taste. Turn off the heat. Add the orange juice and nutmeg. Season with salt and pepper. Ladle into soup bowls and garnish with the chives.

Note: Try serving this delectable soup in a shooter glass as a cocktail.

Serves 16

Photograph on page 10.

In the mid-1950s, Dr. Arturo di Filippi, the man who was responsible for bringing opera to Miami, approached a group of young women to form an opera support group. Thus was born the Young Patronesses of the Opera, a social volunteer organization whose primary goal is to promote opera education and ensure that young people and adults are prepared for what they hear and see on stage.

Cream of Garlic Soup

Many supermarkets now carry prepeeled garlic cloves, which really decreases the preparation time of this fabulous soup. This recipe was collected by one of our members on her travels from the restaurant Bayona.

4 sprigs of fresh parsley
3 sprigs of fresh thyme
1 bay leaf
2 pounds onions, coarsely chopped
2 cups garlic cloves, peeled and chopped
2 tablespoons olive oil
2 tablespoons butter
6 to 7 cups chicken stock
2 cups (1/2-inch) cubed day-old French bread
1 cup half-and-half, or 1/2 cup milk and
  1/2 cup heavy cream
Salt and freshly ground pepper to taste

Wrap the parsley, thyme and bay leaf in a piece of cheesecloth and tie securely with fine string to form a bouquet garni. Sauté the onions and garlic in the olive oil and butter in a large heavy stockpot over medium-low heat for 30 minutes or until the onions are a deep golden brown. Add 6 cups of the stock and the bouquet garni and bring to a boil. Stir in the bread cubes. Simmer for 10 minutes or until the bread is soft. Remove the bouquet garni. Process the soup in a food processor or blender until smooth. Strain the soup into the stockpot, discarding the solids. Stir in the half-and-half and season with salt and pepper. Add the remaining 1 cup stock if needed for the desired consistency. Ladle into soup bowls.

Serves 8

Gazpacho Andaluz

Originally from the Spanish region of southern Andalusia, this flavorful soup is simple to make and always refreshing.

2 slices French or country bread
2 tablespoons sherry vinegar
1 cucumber, peeled and chopped
1 red bell pepper, chopped
2 pounds very ripe tomatoes, peeled and seeded,
　　or 1 (26-ounce) box Pomi chopped tomatoes
1 garlic clove, minced
$1/4$ cup chopped yellow onion
Ice water
Salt and pepper to taste
Sliced cucumber, chopped bell pepper and/or croutons for garnish

Soak the bread in the vinegar in a bowl. Process the soaked bread, cucumber, bell pepper, tomatoes, garlic and onion in a blender until smooth. Add ice water 1 tablespoon at a time until the soup reaches a creamy, slightly thin consistency, processing constantly. Season with salt and pepper. Pour into a container and chill, covered, for 2 hours. To serve, ladle into soup bowls and garnish with diced cucumber, diced bell pepper and/or croutons.

Serves 4 to 6

Multimushroom Soup

The combination of enoki and white mushrooms gives this soup a rich earthy flavor, which is very satisfying.

1 cup leek bulbs, sliced
1 onion, chopped
1 tablespoon butter or margarine
1 (1/2-ounce) package dried enoki mushrooms
  or dried chanterelle mushrooms
8 ounces whole white mushrooms, stems trimmed
16 ounces white mushrooms, sliced
1 1/2 (14-ounce) cans chicken broth or chicken stock
1 cup skim milk
1/4 cup white wine
Salt and freshly ground pepper to taste

Sauté the leeks and onion in the butter in a large heavy saucepan until the onion is translucent. Add the mushrooms and sauté until soft. Add the broth and reduce the heat to low. Simmer for 20 minutes. Remove from the heat to cool slightly. Reserve 1/4 cup of the mushroom mixture for garnish.

Purée the remaining mushroom mixture in batches in a food processor and pour into a large saucepan. Cook over low heat until heated through. Stir in the milk and wine. Season with salt and pepper. Ladle into soup bowls and garnish with the reserved mushroom mixture.

Note: For a thicker soup, use only one can of the broth.

Serves 4

Creamy Baby Green Pea Soup

1 bunch culantro
2 tablespoons butter
1 onion, finely chopped
2 (10-ounce) packages frozen baby green
   peas, thawed and drained

1 (32-ounce) can chicken stock
1/4 cup heavy cream
Salt and pepper to taste
Culantro for garnish

Remove the stems and the tougher part of the culantro leaves so that only the thinner and more delicate pieces remain. Measure 1/4 cup of the delicate culantro pieces, reserving the remaining for another purpose.

Melt the butter over low heat in a large saucepan. Stir in the onion. Cover and cook until the onion is translucent. Stir in the peas, stock and 1/4 cup culantro. Cook over low heat for 15 to 20 minutes or until the peas are soft. Process in a food processor until very creamy. Pour into a large bowl and stir in the cream. Season with salt and pepper. Ladle into soup bowls and garnish with culantro.

Note: Culantro is an herb widely used in cooking in the Caribbean, Latin America, and the Far East. It is a close relative of cilantro or coriander and may be found in specialty food stores.

Serves 4 to 6

Photograph on page 13.

Sunset Bisque

A thick, rich soup with an enjoyable combination of flavors.

1/4 cup (1/2 stick) butter
2 onions, finely chopped
3 ribs celery, chopped
2 tablespoons all-purpose flour
1 teaspoon curry powder

2 green apples, peeled and finely chopped
1 cup chopped cooked chicken
8 cups chicken broth
1 bay leaf
1 cup light cream, chilled

Melt the butter in a skillet. Add the onions and celery and sauté until soft. Stir in the flour and curry powder and cook for 2 minutes, stirring constantly. Process the onion mixture, apples, chicken and 1 cup of the broth in a food processor until smooth. Combine with the remaining broth in a large saucepan. Add the bay leaf and bring to a boil. Remove from the heat and discard the bay leaf. Chill, covered, in the refrigerator. Stir in the cream before serving.

Makes 2 1/4 quarts

Clockwise: Sunset Bisque and Cucumber
Flowers Filled with Crab and Salmon Roe

Chupe de Gallina (Venezuelan Chicken and Corn Chowder)

This tasty traditional Venezuelan soup is served with the corn cobs in pieces. Serve with plenty of queso blanco and Tabasco sauce.

1 (3- to 3¹/2-pound) chicken	1 (15-ounce) can cream-style corn
1 (49-ounce) can chicken stock	1 (12-ounce) can evaporated milk
2 leeks, well cleaned	1¹/2 pounds queso blanco
1 garlic clove, pressed	1 bunch cilantro
5 ears of corn, husks and silks removed	Tabasco sauce (optional)
1 pound potatoes	

Place the chicken, stock, leeks and garlic in a large stockpot. (If the stock does not cover the chicken, add enough water to cover.) Simmer until the chicken is cooked through and falling off the bone. Remove the chicken from the broth and set aside. Cool the broth and discard the leeks.

Cut the ears of corn into 2-inch pieces. Peel the potatoes and cut into 1-inch pieces. Add the potatoes, corn cob pieces and cream-style corn to the cooled broth. Simmer until the potatoes and corn are tender but not mushy.

Cut the chicken into bite-size pieces, discarding the skin and bones. (The chicken pieces should not be too small or they will disintegrate when reheated in the broth.) Add the chicken and evaporated milk to the vegetable mixture and cook until heated through. Cut the cheese into 1/2-inch cubes and chop the cilantro. Ladle the soup into bowls and let your guests add the cheese, cilantro and Tabasco sauce as desired.

Serves 6

Santuzza's Soup

1 pound Italian sausage	2 (10-ounce) cans beef bouillon
1 cup chopped onion	2 cups finely shredded cabbage
2 carrots, chopped	1 (6-ounce) can tomato paste
1 teaspoon basil, chopped	1 teaspoon salt
1 garlic clove, pressed	1/4 teaspoon pepper
2 small zucchini, peeled and sliced	1 (16-ounce) can Great Northern beans
1 (16-ounce) can pear tomatoes, chopped	

Cook the sausage in a large heavy saucepan until brown and cooked through. Add the onion, carrots, basil and garlic and cook over medium heat for 5 minutes. Add the zucchini, tomatoes, bouillon, cabbage, tomato paste, salt and pepper. Bring to a boil and reduce the heat. Simmer, covered, for 1 hour. Add the beans and cook over low heat for 20 minutes. Ladle into soup bowls.

Serves 6

Chupe de Camarones (Seafood Stew)

Chock-full of seafood and vegetables, this soup pleases everyone. For those who prefer a spicier chupe, have Tabasco sauce as an accompaniment.

3 garlic cloves, minced
1 large onion, minced
1 pound yellow potatoes, peeled and cut into $1/2$-inch pieces
$1/4$ cup rice
1 pinch dried oregano
3 tablespoons olive oil
2 cups clam stock or fish stock
3 cups water (optional)
Red pepper flakes to taste
1 large tomato, chopped
1 ear of corn, husks and silks removed
1 cup peas
1 pound medium shrimp, cleaned
1 pound thick white fish (tilapia or cod), cut into 2×2-inch pieces
Salt and freshly ground black pepper to taste
1 cup half-and-half
6 to 8 eggs, poached (optional)
3 to 4 tablespoons chopped parsley
1 tablespoon cilantro (optional)

Sauté the garlic, onion, potatoes, rice and oregano in the olive oil in a large heavy saucepan over medium heat for 5 minutes or until the onion is translucent. Add the stock. Add the water if you desire a thinner soup. Stir in the red pepper flakes and tomato. Bring to a boil and reduce the heat to medium-low. Simmer for 10 minutes.

Cut the corn into five or six pieces. Add the corn and peas to the potato mixture and cook for 5 minutes. Reduce the heat to low and add the shrimp, fish, salt and black pepper. Cook for 5 minutes or until the fish is opaque. (The chupe may be refrigerated for up to 2 days at this point.) Add the half-and-half and cook until heated through. Do not boil. Ladle into soup bowls and top each serving with a poached egg. Sprinkle the top of each serving evenly with the parsley and cilantro.

Serves 6 to 8

Zarzuela de Marisco

A delectable soup full of different flavors. Serve with crusty French bread.

6 slices bacon
1 tablespoon olive oil
3 yellow onions, chopped
2 green bell peppers, chopped
2 carrots, chopped
3 ribs celery, chopped
3 garlic cloves, minced
2 dashes of Tabasco sauce
1 (28-ounce) can Italian-style tomatoes
1 (28-ounce) can crushed tomatoes
1 cup sherry
3 tablespoons lemon juice
1 teaspoon thyme
1 teaspoon dried basil

1 teaspoon sugar
1 teaspoon salt
1 teaspoon freshly ground pepper
1 tablespoon Old Bay seasoning
1 bay leaf
1/4 cup parsley
1 pound crab meat, drained
   and flaked
12 ounces snapper, grouper or
   tilapia fillets
8 ounces medium shrimp, peeled
   and deveined
12 ounces scallops
Hot cooked white rice

Cook the bacon in a large heavy saucepan until crisp. Remove the bacon to paper towels to drain, reserving the drippings in the saucepan. Crumble the bacon and set aside.

Add the olive oil, onions, bell peppers, carrots, celery and garlic to the reserved drippings in the saucepan and sauté for 5 minutes. Stir in the Tabasco sauce, tomatoes, sherry, lemon juice, thyme, basil, sugar, salt, pepper, Old Bay seasoning, bay leaf, parsley and bacon and simmer for 30 minutes. Add the crab meat and fish and cook for 10 minutes. Stir in the shrimp and scallops and cook for 5 minutes or until the shrimp turn pink. Discard the bay leaf. Serve over rice.

Serves 10

Blue Shark

Beautiful and lethal.

1 ounce vodka
1 ounce tequila
1/2 ounce blue Curaçao

Pour the vodka, tequila and blue Curaçao into a shaker two-thirds full of ice cubes. Shake well, strain and serve.

Serves 1

Photograph on page 11.

Blue Lagoon

As pretty to look at as the turquoise sea.

1 1/2 ounces vodka
1/2 ounce blue Curaçao
2 ounces pineapple juice, chilled
Dash of blue Curaçao
Pineapple wedge for garnish

Combine the vodka, 1/2 ounce blue Curaçao and the pineapple juice in a bar glass and stir to mix well. Pour into a highball glass filled with ice. Pour a dash of blue Curaçao on top. Garnish with a pineapple wedge.

Serves 1

Chilled Strawberry Soup

This light and refreshing soup is perfect for Miami's winter strawberry season.

To prepare, process 1 quart strawberries, 1 cup buttermilk and 3/4 cup sugar in a food processor until smooth. Combine 3 cups buttermilk, 2/3 cup sour cream and 3 tablespoons kirsch in a large bowl and mix well. Add the strawberry mixture and stir to mix well. Chill, covered, in the refrigerator. Serve garnished with sprigs of fresh mint. This recipe will serve 6 to 8.

Fun Cocktail Garnishes

Garnishes change sipping a cocktail into a special event. With garnishes you can be as imaginative as you'd like. The only rule is that the garnish should match the flavor of the drink. Basically, never place a cocktail onion in a Cosmopolitan.

For sweet or fruity drinks, consider fresh or frozen strawberries and wheels, wedges, or a combination of pineapple, kiwifruit, mango, star fruit, peach, apple, watermelon, orange, lemon, or lime. Use a colorful wooden pick to make a spinney top, which is a maraschino cherry between two orange wedges. Lemons or limes twist nicely and can be held in place with a wooden pick. With a colorful wooden pick, skewer a melon ball between two pieces of mint. Cranberries, currants, and coconut look pretty floating on the surface of these drinks. Frost cherries or strawberries by dipping them into egg white and sugar for a delicious effect.

Bay Breeze

2 ounces light rum
3 ounces cranberry juice
1 ounce pineapple juice

Combine the rum, cranberry juice and pineapple juice in a bar glass and stir to mix well. Pour into a highball glass filled with ice cubes and stir gently.

Serves 1

Photograph on page 27.

Caribbean Cosmopolitan

The sophisticated drink with a tropical twist.

1 1/2 ounces Bacardi Limon rum
1 ounce cranberry juice
1 ounce Cointreau
1/2 ounce fresh lime juice
Strips of orange peel for garnish

Combine the rum, cranberry juice, Cointreau and lime juice in a shaker with ice cubes and shake to mix well. Strain into a chilled martini glass. Garnish with orange peel.

Serves 1

Photograph on page 10.

Champagne Flirtini

So many delicious flavors!

4 fresh raspberries
1 1/2 ounces raspberry-flavored vodka
1/2 ounce Cointreau
Splash of fresh lime juice
Splash of cranberry juice
Spash of pineapple juice
Dry Champagne, chilled

Muddle the raspberries in the bottom of a chilled Champagne flute. Pour the vodka, Cointreau, lime juice, cranberry juice and pineapple juice into a shaker two-thirds full of ice cubes and shake well. Strain into the prepared Champagne flute and top off with the Champagne.

Serves 1

Photograph on page 225.

Champagne Kiss

4 ounces Champagne
1 ounce Grand Marnier
Fresh fruit for garnish

Pour the Champagne and Grand Marnier into a wine goblet filled with crushed ice and stir gently. Garnish with fresh fruit.

Serves 1

Photograph on page 213.

Fun Cocktail Garnishes
(continued)

For savory or vegetable drinks, peel off ribbons of carrot or chile and soak the ribbons in ice water for decorative curls. Grape tomatoes, black or green olives, cocktail onions, herbs, and paprika are festive. Before slicing it, score a cucumber with a fork and then slice into thin wheels. Scallions, celery sticks with leaves, cucumber slices, stems of lemongrass, and even bamboo sprigs make great stirrers.

For chocolate drinks, use whipped cream, chocolate sprinkles, whole or crushed peppermints, or chocolate shavings or curls.

Spirits Supply

When deciding how much to buy, it's important to be aware of your guests' preferences and to make allowances for the time of day and the occasion. A luncheon during the middle of a work-day, or an early dinner the night before a workday would require at the most a half bottle of wine per person; most people will drink a glass before the meal and possibly one more glass with the meal. There are six glasses in a bottle of wine or bubbling spirits, or eight if you are making cocktails.

For a weekend party, allow one bottle of wine per person. For cocktails, liquor, and punches with liquor, allow two to three drinks per person for a two-hour party. There are sixteen measures in a fifth of liquor, so one bottle will serve a little over five people. For Champagne or other bubbling spirits, allow for two to three drinks per person, less if you are not serving it throughout the party. Don't forget your guests who won't be drinking! Have plenty of sparkling water and soft drinks. For picnics and barbecues, have plenty of small water bottles on ice.

Mojito

Everyone agrees; mojitos are the most refreshing drink ever.

2 sprigs of fresh mint
2 teaspoons sugar
3 tablespoons fresh lime juice
1 1/2 ounces light rum or mango-flavored rum
Club soda, chilled
1 sprig of fresh mint for garnish
Lime slice for garnish

Crush two sprigs of mint with a fork in a tall thin glass to coat the inside. Add the sugar and lime juice and stir to mix well. Top with ice. Add the rum and mix well. Top off with club soda. Garnish with one sprig of mint and the lime slice.

Serves 1

Photograph on page 36.

Strawberry Mojitos

Miami is known as the mojito capital; this is one of our best.

10 fresh strawberries
4 sprigs of fresh mint
4 lime wedges
1 shot Crème de Fraise des Bois
3 shots premium white rum
2 splashes of soda water
2 sprigs of fresh mint for garnish

Muddle the strawberries, four sprigs of mint, the lime and Crème de Fraise des Bois hard in a shaker. Add the rum and then fill the shaker with ice. Shake to mix well. Double strain through a sieve into two Collins glasses filled with cracked ice. Top each with a splash of soda water and garnish each with a sprig of mint.

Serves 2

Photograph at right.

Mango Margarita

Try not to use gold tequila when making this pretty margarita; it is too mild.

Salt for dipping glass
2 ounces tequila
3/4 ounce Grand Marnier
1 ounce fresh mango nectar
3/4 ounce fresh orange juice
3/4 ounce fresh lime juice
1 teaspoon simple syrup
1 cup ice cubes

Lightly rim the edge of a margarita glass with salt. Process the tequila, Grand Marnier, mango nectar, orange juice, lime juice, simple syrup and ice cubes in a blender until the ice is crushed. Pour into the prepared glass and serve.

Serves 1

Frosting Rims

A margarita isn't a margarita without a salty coating. Unfortunately frosting a glass the wrong way will cause salt and juice to fall in your margarita, making it way too salty. The same holds true for chocolate on chocolate martinis and sugar on other drinks.

To properly rim a glass for a margarita, use a piece of fruit to wet only the exterior rim of the glass. Turn the glass upside down over a sink or plate and sprinkle the salt by hand or with a salt shaker, twirling the glass, so that only the exterior rim is coated.

If you are coating glasses with chocolate or sugar, wet the exterior edge of the glass with some of the liquid you will be using in the drink. For a pretty effect, try matching the sugar to the color of a sweetened cocktail by mixing it with a drop of food dye or colored syrup, such as grenadine. Prepare the glasses in advance of your party so you will have them when you need them.

Special Martinis

Martinis have evolved since the simple combination of vodka or gin and vermouth. Many vodka and gin drinks which are called martinis have varied ingredients. If you like chocolate, try combining one ounce white crème de cacao and two ounces vodka with a chocolate chip garnish. If you love the flavor of apple, mix one ounce each apple juice, sour apple schnapps and vodka to create the always-popular apple martini with a thin apple slice garnish.

Kwitini

*1/2 kiwifruit
1/2 teaspoon simple syrup
3 ounces vodka or citrus-flavored vodka
Slice of kiwifruit for garnish*

Muddle the kiwifruit with the simple syrup in a cocktail shaker. Add ice and the vodka and shake well. Strain into a chilled cocktail glass and garnish with a slice of kiwifruit.

Serves 1

Photograph on page 27.

South Beach Martini

An Ocean Drive specialty.

*2 ounces orange-flavored vodka
2 ounces citrus-flavored vodka
3/4 ounce Cointreau
3/4 ounce fresh lime juice
Orange twist or lime twist for garnish*

Pour the vodka, Cointreau and lime juice into a cocktail shaker filled two-thirds full of ice cubes. Shake well and strain into a chilled cocktail glass. Garnish with an orange twist or lime twist.

Serves 1

Millionaire Martini

When only the best will do.

Splash of dry vermouth
3 ounces highest quality gin, such as Bombay Sapphire
2 jalapeño-stuffed olives or pimento-stuffed olives for garnish

Rinse a chilled martini glass with the vermouth and pour out any excess. Pour the gin into a mixing glass filled two-thirds full of ice cubes and stir. Strain into the martini glass and garnish with the olives.

Serves 1

Summer Sangria

The perfect drink for a lazy summer day or a lively party.

1/4 cup water
1/4 cup sugar
2 bottles red Spanish table wine
1 cup brandy
1/2 cup triple sec
1 orange, sliced
1 lemon, sliced
1 plum, cut into wedges
6 strawberries
1 bottle club soda

Heat the water and sugar in a small saucepan until the sugar dissolves. Remove from the heat and let stand until cool. Combine the simple syrup, wine, brandy, triple sec, orange, lemon, plum and strawberries in a large container and mix well. Cover tightly and chill for at least 24 hours. To serve, pour the Sangria into a glass with a piece of a fruit, filling the glass three-quarters full. Fill the remainder of the glass with the club soda.

Serves 6

Cuban Coffee

Drinking Cuban coffee is a daily ritual for most Cuban-Americans and many other Miamians. You will see lines of people waiting on the sidewalks to buy their Café Cubano at lunch counters and juice and coffee bars facing busy commercial streets all around Miami. Cuban coffee is served in tiny paper cups and is drunk in one quick gulp. Why not drink it slowly? Café Cubano is brewed at double the strength of American coffee and is thick and sweet, with one teaspoon of sugar for each demitasse cup.

To make Café Cubano, add 1 teaspoon sugar to the glass carafe for every serving. The coffee will pour over the sugar and easily dissolve it. Stir briskly before serving to dissolve any remaining grains of sugar.

Pineapple Batido

With Miami's sultry weather, batidos (bah-TEE-dos) have long been popular. Batidos are blended fruit, milk, and ice drinks which are not made with ice cream or yogurt like milk shakes or smoothies. They are sold at juice bars throughout Miami and are available in a stunning variety of fruit combinations as well as in chocolate and vanilla. They are very healthful when made with skim or fat-free milk and fresh fruit. You can make batidos with any fresh fruit, canned fruit, frozen fruit, or fruit purée that you prefer. Batidos have also been known to be alcoholic, particularly with the addition of light rum and Coco Lopez.

1 cup skim milk
1 cup chopped fresh pineapple
1/2 cup crushed ice
Confectioners' sugar to taste

Process the milk, pineapple, ice and confectioners' sugar in a blender or a food processor until smooth. Pour into two chilled glasses and serve immediately.

Serves 2

Iced Cappuccino Cubano

1 1/2 cups very strong brewed coffee
1/2 cup sweetened condensed milk
1/2 cup half-and-half
1/2 teaspoon vanilla extract

Combine the coffee and condensed milk in a medium bowl and mix well. Whisk in the half-and-half and vanilla. Pour into glasses filled with ice.

Serves 2

Iced Mint Tea for a Crowd

7 regular-size tea bags
12 sprigs of fresh mint
Grated zest of 3 lemons
2 quarts boiling water
1 cup fresh lemon juice (juice of about 7 lemons)
2 cups sugar
Fresh mint leaves and lemon slices for garnish

Place the tea bags, mint sprigs and lemon zest in a large glass container. Add the boiling water and steep for 12 minutes. Discard the tea bags. Add the lemon juice and sugar and stir until the sugar dissolves. Strain the tea into a large pitcher, discarding the solids. Add water to reach the desired strength. Serve over ice and garnish each serving with mint leaves and lemon slices.

Makes about 1 gallon

Cuban Coffee (continued)

You may wish to make a Colado, which is a large "to-go" cup of Cuban coffee with a lid and several small espresso cups. It is to be shared with friends, often in the midmorning and midafternoon for that JOLT to get you through the day.

Bustelo and Pilon are popular brands of Cuban coffee. If you can't find these brands, Colombian coffee finely ground may be substituted.

Café con Leche is two parts Cuban coffee with one part steamed milk. It is known as the "quiet cousin" of Café Cubano and is often served with toasted bread or Cuban crackers for a typical Cuban breakfast.

Reunion Tropicál

A large family get-together is really a Reunion Tropicál on this beautiful day in Fairchild Tropical Botanic Gardens. Making music, playing dominoes, and sharing family stories while eating a delicious leisurely meal are all planned for this wonderful afternoon.

A family gathering in any culture is a cause for celebrating, but in Miami it is the reason for a "Reunion Tropicál." Under warm sun and among gorgeous flowers and reflecting ponds, generations come together to share stories, music, customs, and of course, food and drink. Outdoor picnics are a delight for the senses whether in your own back yard or here at the Victoria Amazonica Pool in Fairchild Tropical Botanic Gardens.

To add layers of excitement to the party the family is using multicolored dinner plates by Fiesta Ware. Vibrant fuchsia bougainvillea, coconut seeds, split-leaf philodendron, and tropical fruits are used to enhance the setting. A woven mat of palm leaves provides comfort, and rattan baskets serve to hold the platters of food. A gathering of pillows is arranged in the perfect location for Abuela's (Grandmother's) stories.

Everyone has brought a cooler with their favorite dishes. As the sweet smell of cigars and grilling flank steak fills the air, the family enjoys the Cold Hot Shrimp. Some are enjoying frosty Mojitos, while others grab a Mexican beer or a malta soft drink chilling in the old washtub. After dinner the adults enjoy the sweet fruitiness and chocolate of Passion Fruit Pie, and the children enjoy Irresistible Cookies.

There is time for a game of dominoes while traditional songs are played, sung, and enjoyed by all. As the sun starts to set a CD player appears, and tunes with a lively Latin beat ring out. No one can resist dancing, and the generations mix as grandchildren dance with grandparents, parents with children.

Reunion Tropicál is a time for family to join together and celebrate life while sipping cool rum drinks laced with memories. It is a time to introduce special boyfriends or girlfriends and to make plans for the future. This celebration beats with the heart and soul of the family.

Appetizers

Menu

*Cold Hot Shrimp, Grilled Flank Steak with Chimichurri Sauce, Plantain
Chips and Black Bean Salad with Chipotle Vinaigrette will be enjoyed
by the whole family. Mojitos are ready on a wooden board and
Mexican beer and Malta soft drinks are in the metal washtub.*

Crotons, bougainvillea, poinciana blossoms, and tropical fruits frame the background of the Victoria Amazonica Pond. Passion Fruit Pie and Irresistible Cookies are for dessert. Some family members will eat the Mango and Jicama Salad for dessert; others will enjoy it with the main meal.

Work Plan

SEVERAL DAYS BEFORE

Prepare Irresistible Cookies and freeze or
    store in an airtight container.

THE DAY BEFORE

Prepare Black Bean Salad with Chipotle
    Vinaigrette. It can be left out of
    refrigeration if covered tightly.
Prepare My Girlfriend's Salad Dressing
    and refrigerate.
Prepare Chimchurri Sauce and marinate
    the flank steak.
Prepare Plantain Chips and store in
    airtight container.
Prepare Passion Fruit Pie and refrigerate.

ON THE DAY

Prepare a Tomato, Cucumber and Hearts
    of Palm Salad, refrigerate, and do not
    add dressing.
Prepare Cold Hot Shrimp and refrigerate.
Prepare Festive Fruit Salsa, can be left
    out of refrigeration if tightly covered.
Prepare Mango and Jicama Salad.

JUST BEFORE SERVING

Toss Tomatoes, Cucumbers and Hearts
    of Palm Salad with My Girlfriend's
    Salad Dressing.
Grill flank steak.
Make Mojitos.

Cucumber Flowers Filled with Crab and Salmon Roe

This appetizer is especially pretty when the cucumber strips are laid closely together on the serving platter and the cucumber flowers are set on the strips.

2 English cucumbers
8 ounces white lump crab meat,
   shells removed and meat chopped
2 tablespoons finely chopped pimento
1/2 cup finely chopped onion
1 rib celery, finely chopped
1/2 cup sour cream
1 teaspoon Dijon mustard
2 or 3 drops of Worcestershire sauce
1 tablespoon chopped dill weed
1 ounce red salmon caviar

Peel each cucumber in long strips and lay the strips in overlapping rows on a serving platter. Scoop out a small trench along the length of each peeled cucumber using a zester. Rotate the cucumber so that the first trench is directly below where you will scoop another trench along the length of the cucumber. Rotate the cucumber so that the next trench you scoop will be equidistant from the other two trenches. Scoop another trench across from that trench, so that all four trenches are equidistant from each other. If your cucumber is thick enough, scoop another four trenches, taking care to rotate the cucumber so that the trenches are equally spaced from each other. Cut each cucumber into 1/2-inch slices to form a flower-like design. Scoop out a small amount of the center of each cucumber slice, taking care not to scoop all the way through.

Combine the crab meat, pimento, onion, celery, sour cream, mustard, Worcestershire sauce and dill weed in a bowl and mix well. Dollop a small amount of the mixture onto the center of each cucumber flower. Sprinkle each with a small amount of the caviar. Place on the serving platter with the cucumber strips.

Makes 20 appetizers

Wine Recommendations: Albariño, Sancerre, or Chardonnay

38

Wrapped Shrimp with Roasted Red Pepper Aïoli

The red pepper aïoli provides an appealing contrast to the shrimp.

ROASTED RED PEPPER AÏOLI
  1 red bell pepper
  1 egg yolk
  1/4 teaspoon chopped garlic
  1/2 cup canola oil
  Salt and pepper to taste

SHRIMP
  16 (21- to 25-count) shrimp with tails, peeled and deveined
  Salt and pepper to taste
  16 won ton wrappers
  1 egg white
  2 tablespoons vegetable oil
  1 bunch parsley for garnish

To prepare the aïoli, roast the bell pepper over an open flame until charred on all sides. Cover with plastic wrap and let stand until cool. Unwrap the cooled bell pepper. Peel and remove the stem and seeds. Finely chop the bell pepper. Whisk the egg yolk and garlic together in a small bowl. Drizzle in the oil gradually, whisking constantly to form mayonnaise. Stir in the bell pepper. Season with salt and pepper.

To prepare the shrimp, season the shrimp with salt and pepper. Wrap the head of each shrimp with a won ton wrapper to form a square envelope shape. Brush the edges with the egg white and press to seal. Fry in the oil in a skillet for 1 1/2 to 2 minutes or until golden brown. Drain on paper towels. Place on a serving platter and garnish with the parsley. Serve with the aïoli.

Note: If you are concerned about using raw egg yolks, use eggs yolks from eggs pasteurized in their shells, which are sold at some specialty food stores, or use an equivalent amount of pasteurized egg substitute.

Serves 4

Wine Recommendations: Riesling, Sauvignon Blanc, Chablis, or Pinot Grigio

Early Party Planning for a Large Party

Planning for a large party should be done well in advance to make sure you have everything and everyone you need for your big event. The following is a list that will take you up to the week before the party:

Decide what type of party will work best for you, such as barbecue or a cocktail party. Choose the food serving setup, whether it will be buffet or served, and determine if you will have seating for everyone.

If you wish, choose a theme and plan invitations and decorations around the theme.

Plan your menu.

If you are having live entertainment, reserve your performers.

Take an inventory of your serving utensils, dishes, flatware, glasses, napkins, and other linens.

Shrimp and Avocado Nori-Maki

Rolling sushi does take practice, but once you have learned how the possibilities are endless for creating sushi with different fillings. It is also much fresher and far less expensive to prepare at home than to purchase sushi from supermarkets or restaurants. This recipe calls for cooked shrimp so it does not spoil easily.

3 cups sushi rice or other short-grained white rice
3¹/2 cups water
¹/4 cup rice vinegar
¹/4 cup sugar
1 large avocado
2 tablespoons lemon juice
4 nori sheets
1 or 2 seedless cucumbers, peeled and
    cut into ¹/4×8-inch slices lengthwise
12 medium shrimp, cooked, peeled,
    deveined and cut into small pieces
Wasabi or soy sauce for dipping
Pickled ginger (gari)

Rinse the rice in a colander under cold running water until the water runs clear with no milky residue. Drain the rice well. Combine the rice and water in a heavy saucepan. Cover tightly and bring to a boil over medium-high heat. (Make sure the water is boiling but do not uncover the saucepan.) Reduce the heat to low and cook for 8 minutes. Remove from the heat and cover the top of the saucepan with a towel. Let stand for 10 minutes to cool. Simmer the vinegar and sugar in a small saucepan until the sugar is dissolved. Remove from the heat to cool.

Stir the rice with a dampened wooden spatula or dampened wooden spoon until a rice grain yields to pressure when pinched. Spread the rice evenly in a 10×15-inch pan. Cover with a damp cloth if the vinegar mixture has not cooled.

Slide the spatula or spoon through the rice in a slicing motion to separate the grains while slowly adding the cooled vinegar mixture. Gradually spread the rice in the pan. Let stand for 20 minutes or until the rice reaches room temperature. Spoon the rice into a bowl and cover with a cloth. Let stand until needed or for up to 3 hours. (This should not be refrigerated and cannot be made a day ahead.)

Peel the avocado and remove the pit. Rub the avocado with just enough of the lemon juice to cover to prevent browning. Cut the avocado into ¹/4×8-inch slices. (If you cannot cut the slices this long, cut into slices 4 inches long.)

Shrimp and Avocado Nori-Maki *(continued)*

Place a bamboo sushi mat on a work surface with the slats running crosswise. Lay one nori sheet shiny side down on the mat and place 3/4 cup of the rice on top. Spread the rice over the nori sheet with damp fingers, leaving a 3/4-inch empty border on the edge closest to you and a 3/4-inch empty border on the farthest edge from you. Press down firmly on the rice. Lay one of the long cucumber slices horizontally across the middle of the rice. Lay one 8-inch or two 4-inch avocado slices on top of the cucumber slice. Spread one-fourth of the shrimp pieces on top of the avocado.

Beginning with the edge nearest you, lift up the mat with your thumbs and then roll the mat over so that the upper and lower edges of the rice meet. Gently squeeze along the length of the roll, gently pulling away the edge of the mat farthest from you to tighten. Open the mat and roll the cylinder forward to seal with the nori border. Place the cylinder seam side down on a cutting board. Repeat this process until you have made four cylinders.

Let the cylinders stand until cool. Wipe a sharp serrated knife with a damp cloth and cut the cylinders into sections. Serve immediately with wasabi, soy sauce and/or pickled ginger.

Makes 30 to 36 pieces

Wine Recommendations: Riesling, Sake, Pinot Grigio, or Sauvignon Blanc

The Roberta Rymer Balfe Leadership Golden Patron Award was given to the Young Patronesses of the Opera in 1993 for having made a lifetime contribution of over $1 million to the Greater Miami Opera. Because of its many achievements, YPO continues to be one of the most active and successful groups in the arts community.

Early Party Planning for a Large Party *(continued)*

Order or call early to borrow any items that are not readily available such as tents, tables, chairs, linens, party favors, or special centerpiece vases. If you plan to rent more readily available items such as dishes, glasses, flatware, or serving utensils, place your order(s) early.

If you are planning to order flowers, meet with your florist. Show him/her pictures of arrangements you'd like to use and discuss ideas.

Make arrangements for extra help.

Based on your inventory and your menu, borrow or purchase items that you don't plan to rent and that are usually less expensive and more readily available such as napkins, glasses, plates, dishes, and serving pieces.

Draw up your shopping list for food and drinks.

Cold Hot Shrimp

Everyone loves these spicy shrimp. Add a little extra garlic, and it will work as a cold tapas dish.

4 cups water
2 scallions, chopped
3 garlic cloves, pressed
Salt and freshly ground black pepper
   to taste
2 bay leaves
4 small ribs celery, finely chopped
1 pound medium shrimp with tails, peeled
   and deveined
2 scallions, chopped

1/2 cup finely chopped Vidalia or other
   sweet onion
2 tablespoons olive oil
1/4 cup lemon juice
1/4 cup chili sauce
1/4 cup ketchup
1 tablespoon finely grated horseradish
1 tablespoon mustard
1 teaspoon paprika
Dash of cayenne pepper, or to taste

Bring the water to a boil in a small saucepan. Add two scallions, the garlic, salt, black pepper, bay leaves and celery. Cover and simmer for 15 minutes. Add the shrimp and simmer for 4 minutes or until the shrimp turn pink. (Do not overcook.) Drain in a colander; discard the bay leaves. Stir gently and place in a bowl. Let stand to cool.

Combine two scallions, the onion, olive oil, lemon juice, chili sauce, ketchup, horseradish, mustard, paprika and cayenne pepper in a small bowl. Pour over the shrimp mixture and mix well with a wooden spoon. Marinate, covered, in the refrigerator for 8 to 10 hours. Place the shrimp and sauce in a glass bowl arranged in a larger bowl of cracked ice. Serve with wooden picks.

Serves 6

Wine Recommendations: Sauvignon Blanc, Riesling, Pinot Grigio, Sancerre, or Gewürztraminer

Sea Bass Ceviche with Plum Tomatoes

Sea bass is now very popular and may be difficult to find. If you cannot find sea bass, use any other white fish.

1 1/2 pounds Chilean sea bass
1/4 cup vegetable oil
1 teaspoon lemon zest
1/4 teaspoon turmeric
Juice of 2 lemons
1/2 cup fresh lime juice
1 tablespoon salt
4 plum tomatoes, seeded and chopped
1/2 red onion, sliced into half-moon shapes

Place the fish on a tray and freeze for 1 to 2 hours or until very firm but not frozen. Combine the oil, lemon zest and turmeric in a small saucepan. Cook over low heat for 10 minutes. Remove from the heat and let stand for 1 hour before using.

Place 3 tablespoons of the lemon oil in a nonreactive bowl, reserving the remaining lemon oil for another purpose. (The remaining lemon oil can be stored for up to 2 weeks in the refrigerator.) Add the lemon juice, lime juice and salt and mix well. Remove the fish from the freezer and cut crosswise into very thin slices using a sharp knife. Stir the fish, tomatoes and onion into the marinade. Marinate for 25 minutes. (Do not marinate for any longer or the fish will become mushy.) Serve immediately.

Serves 12

Wine Recommendations: Chardonnay, Fumé Blanc, Muscadet, Albariño, or Sauvignon Blanc

Grouper Ceviche with Mango and Chiles

Timing is everything with ceviche! The fish should be very fresh and should not marinate too long or it will become mushy.

1 1/2 pounds grouper fillets, skin removed
1/2 cup fresh lime juice
1 tablespoon salt
1/2 cup fresh lemon juice
Hot red pepper sauce to taste
2 jalapeño chiles, seeded and minced
1 cup finely chopped mango
10 large basil leaves, finely chopped
1/2 red onion, sliced into half-moon shapes

Place the fish on a tray and cover with plastic wrap. Freeze for 2 hours or longer. Uncover the fish and chop into 3/4-inch pieces using a sharp knife. Toss the fish with the lime juice and salt in a bowl. Marinate in the refrigerator for 1 hour.

Combine the lemon juice, hot sauce, jalapeño chiles, mango, basil and onion in a glass bowl and mix well. Stir in the fish just before serving. Serve on a lettuce-lined platter, with crackers as a dip or in a cocktail glass with crackers on the side.

Serves 12

Wine Recommendations: Fumé Blanc, Sauvignon Blanc, Chablis, Albariño, Viño Verde, or Pinot Grigio

Pepper Pungency

If you would like to substitute one type of chile pepper for another in a recipe, it is a good idea to know how each pepper falls on the Scoville scale, which was developed to determine the pungency of each type of pepper. The heat of each pepper is determined by the amount of capsaicin, which is found mainly in the membranes and seeds of each pepper. The tiny Scotch Bonnet chile, used frequently in Caribbean cooking, is more than forty times more pungent than the larger Anaheim chile, so many recipes call for a very small amount of Scotch Bonnet chile.

If a friend or family member asks you to change the peppers in a dish, remember that no two people taste pungency the same way. The riper the pepper, the more pungent it will be!

Scallop and Tangerine Ceviche with Pickled Jalapeño Chiles

The pickling makes the jalapeño chiles milder than normal. Prepare the pickled chiles a day in advance. Serve this attractive ceviche on endive leaves or in hollowed out oranges.

PICKLED JALAPEÑO CHILES
1/4 cup white vinegar
2/3 tablespoon sugar
2/3 tablespoon salt
2 jalapeño chiles, thinly sliced
1 tablespoon finely chopped shallot

CEVICHE
1 1/2 pounds large sea scallops, cut into quarters
1/2 cup fresh lime juice
1/2 tablespoon salt
1/2 cup fresh tangerine juice
1 tablespoon finely chopped oregano
1 tablespoon finely chopped cilantro
3 shallots, thinly sliced

To prepare the pickled jalapeño chiles, combine the vinegar, sugar, salt, jalapeño chiles and shallot in a bowl and mix well. Store, covered, in the refrigerator for 24 hours or up to 1 month.

To prepare the ceviche, combine the scallops, lime juice, salt, tangerine juice, oregano, cilantro, shallots and 1 tablespoon of the pickled jalapeño chiles in a bowl and mix well. Marinate, covered, in the refrigerator for 1 hour. (Do not marinate for any longer or the scallops will become mushy.) Serve in martini glasses, on pieces of endive, or in a bowl with crackers on the side.

Serves 12

Wine Recommendations: Sauvignon Blanc, Gewürztraminer, Muscadet, Albariño, or Pinot Grigio

Gravlax with Mustard Sauce

*Gravlax, or cured salmon, should marinate for three to four days.
With a little practice, you'll be able to cut elegant red ribbons
of gravlax.*

GRAVLAX

1 (4- to 5-pound) salmon, cut into halves with the skin on
1/4 cup coarse salt
1/4 cup sugar
2 tablespoons coarsely ground pepper
2 large bunches of dill weed
1/2 cup vodka

MUSTARD SAUCE

1/4 cup Dijon mustard
1 teaspoon dry mustard
3 tablespoons sugar
3 tablespoons wine vinegar
1/3 cup light vegetable oil
1 small bunch dill weed, chopped

ASSEMBLY

Sprigs of fresh dill weed and lemon wedges for garnish

To prepare the gravlax, place half the fish skin side down in a
glass dish or other nonreactive dish large enough to hold the length of
the fish. Sprinkle with the salt, sugar and pepper. Spread the dill weed
over the seasonings. Pour the vodka over the top. Place the remaining fish
skin side up on top of the bottom half. Cover the fish (not the dish) with
plastic wrap and weigh down with a plastic-covered brick, a bag of sugar
or flour, bags of dried beans or some other product to use as a weight.
Marinate in the refrigerator for 3 to 4 days, turning the fish every 24 hours.

To prepare the mustard sauce, combine the Dijon mustard, dry
mustard, sugar and vinegar in a bowl and mix well. Whisk in the oil
1 tablespoon at a time until thick. Stir in the dill weed.

To assemble and serve, remove the fish from the dish and drain.
Wipe off the seasonings and dill weed. Cut the fish very thinly at
an angle and garnish with dill weed and lemon wedges. Serve with small
slices of wheat bread or Pumpernickel bread and the mustard sauce.

Serves 20

Wine Recommendations: Champagne, Gewürztraminer, Sauvignon Blanc,
or Chenin Blanc. May also serve with Akvavit.

Pepper Pungency (continued)

*According to the Scoville scale,
the following peppers range
from the mildest to the hottest:*

Bell and Pimento—
   0 units

Pepperoncini—
   100 to 500 units

Anaheim, Mulato—
   500 to 1,000 units

Poblano—
   1,500 to 3,000 units

Jalapeño—
   3,500 to 4,500 units

Serrano—
   7,000 to 25,000 units

Arbol—
   15,000 to 30,000 units

Tabasco, Cayenne—
   30,000 to 50,000 units

Thai—
   50,000 to 105,000 units

Jamaican—
   100,000 to 200,000 units

Habanero—
   300,000 units

Scotch Bonnet—
   350,000 to 600,000 units

Fresh Salmon Tartare

This refreshing appetizer can be combined with greens to make a delicious salad.

1 (3-pound) salmon fillet
1 tablespoon chopped fresh dill weed
1 tablespoon grated lemon zest
1/4 cup sour cream
1 tablespoon Dijon mustard
2 tablespoons lemon juice
Salt and pepper to taste
Lemon slices and dill weed for garnish

Remove the skin from the salmon. Chop the salmon into small pieces and set aside. Combine the chopped dill weed, lemon zest, sour cream, mustard, lemon juice, salt and pepper in a bowl and mix well. Add the salmon and mix well. Shape the salmon mixture into a mound on a serving plate. Garnish with lemon slices and dill weed. Serve with toast or small pieces of pumpernickel bread.

Makes 6 cups

Wine Recommendations: Sauvignon Blanc, Chardonnay, Chablis, or Pouilly Fuissé

Photograph on page 13.

During the 1994 opera season, *the Greater Miami Opera and the Opera Guild, Inc. of Fort Lauderdale formed the Florida Grand Opera, Inc., making FGO the tenth-largest opera company in the United States. Since 1994 the Young Patronesses of the Opera have donated over $800,000 to the Florida Grand Opera, Inc. and its programs.*

Steak and Cebollitas Summer Rolls

This mouthwatering appetizer is a meal in itself. Please see the recipe for Cebollitas (page 72), which are pickled onions.

8 ounces sirloin steak, trimmed
Salt and pepper to taste
1/2 cup mayonnaise
2 tablespoons wasabi sauce
8 or more (8-inch) rice paper rounds
1 cup crumbled Gorgonzola cheese
1 cup Cebollitas, drained (page 72)
1 1/2 cups chopped arugula or less bitter salad greens

Preheat the grill or preheat the broiler. Season the steak with salt and pepper. Place on a grill rack or on a rack in a broiler pan and grill over medium-high heat or broil to 145 degrees on a meat thermometer for medium-rare. Cut the steak into thin strips. Mix the mayonnaise and wasabi sauce in a small bowl.

Place a double thickness of damp paper towels on a work surface and fill a shallow baking pan with warm water. Check the rice paper rounds and use only those that do not have holes. Soak one rice paper round at a time in warm water for 30 to 60 seconds or until pliable; do not allow them to become too soft. Carefully remove to the paper towels.

Arrange three slices of steak in a row across the bottom third (the part nearest you) of one soaked rice paper. Spread 2 tablespoons of the cheese, 2 tablespoons of the Cebollitas and 2 tablespoons of the arugula on top of the steak. Spread 1 tablespoon of the wasabi mayonnaise on top. Fold the bottom of the rice paper over the filling and begin rolling up tightly, stopping at the halfway point. Arrange 1 more tablespoon of the arugula along the crease. Fold in the ends and continue rolling. Place seam side down on a platter and cover with damp paper towels. Repeat to make seven more rolls. Serve the rolls whole or cut into halves diagonally. Cut into small pieces to serve as appetizers.

Note: These rolls can be made 2 hours ahead and chilled, covered with damp paper towels and then with plastic wrap. Bring to room temperature before serving.

Makes 8 whole rolls

Wine Recommendations: Zinfandel, Beaujolais, Chianti, or Malbec

Ginger Pork Dumplings

Pot stickers, dumplings, whatever you choose to call them—they are fabulous!

DIPPING SAUCE

1/2 cup light soy sauce

1 teaspoon sesame oil

1/4 cup water

3 tablespoons sugar

1/8 to 1/4 teaspoon crushed red pepper

DUMPLINGS

1 pound ground pork

2 tablespoons finely chopped ginger

3 tablespoons finely chopped scallions

2 ounces water chestnuts, finely chopped

1 teaspoon light brown sugar

1 teaspoon salt

2 tablespoons light soy sauce

1 tablespoon rice wine

2 teaspoons sesame oil

1 teaspoon cornstarch

40 square won ton wrappers

To prepare the sauce, combine the soy sauce, sesame oil, water, sugar and red pepper in a bowl and mix well.

To prepare the dumplings, combine the pork, ginger, scallions, water chestnuts, brown sugar, salt, soy sauce, rice wine, sesame oil and cornstarch in a bowl and mix well. Place one won ton wrapper on a flat board. Place 1 teaspoon of the pork filling into the center of the wrapper. Moisten the edge of the wrapper with water using a brush or your fingertips and fold into a triangle. Bring the two outer tips together in the middle and pinch firmly to seal. Repeat with the remaining won tons and filling. (Store any remaining filling in an airtight container in the refrigerator or freezer for later use.)

Steam the dumplings in a lightly oiled basket for 12 to 15 minutes or until cooked through. Serve with the dipping sauce.

Makes 40 dumplings

Wine Recommendations: Riesling or Gewürztraminer

Corn Bread Appetizers with Corn, Black Bean and Manchego Cheese Topping

The corn bread alone is delicious; with the topping it is fabulous.

MANCHEGO CHEESE CORN BREAD

1/2 cup finely ground yellow cornmeal
1/2 cup all-purpose flour
1/2 teaspoon baking soda
1 teaspoon salt
2 eggs
1/3 cup shortening, melted
1 cup plus 2 tablespoons buttermilk
1 cup (4 ounces) shredded manchego cheese

APPETIZERS

1 tablespoon unsalted butter
1 cup fresh corn kernels, or 1 cup drained thawed frozen corn kernels
1 jalapeño chile, seeded and chopped
1 cup black beans, drained (see Note below)
2 tablespoons lime juice
1 cup (4 ounces) shredded manchego cheese
1/2 cup coarsely chopped cilantro for garnish

To prepare the corn bread, preheat the oven to 375 degrees. Mix the cornmeal, flour, baking soda and salt together in a medium bowl. Combine the eggs, shortening and buttermilk in a bowl and mix well. Stir in the cheese. Fold into the cornmeal mixture. Pour into a lightly greased 11×14-inch glass baking dish. Bake for 20 minutes or until a wooden pick inserted in the center comes out clean. Cool and then cut into 1 1/2-inch squares.

To prepare the appetizers, increase the oven temperature to 450 degrees. Melt the butter in a large skillet over medium heat. Add the corn and jalapeño chile and sauté for 3 minutes. Remove from the heat to cool. Stir in the black beans and lime juice. Place the corn bread squares on an ungreased baking sheet. Gently dollop 1 tablespoon of the black bean mixture on each corn bread square, mounding in the middle and being careful not to spread the mixture to the sides. Top evenly with the cheese. Bake for 2 minutes or until the cheese melts. Garnish with the cilantro.

Note: If you are using canned black beans for this recipe, sauté 1/2 cup chopped green bell pepper, 1/2 cup chopped red bell pepper, 3/4 cup chopped onion, 1 garlic clove, minced, 1/4 teaspoon cayenne pepper and 1/4 teaspoon cumin in 1 tablespoon vegetable oil in a skillet and stir into the black beans before adding to the recipe.

Makes about 68 squares

Wine Recommendations: Gewürztraminer, Rioja, Albariño, Dão, or White Zinfandel

West Indian Empanadas

Directions are given for preparing these delicious empanadas the traditional way as well as a low-fat way. These empanadas are filled with a type of picadillo flavored with West Indian spices.

PICADILLO FILLING
    8 ounces ground beef
    8 ounces ground pork
    1 onion, chopped
    2 garlic cloves, minced
    1/2 to 1 teaspoon ground thyme
    1/2 teaspoon cumin
    1/2 teaspoon allspice
    1/2 cup tomato juice or vegetable juice cocktail
    3 tablespoons red wine
    3 tablespoons raisins, soaked and drained
    6 pimento-stuffed green olives, chopped
    Salt and pepper to taste
    2 to 4 tablespoons dry bread crumbs (optional)

EMPANADAS
    40 empanada wrappers or won ton wrappers, thawed
    2 eggs, lightly beaten for the traditional way,
        or 2 egg whites, lightly beaten for the low-fat way
    18 tablespoons (about) vegetable oil for the traditional way

To prepare the filling, brown the ground beef, ground pork, onion and garlic in a large saucepan, stirring until the ground beef and ground pork are crumbly; drain. Add the thyme, cumin, allspice, tomato juice, wine, raisins, olives, salt and pepper. Simmer for 10 minutes, stirring constantly. Process in a food processor until coarsely ground, adding the bread crumbs if the filling is too thin. Adjust the seasonings to taste. Chill, covered, in the refrigerator.

To prepare the empanadas the traditional way, place one wrapper on a work surface and brush the edges with the eggs. Spoon 1 heaping tablespoon of the chilled filling onto the center and fold the wrapper over the filling to form a small triangle. (Fold into a half-moon shape if using round wrappers.) Press the edges together to seal and crimp with a fork. Repeat with the remaining wrappers and filling. Heat 3 tablespoons of the oil in a large nonstick skillet over medium heat. Fry four empanadas at a time for 1 1/2 minutes per side or until brown. Remove to a plate lined with paper towels to drain. Repeat with the remaining empanadas, adding 3 tablespoons oil (or more) per batch. (To prepare like dumplings, fry for 30 seconds on each side. Steam for 4 to 5 minutes and then fry again.)

To prepare the empanadas the low-fat way, preheat the oven to 400 degrees. Coat a nonstick baking sheet with nonstick cooking spray. Lightly brush the edge of each wrapper with the egg whites. Place a tablespoon of the filling in the center of each and fold the wrappers in half to make a triangular pastries or half-moon shapes if using round wrappers. Press the edges together to seal and crimp with a fork. Place on the prepared baking sheet and coat the tops with nonstick cooking spray. Bake for 6 to 8 minutes or until crisp and golden brown.

Note: Empanadas can be prepared ahead. Arrange in a single layer on a foil-lined baking sheet and cover with plastic wrap. Chill for up to 6 hours or freeze for up to 3 days. If frozen, thaw the empanadas before continuing with the recipe.

Makes 40 empanadas

Wine Recommendations: Cabernet Sauvignon, Cabernet Franc, Syrah, Chianti, Beaujolais, or Montepulciano

Corn Soufflés with Sherry Béchamel Sauce

Plan to make an impression with these beautiful individual appetizers at a seated dinner. This is a Venezuelan appetizer and is usually made with Guyana cheese, although you can substitute another hard cheese.

SOUFFLÉS
1 cup white cornmeal
2³/4 cups boiling water
1 tablespoon sugar
1 teaspoon salt
2 tablespoons butter
2 egg yolks, lightly beaten
2 egg whites, stiffly beaten
4 ounces hard cheese such as Guyana,
    manchego or Parmesan, cut into
    6 small wedges and chilled

SHERRY BÉCHAMEL SAUCE
1 tablespoon butter
³/4 to 1 tablespoon all-purpose flour
¹/2 cup milk
¹/2 to 1 teaspoon sherry

ASSEMBLY
¹/4 cup high-quality olive oil
Chopped parsley for garnish

To prepare the soufflés, preheat the oven to 450 degrees. Stir the cornmeal into the boiling water in a saucepan. Reduce the heat to low and add the sugar, salt and butter. Cook until the mixture is thick and creamy, stirring constantly. Stir in the egg yolks. Fold in the egg whites. Fill six to eight lightly buttered popover or soufflé dishes one-third from the rim with the cornmeal mixture. Place a wedge of the cheese on top of each. Fill with the remaining cornmeal mixture. Place the dishes on a baking sheet and bake for 8 to 10 minutes or until the tops are golden brown.

To prepare the sauce, melt the butter in a saucepan over low heat. Stir in the flour gradually. Add the milk and sherry. Simmer until thickened and smooth, whisking constantly.

To serve, lightly cover each appetizer plate with the olive oil. Remove the soufflé dishes from the oven and let stand for 5 minutes to cool. Slide a knife carefully around the edge of each dish and unmold onto the prepared appetizer plates. Dollop each with the sauce. Garnish with the parsley.

Note: The soufflés should ooze cheese when cut.

Serves 6 to 8

Wine Recommendations: Chardonnay, Sauvignon Blanc, Pouilly Fuissé, Chablis, or Albariño

Tasty Crostini

This recipe is for a delicious crostini which can be served either baked or cold. If you decide to bake it, it tastes best when served immediately. Bake a few at a time and pass them around to your guests.

1 narrow white French baguette
5 thin slices Black Forest ham
1 cup high-quality mayonnaise
1 cup (4 ounces) finely grated Gruyère cheese
1 (14-ounce) can artichoke hearts, drained and finely chopped
2 garlic cloves, finely chopped
3 scallions, chopped into small pieces
1/4 cup sliced almonds

To prepare baked crostini, preheat the oven to 375 degrees. Cut the baguette into 1/4-inch slices. Place on a baking sheet and bake for 5 minutes. Chop the ham into fine pieces. Combine the mayonnaise, cheese, artichoke hearts, garlic and ham in a bowl and mix well. (The mixture can be chilled at this point and the baked bread wrapped and stored until prepared for baking later in the day.) Preheat the oven to 425 degrees. Spread the ham mixture evenly over the toasted sides of the baguette slices. Top each crostini alternately with two or three scallion pieces or two almond slices. Place on a baking sheet and bake on the top oven rack for 5 minutes. Serve immediately.

To prepare cold crostini, preheat the oven to 375 degrees. Cut the baguette at an angle into twelve 1/4×3-inch slices. Place on a baking sheet and bake for 5 minutes. Remove from the oven. Reduce the oven temperature to 250 degrees. Spread the almonds on a baking sheet and bake for 4 minutes or until golden brown. Combine the garlic, cheese and mayonnaise in a saucepan. Cook over low heat until the cheese is melted, stirring constantly. Remove from the heat to cool slightly. Spread a thick layer of the cheese mixture on the toasted side of each baguette slice. Cut the ham into twelve pieces. Fold one piece of ham around a spoonful of the artichoke hearts and place on each crostini. Top each crostini with two scallion pieces and two toasted almond slices. Serve immediately.

Makes 20 to 24 warm crostini or 8 to 12 cold crostini

Wine Recommendations: Fumé Blanc, Chardonnay, or Sauvignon Blanc

Photograph on page 53.

From Spain to Miami–Tapas Parties

Tapas have long been popular in Miami. Tapas are appetizers which can precede the meal or be a group of small meals served as the main meal. A true tapas party includes Spanish cheeses, olives, marcona almonds, and usually a dish with chorizo sausage or chorizo served on its own. Tapas are finger food and traditionally are eaten on small round tapas plates. For tapas recipes, please consider Arepas with Cebollitas (page 72); West Indian Empanadas (page 52); Corn Bread Appetizers with Corn, Black Bean and Manchego Cheese Topping (page 51); Manchego Crostini (page 56); Cold Hot Shrimp (page 42); Mussels Picante (page 189); Caponata (page 58) stuffed in cherry tomatoes; and of course, Summer Sangria (page 30).

Tapas are accompanied with sangria, cocktails, and most often with Sherry. Sherry is a fortified wine, which means a little extra alcohol has been added to it. There are a variety of Sherries.

Manchego Crostini

Plan to make the topping and toast the baguette slices early on the day of the party or even the day ahead. Assemble the crostini before your party. When your guests arrive, bake and serve.

3 plum tomatoes
1 (8-ounce) white French baguette
1 3/4 cups (7 ounces) finely shredded manchego cheese
1/2 cup mayonnaise
2 garlic cloves, finely chopped
3 scallions

Cut the tomatoes into halves lengthwise and cut off the ends. Remove the seeds and inner membranes and pat dry. Finely chop the tomatoes.

Preheat the oven to 375 degrees. Cut the baguette into 1/4-inch slices. Place on a baking sheet and bake for 5 minutes. Combine the tomatoes, cheese, mayonnaise and garlic in a bowl and mix well. (The mixture can be chilled at this point and the baked bread wrapped and stored until prepared for baking later in the day.)

Preheat the oven to 425 degrees. Chop the scallions into small oval pieces, discarding the ends at the top and bottom of each scallion. Spread the cheese mixture evenly over the toasted sides of the baguette slices. Top each with two or three scallion pieces. Place on a baking sheet and bake on the top oven rack for 5 minutes. Serve immediately.

Note: If your baguette is smaller, you may have leftover topping. You may decide to use the topping for another use, or you may buy an additional baguette.

Makes 40 to 45 crostini

Wine Recommendations: Chardonnay, Albariño, Rioja, Dão, Fumé Blanc, or Sauvignon Blanc

Caramel Brie in Challah

This simple recipe is deliciously rich and serves well for brunch as well as for an appetizer.

2 round loaves challah
1 (12-ounce) wheel Brie cheese, rind removed
1/2 cup (1 stick) butter
1/2 cup packed light brown sugar
1/2 cup granulated sugar
1/2 cup heavy cream
1/4 teaspoon ground nutmeg
2 tablespoons sliced pecans, toasted

Preheat the oven to 325 degrees. Hollow out the center of one loaf of the bread and fit the cheese snugly in the center, leaving a 1-inch wall of the bread above it. Cut the center and remaining loaf of bread into bite-size squares to use for dipping.

Melt the butter, brown sugar and granulated sugar in a saucepan over low heat, stirring constantly. Add the cream gradually, stirring constantly until the mixture is blended and smooth. Stir in the nutmeg. Cook until the mixture is caramelized and turns golden brown. Pour over the cheese until the caramel is 1/2 inch from the top of the bread, reserving the remaining caramel for the top. Bake for 15 minutes or until the cheese softens. Place on a serving platter and pour the reserved caramel into the center, allowing it to spill over and down the sides of the bread. Sprinkle with the pecans. Serve immediately with the bread squares.

Serves 8 to 10

Wine Recommendations: Beaujolais, Chianti, or Cabernet Franc

From Spain to Miami— Tapas Parties *(continued)*

The most commonly used Sherry for tapas are the Fino Sherries, which are light, dry, and pale in color and are best served chilled in Sherry Copita glasses or on the rocks.

Oloroso Sherries, which are a dark amber color, have a nutty sweet flavor and go well with cheese, nuts, and creamy desserts. If you would like a Spanish wine other than a Sherry, consider a Cava, Spain's most famous sparkling wine, or a Rioja, a soft red wine with berry flavors that will be a great match for the more strongly flavored tapas.

Count on four to six appetizers per person if you are serving a meal. If you are just serving appetizers with cocktails, plan on serving twelve pieces per person.

A portion of meat or chicken per person is 1/3 pound; the portion of fish per person is 1/2 pound.

Unless you know differently, always assume that some of your guests will be vegetarian.

A portion of vegetables, rice, pasta, or salad is 1/2 cup.

A three-layer cake will serve fifteen; a two-layer cake will serve twelve.

A 9×13-inch pan of bar cookies will provide twenty-eight cookies.

A 9-inch pie or tart as dessert will serve eight to ten.

Always plan to serve some items at room temperature so you can easily focus on the few items that must stay hot or cold.

Caponata

For a tapas party, finely chop the eggplant, onion, mushrooms, bell peppers, and olives and stuff into cherry tomatoes. If you are not stuffing cherry tomatoes, you can chop these vegetables as directed in the recipe and serve with crackers, flatbread, or toast. This dish can also be served as an accompaniment to pork or to an oily fish such as grouper.

2 medium to large eggplant
1 teaspoon salt
1 large red onion, finely chopped
2 ribs celery, chopped
1/2 cup chopped fresh mushrooms
1/2 green bell pepper, chopped
1/2 red bell pepper, chopped
2 large garlic cloves, minced
1/3 cup olive oil
1/3 cup (or less) water
1/2 cup chopped stuffed green olives
1/4 cup chopped kalamata or gaeta olives
1/4 cup drained capers
1 tomato, chopped
2 tablespoons red wine vinegar
1/2 teaspoon ground pepper
1/2 teaspoon chopped fresh oregano, or
    slightly more if using dried

Cut the eggplant into large pieces. Place the eggplant in a strainer and sprinkle with the salt. Let stand in the strainer for 1 hour or longer to allow the bitter juices of the eggplant to drain. Place the eggplant on a paper towel and blot to dry. Chop the eggplant.

Sauté the eggplant, onion, mushrooms, bell peppers and garlic in the olive oil in a large saucepan until the vegetables become translucent. Add the water and simmer for 10 minutes. Stir in the green olives, kalamata olives, capers, tomato, vinegar, pepper and oregano. Simmer for 25 minutes, stirring frequently. Remove from the heat to cool.

Note: Caponata can be frozen for up to 2 months.

Makes 3 cups

Wine Recommendations: Sherry if serving with tapas; Fumé Blanc, Sauvignon Blanc, Pinot Noir, Montepluciano, Chianti Classico, Baudol, or Barolo

Sun-Dried Tomato Mousse

Everyone enjoys this creamy and satisfying cocktail party staple.

I cup (2 sticks) unsalted butter, softened
I6 ounces cream cheese, softened
1/2 cup oil-pack sun-dried tomatoes, drained and chopped
I garlic clove, pressed
I (6-ounce) can tomato paste
Leaves from I bunch basil, chopped
2 teaspoons salt
1/2 teaspoon freshly ground pepper
1/4 cup pine nuts, toasted
4 to 6 basil leaves and salad greens for garnish

Cream the butter in a mixing bowl until smooth but not fluffy. Add the cream cheese and mix well. Stir in the sun-dried tomatoes, garlic, tomato paste, chopped basil leaves, salt and pepper. Do not overmix. Spoon into a 6-inch springform pan and chill for 8 hours.

To serve, remove the mousse from the pan by placing the pan in hot water for 10 to 20 seconds. Release the side of the pan and invert the mousse onto a serving platter. Smooth the top with a warm knife. Sprinkle the pine nuts evenly on top and garnish with the fresh basil leaves. Garnish the platter with salad greens. Serve with water crackers or breadsticks.

Note: Allow at least 9 hours to prepare this recipe prior to serving.

Makes 3 1/2 cups

Wine Recommendations: Pouilly Fumé, Sancerre, Chianti, Prosecco, or Sauvignon Blanc

Although some brands of commercial (not from concentrate) orange juice may work as a substitute for fresh orange juice, bottled lemon and lime juice are never a good substitute. Bottled Key lime juice can be substituted, but the quality will not be as high as freshly squeezed Key limes. Persian limes are the most common type of lime sold in supermarkets. One Persian lime produces about 1 1/2 tablespoons of juice. Key limes produce only about 1 tablespoon of juice, so be sure to buy in quantity when making Key lime pie.

Haas Avocado Guacamole

The Haas avocado has a rough, almost black skin. In spite of its outward appearance, it is the most popular avocado because of its small pit and smooth, buttery texture.

Juice of 1 lemon
4 ripe Haas avocados
1/2 cup plus 1 tablespoon chopped red onion
7 to 9 dashes of Tabasco sauce
2 garlic cloves, pressed
1 teaspoon Maldon's sea salt, or to taste
1 teaspoon freshly ground pepper, or to taste
4 Roma tomatoes, seeded and chopped
Chopped cilantro for garnish

Pour the lemon juice in a large bowl. Peel the avocados and scoop the flesh from the avocados into the lemon juice, tossing gently to coat. Add the onion, Tabasco sauce, garlic, 1 teaspoon sea salt and 1 teaspoon pepper. Slice the avocados with two knives until chopped. Stir in the tomatoes gently. Taste and adjust seasonings if needed. Garnish with cilantro. Serve immediately.

Note: To keep the avocados green, store by placing plastic wrap directly on top of the mixture.

Makes 4 cups

Wine Recommendations: Riesling or Pinot Grigio. Serve also with margaritas.

*Clockwise: Old Florida Caviar,
Haas Avocado Guacamole,
and Gazpacho Andaluz*

Old Florida Caviar

A favorite on a warm evening. Serve with large corn chips or with larger Plantain Chips (page 63) to scoop up the dip.

2 tomatoes, seeded and chopped
1 bunch green onions, sliced
5 tablespoons fresh lime juice
2 tablespoons olive oil
3 garlic cloves, minced
1/2 teaspoon cumin
1 teaspoon salt

1 drop of Tabasco sauce, or
  1/2 teaspoon freshly ground pepper
  (optional)
1 (16-ounce) can black-eyed peas, rinsed
  and drained
2 tablespoons chopped fresh cilantro
Lettuce leaves

Combine the tomatoes, green onions, lime juice, olive oil, garlic, cumin, salt and Tabasco sauce in a bowl and mix well. Stir in the peas gently. Cover and chill for 4 hours or longer. Stir in the cilantro when ready to serve. Spoon into a serving bowl lined with lettuce leaves.

Makes 21/2 cups

Wine Recommendations: Beaujolais, Muscadet, Albariño, or Zinfandel

Photograph on page 61.

Red Pepper Pesto Dip

Serve with toasted whole wheat pita chips, crackers, or vegetables.

1 garlic clove, pressed
1/4 teaspoon salt
1/2 cup drained bottled roasted
  red peppers
6 tablespoons toasted almonds or
  untoasted walnuts
1 teaspoon pomegranate molasses, or
  2 teaspoons lemon juice

1/2 teaspoon salt
1/4 to 1/2 teaspoon black pepper
1/2 teaspoon cumin
1/8 teaspoon cayenne pepper
1/2 cup extra-virgin olive oil
Parsley for garnish

Mix the garlic with 1/4 teaspoon salt in a small bowl. Process with the red peppers, almonds, molasses, 1/2 teaspoon salt, the black pepper, cumin and cayenne pepper in a food processor for 1 minute or until smooth. Add the olive oil gradually, processing constantly. Spoon into a serving bowl and garnish with parsley.

Makes 1 cup

Wine Recommendations: Chianti Classico, Merlot, or Zinfandel

Curried Vegetable Dip

Juice of 1/2 lemon
1/2 onion, chopped
1 garlic clove, minced
1 teaspoon salt
1/2 teaspoon black pepper
1/4 teaspoon dry mustard
1 tablespoon ketchup
1 teaspoon curry powder

1 tablespoon mayonnaise
1 tablespoon paprika
1/4 teaspoon red pepper
1/2 teaspoon dried parsley
1 tablespoon horseradish
1/4 teaspoon celery seeds
2 cups mayonnaise

Process the lemon juice, onion, garlic, salt, black pepper, dry mustard, ketchup, curry powder, 1 tablespoon mayonnaise, the paprika and red pepper in a food processor or blender for several minutes. Add the parsley, horseradish and celery seeds and pulse until blended. Add 2 cups mayonnaise and pulse until blended. Spoon into a storage container and store, covered, in the refrigerator for up to 2 weeks. Serve with carrot sticks, celery sticks, broccoli pieces, cherry tomatoes and cauliflower pieces.

Makes 2 1/2 cups

Wine Recommendations: Chardonnay, Chenin Blanc, Fumé Blanc, Gewürztraminer, Riesling, or Sauvignon Blanc

Photograph on page 45.

Plantain Chips

6 green plantains
6 cups vegetable oil

2 teaspoons salt

Cut off the ends of the plantains and score the skin four or five times. Soak the plantains in a large bowl of cold water for 10 minutes. Peel with a vegetable peeler and your fingers. Rinse the peeled plantains and pat dry. Cut diagonally into narrow pieces about 1/8 inch thick.

Heat the oil in a heavy saucepan until small bubbles form when a piece of plantain is dropped into the oil. Add the plantains and fry until crisp and golden brown. Remove with tongs to several layers of paper towels to drain. Sprinkle with the salt.

Serves 10

Photograph on page 36.

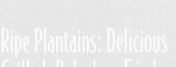

Ripe Plantains: Delicious Grilled, Baked, or Fried

Everyone adores cooked, ripe plantains as a side dish for roasted meats. The plantain is a member of the banana family and has a thicker skin than a common banana. Since the skin is thicker, it is harder to peel when green.

To bake, fry, or grill ripe plantains, choose only very black plantains with no mildew on the skin. To fry a ripe plantain, peel the skin and cut the fruit diagonally into slices. Heat vegetable oil in a skillet until small bubbles form when a piece of plantain is dropped into the oil. Add the plantains and fry for 2 to 3 minutes or until golden brown. Ripe plantains can also be baked in a covered dish in a 350-degree oven for 30 to 35 minutes. If you prefer them grilled, preheat the grill. Cut the plantains into large diagonal slices and place in a lightly greased grill basket. Grill over direct heat until lightly seared and then grill over indirect heat until cooked through.

Mango Tips

A ripe mango will have a fruity aroma at the stem end and will feel slightly soft, like a ripe peach. Mangos will ripen at room temperature or in a paper bag and will keep for up to a week at room temperature and longer in a refrigerator.

Cutting a mango is a challenge! To chop mangoes for salsas, pare the skin off with a sharp knife since a peeler will not be strong enough for the tough, leathery skin. Cut into halves lengthwise and remove the large seed. Gently pare away the tougher flesh that was around the seed.

Tropical Fruit and Pepper Salsa

A tasty salsa with a little bit of everything.

1 cup chopped ripe papaya
1 cup chopped ripe pineapple
2 tangerines, sectioned
1/2 red bell pepper, finely chopped
1/2 yellow bell pepper, finely chopped
2 green onions, thinly sliced
2 tablespoons cilantro, chopped
Juice of 2 limes
Salt and pepper to taste
1 to 2 tablespoons finely chopped seeded Anaheim chile or
   long green chile

Combine the papaya, pineapple, tangerines, bell peppers, green onions, cilantro, lime juice, salt and pepper in a bowl and mix well. Stir in the chile a little at a time, tasting to check for desired spiciness. Serve chilled or at room temperature.

Serves 8

Festive Fruit Salsa

Many South Florida cooks have their own favorite fruit salsa recipes. As with every salsa, add the cilantro and chiles in proportions that please you.

2 cups chopped fresh papaya
1 cup chopped fresh pineapple
1/2 cup chopped red onion
2 to 6 tablespoons chopped cilantro leaves
2 tablespoons olive oil
2 tablespoons lime juice
1 to 2 teaspoons chopped jalapeño chiles

Combine the papaya, pineapple, onion, cilantro, olive oil, lime juice and jalapeño chiles in a bowl and mix well. Serve chilled or at room temperature.

Serves 8

Avocado, Mango and Papaya Salsa

Your guests will love this salsa with chips or as a side dish with grilled fish.

1 cup finely chopped mango, drained
1 cup finely chopped papaya, drained
2 firm California avocados, chopped
1/4 cup fresh cilantro, chopped
1/4 cup finely chopped red onion
1 jalapeño chile, seeded and finely chopped
2 tablespoons fresh lime juice, or to taste

Combine the mango, papaya, avocados, cilantro, onion, jalapeño chile and lime juice in a bowl and mix well.

Note: Pineapple can be substituted for the mango or papaya.

Serves 8

Pineapple Salsa

Pineapple works well with other fruit in almost every salsa, but here it stands on its own.

1 tablespoon vegetable oil
1 cup chopped red onion
1 red bell pepper, chopped
2 tablespoons brown sugar
1 pineapple, cored and chopped
1/4 cup fresh lime juice
2 tablespoons chopped cilantro

Heat the oil in a saucepan over medium heat. Add the onion and bell pepper and sauté for 2 minutes. Add the brown sugar and heat until dissolved, stirring constantly. Remove from the heat and add the pineapple, lime juice and cilantro. Serve chilled or at room temperature.

Serves 8

Mango Tips (continued)

You may also simply cut the mango into halves, remove the seed and gently pare away the flesh which held the seed. Then cut the flesh in a grid pattern so you have small chunks of mango which then can be gently scooped out individually with a spoon.

Sweet, juicy mango is not only low in calories and filled with vitamins, minerals, anti-oxidants, and fiber, it also contains enzymes which aid digestion and can create a feeling of well-being. Unfortunately, it can cause an allergic reaction when you are handling the fruit, so wear gloves or rinse your hands afterward.

Romantic Interlude in the Tropics

Breads and Brunch

Miami's balmy nights are made for romance. As the sun sets and the night comes alive, the sky fills with stars. The full moon's golden light is reflected on the water and paints the lush landscape. The fragrance of orchids, night-blooming jasmine, and ginger perfume the air. Miami's verdant backyards and gardens are the perfect backdrop for any romantic celebration.

In a secluded garden spot a table is set for an intimate dinner for two. High-backed rattan chairs with inviting bright pink and orange cushions surround a table covered in a ribboned silk organza cloth. Adding to the Caribbean colonial feel, polished mahogany hurricane candles reflect off the gleaming silver trays and sparkling crystal serving bowls at this enchanting garden dinner. Whimsical brass monkeys host the table which is set with—what else?— "Monkey Business" china, placed on brown wicker chargers.

Using the surrounding natural vegetation, the pineapple-shaped centerpiece is covered with orchids, and the napkin rings are made from woven pandanus with decorative pineapples. Ginger pods and tree orchids add drama to the landscape.

To prolong the intimacy, the couple serve themselves from an old mahogany sideboard set up nearby. Beautiful vanda orchids, pin cushion protea, and ponsidium fill the vintage banana leaf pitcher and make a captivating centerpiece. Stone Crab Salad with Lime and Orange Vinaigrette starts the repast. The couple then leisurely enjoys the main course of this Caribbean dinner while they share a bottle of Riesling.

The sideboard now holds Versatile Key Lime Tartlets with fruit as well as a choice of aged rums. A Bahamian window shutter embellished with decorative pineapples and more orchids makes a pleasing backdrop for our dessert. A tart, some fruit, and a sip of twelve-year-old rum completes the meal.

Both stimulated and relaxed by their tropical dinner, seductive surroundings, and each other, the couple retires for the evening.

A romantic dinner for two is set up in a lovely lush garden in Coconut Grove. Standing mahogany hurricane candles provide soft light.

Menu

Stone Crab Salad with Lime and
Orange Vinaigrette *page 113*

Jamaican Johnnycake *page 73*

Jamaican Jerk Chicken *page 171*

Jamaican Pigeon Peas, Wild Rice and
Pepper Salad with Apple Cider
Vinaigrette *page 128*

Versatile Key Lime Tartlets with Fruit
page 238

Riesling

Aged Rum for Dessert

*The hostess has chosen to serve the
Jamaican Pigeon Peas, Wild Rice and
Pepper Salad with Apple Cider Vinaigrette in
a handsome crystal pedestal bowl. Jamaican
Jerk Chicken is served in a large "Monkey
Business" china platter. Large tea leaves
serve as a runner. A vintage banana leaf
pitcher holds vanda orchids, pin cushion
protea, and ponsidium.*

*Stone Crab Salad with Lime and Orange Vinaigrette with Jamaican Johnnycake is the first
course of this fabulous dinner. The native orchids in the centerpiece, the pillows and napkins
are all a bright tropical pink and orange. Whimsical brass monkeys host the table.*

Work Plan

THE DAY BEFORE

Chill Riesling for entrée.
Purchase stone crabs; don't have
   them cracked.
Chill stone crabs.
Prepare Lime and Orange Vinaigrette.
Marinate Jamaican Jerk Chicken.
Prepare Versatile Key Lime Tartlets
   and refrigerate.

ON THE DAY

Bake Johnnycake.
Prepare Jamaican Pigeon Peas, Wild Rice and
   Pepper Salad with Apple Cider Vinaigrette,
   but do not add cilantro; refrigerate.

Grill Jamaican Jerk Chicken. Cover and
   do not refrigerate until needed.
Peel the avocados for the Stone Crab Salad
   and toss them with some Lime and
   Orange Vinaigrette to prevent browning.

JUST BEFORE SERVING

Stir the cilantro into Jamaican Pigeon Peas,
   Wild Rice and Pepper Salad and place
   on a platter of greens to serve.
Crack the stone crabs and assemble the
   Stone Crab Salad in a glass bowl or
   on serving plates.

French Baguette

This delicious classic bread is the perfect accompaniment for many of our recipes. It could especially be used in Tasty Crostini (page 55) and Manchego Crostini (page 56).

1 envelope dry yeast
1/3 cup warm water
1/4 teaspoon sugar
3 1/2 cups all-purpose flour
2 teaspoons salt
1 cup (or more) cold water

Dissolve the yeast in the warm water in a cup or small bowl, stirring gently. Mix the sugar, flour and salt together in a large bowl. Stir in the yeast mixture. Add the cold water gradually, stirring until the mixture leaves the side of the bowl to form a moist ball. Knead the dough with lightly floured hands on a lightly floured surface for 5 minutes or until the dough is firm and nonsticky, continuing to lightly flour the surface as needed. If the dough is too dry, gradually add additional cold water. Place the dough in a greased bowl, turning to coat. Cover and let rise in a warm place for 1 hour.

Place the dough on a lightly floured surface and knead for 2 minutes. Divide the dough into two equal portions. Roll each portion into a long narrow cylindrical loaf. Place the loaves side by side on a lightly greased and floured baking sheet. Cut 1/4-inch-diagonal slashes 2 inches apart on the surface of each loaf. Cover and let rise for 1 hour.

Preheat the oven to 400 degrees. Bake the loaves for 20 minutes or until light golden brown. Cool on a wire rack.

Note: For a crisper crust, place a baking pan filled with 1 inch of hot water on the bottom oven rack under the baking sheet while baking the loaves.

Makes 2 loaves

Potato Crescent Knot Dinner Rolls

A light and tasty dinner roll that will complement many meals.

1 envelope dry yeast
1/4 cup warm water
1 egg
1/4 cup sugar
1/2 cup mashed potatoes
1/2 cup milk
1/2 cup (1 stick) butter, softened
1/2 teaspoon salt
3 to 31/2 cups all-purpose flour
1/4 cup (1/2 stick) butter, melted

Dissolve the yeast in the warm water in a cup or small bowl. Combine the egg and sugar in a large bowl and mix well. Add the potatoes, milk, 1/2 cup butter and the salt and mix well. Add the yeast mixture and 2 cups of the flour and mix well. Add the remaining flour gradually, stirring until the dough pulls from the side of the bowl. Shape the dough into a ball and knead on a lightly floured surface for 5 minutes or until smooth and elastic. Place the dough in a greased bowl, turning to coat the surface. Cover and let rise in a warm place for 1 hour or until doubled in bulk.

Lightly grease and flour two baking sheets. Remove the dough from the bowl and knead on a lightly floured surface. Divide the dough into twenty four portions. Roll each portion on a lightly floured surface into an 8-inch length to resemble a rope. Tie each rope into a bow knot and place on the prepared baking sheets. Let rise for 30 minutes or until doubled in bulk.

Preheat the oven to 375 degrees. Brush the rolls with 1/4 cup butter. Bake for 20 minutes or until golden brown. Remove to a wire rack to cool.

Makes 2 dozen

Photograph on page 109.

Sunshine Syrup

Heat 4 cups fresh orange juice in a saucepan until warm. Melt 1 cup (2 sticks) butter in a large saucepan over medium heat. Stir in 1 cup all-purpose flour. Reduce the heat to low and cook for 3 minutes, stirring constantly. Add the orange juice. Cook until the flour mixture is dissolved, stirring constantly. Stir in 3/4 cup sugar and the zest of 2 oranges. Simmer over low heat for 5 minutes. Serve over pancakes. This recipe makes about 1 quart.

Arepa Flour

Arepa flour is milled from cooked, dried corn kernels and is much finer than cornmeal and slightly coarser than all-purpose flour. It is usually sold as masarepa and can be made from either yellow or white corn. It should also be used for cuchapas and empanadas. Many cooks prefer it for spoon bread and corn bread, because it stays moister and is less gritty than cornmeal. You can buy it in Hispanic or gourmet markets or on-line through Goya.com or sabiasque.com.

Arepas with Cebollitas

Arepas are cheesy cornmeal pancakes and are delicious by themselves or with toppings. They are especially popular in Columbia, Nicaragua, and of course, Miami. Ours are topped with cebollitas, Nicaraguan pickled onions. Slow-cooked or pulled pork also makes a delicious topping for arepas. To vary the taste of the arepas, try other medium-soft cheeses.

CEBOLLITAS
- 1 red onion, chopped
- 1 or 2 Scotch bonnet chiles or other strong chiles, seeded and chopped
- 1/2 cup white vinegar
- 1 teaspoon fresh oregano, minced
- 1/2 teaspoon salt, or to taste
- 1/2 teaspoon sugar (optional)

AREPAS
- 1 1/2 cups milk
- 1/4 cup (1/2 stick) butter, cut into pieces
- 1 1/2 cups white arepa flour (see sidebar at left)
- 1 tablespoon sugar
- 1 teaspoon salt
- 1 cup (4 ounces) shredded white cheese, such as queso blanco or mozzarella cheese
- Vegetable oil for frying

To prepare the cebollitas, combine the onion, chiles, vinegar, oregano, salt and sugar in a bowl and stir until the sugar is dissolved. Chill, covered, for 12 hours or longer before serving, stirring occasionally. Cebollitas may be stored in the refrigerator for 3 weeks.

To prepare the arepas, bring the milk to a simmer in a saucepan and remove from the heat. Add the butter and stir until melted. Whisk the flour, sugar, salt and cheese in a large bowl. Add the milk mixture a small amount at a time, stirring to form a firm, slightly moist dough. Cover and let stand for 5 minutes.

Shape 1 tablespoon of the dough at a time into balls, adding more of the milk mixture if the dough becomes too stiff or the edges crack. Flatten each ball into a circle 1 3/4 inches in diameter and place on waxed paper or baking parchment.

Heat 1 tablespoon oil in a 12-inch skillet over medium-low heat. Cook the arepas in batches for 4 to 5 minutes on each side or until golden, turning once and adding additional oil as needed. Remove the arepas to a baking sheet. Arepas can be cooled and warmed later. You can also cook until partially cooked through. Just before serving, bake, covered, in a 350-degree oven until cooked through. Serve arepas topped with room temperature or chilled cebollitas.

Serves 8

Jamaican Johnnycake

The coconut and cinnamon makes this the perfect bread for Jamaican Jerk Chicken (page 111).

1 tablespoon butter
1 1/2 cups all-purpose flour
1 3/4 cups yellow cornmeal
2 teaspoons baking powder
1/2 teaspoon salt
1/2 teaspoon cinnamon
1 to 4 teaspoons nutmeg
1/2 teaspoon ground cloves
1/3 cup unsweetened coconut milk
1/3 cup milk
2/3 cup butter, softened
1/4 cup sugar
4 eggs
1 cup shredded coconut

Preheat the oven to 375 degrees. Grease two 5x8-inch loaf pans with 1 tablespoon butter and flour the bottom of each. Sift 1 1/2 cups flour, the cornmeal, baking powder, salt, cinnamon, nutmeg and cloves into a bowl. Stir in the coconut milk and milk gradually.

Cream 2/3 cup butter and the sugar in a mixing bowl until light and fluffy. Beat in the eggs one at a time. Stir in the flour mixture and coconut. Pour into the prepared pans and bake for 35 minutes or until golden brown and wooden picks inserted in the centers come out clean. Cool in the pans for 5 minutes. Invert onto wire racks to cool completely.

Makes 2 loaves

Working with Phyllo

With a little practice, phyllo dough is easy to use and is wonderful for all sorts of strudel and turnover combinations. Thaw frozen phyllo in the refrigerator for 3 to 10 hours before using. Since phyllo dough dries out quickly, prepare the filling mixture while the phyllo is defrosting.

When you remove the dough from the package, carefully unroll it so it won't tear. Be sure to handle phyllo gently and cover it with a damp towel as you are using it.

If your phyllo dough does tear, do not brush it with water. Brush torn areas with butter, patch with small pieces of dough, and brush again with butter to seal the patch. Since all phyllo dishes are made with melted butter or olive oil, always bake them on a pan which will allow the butter or oil to drain off.

If you wish to store leftover phyllo sheets, cover the sheets with plastic wrap. The phyllo should be thoroughly sealed. Store in the refrigerator for up to a week or refreeze for up to 3 months.

Sociable Apple Strudel

This strudel is a wonderful dish to make with friends before the holidays. This recipe will make six strudels, so each friend can take one home to freeze and serve when they need it. Multiethnic Miami also has cooks from Croatia, which is where this recipe originated.

15 ounces golden raisins or dried cranberries
1 tablespoon Kir or fruit brandy (optional)
3/4 cup plain bread crumbs
3/4 cup all-purpose flour
3 pounds Granny Smith apples
Lemon or lime juice

1 package fresh phyllo dough, or 1 1/2 packages frozen phyllo dough
1 cup (2 sticks) butter, melted
6 tablespoons granulated sugar
8 ounces chopped walnuts
Confectioners' sugar

Preheat the oven to 425 degrees. Marinate the raisins in the Kir in a bowl. Mix the bread crumbs and flour together. Peel the apples and cut into small chunks. Squeeze lemon juice over the apples to prevent browning. Unroll the phyllo dough onto a baking sheet and cover with a damp dish towel to prevent drying out. Lay a clean dish towel on a work surface. Place two sheets of the phyllo dough on the cloth so that they are lined up at the top and bottom but do not overlap for about 2 inches on each side. Brush the phyllo dough with some of the melted butter. Lay another two sheets of phyllo dough over the first two sheets and place a final phyllo sheet in the center. Brush with some of the melted butter. Lay one-sixth of the apples in a mound from left to right, beginning about 2 inches from the top and bottom edges and 1 inch from the sides. Sprinkle the apples with 1 tablespoon of the granulated sugar, 2 tablespoons of the bread crumb mixture, 2 tablespoons of the walnuts and 2 tablespoons of the raisins. Fold the sides of the phyllo dough near the apples toward the center. Roll the phyllo dough over just enough to cover the apples, using the dish towel, and brush with some of the butter. Repeat until the entire strudel is brushed with butter. Repeat the process five times to make six strudels.

Reduce the oven temperature to 350 degrees. Carefully place each strudel seam side down on a baking sheet lined with foil. Bake for 20 minutes or until golden brown. Sprinkle with confectioners' sugar before serving. Serve warm with or without vanilla ice cream.

Note: You may wrap the foil loosely around the strudels and freeze. Do not thaw before baking. Bake, uncovered, for 20 minutes or until golden brown.

Makes 6

Guava Empanadas

Empanadas, or fried turnovers, are enjoyed throughout Latin America and much of the Caribbean. Many Miamians won't start the day without a guava empanada and a Café Cubano (page 32).

2 cups all-purpose flour
1/2 teaspoon salt
2 tablespoons shortening
1 egg
1/2 cup milk
5 ounces guava paste
3 ounces cream cheese, softened
1 to 3 tablespoons sugar (optional)
2 eggs, lightly beaten
Cinnamon-sugar (optional)

Process the flour and salt in a food processor to combine. Add the shortening a tablespoonful at a time, pulsing until the mixture resembles coarse cornmeal. Add the egg and pulse to mix. Add the milk 1 tablespoonful at a time until the dough sticks together, processing constantly. Scrape the dough into a sealable plastic bag and seal the bag. Flatten in the bag into a disc shape and chill for 30 minutes. Roll the dough 1/8 inch thick on a lightly floured surface. Cut into 3-inch circles with a round cookie cutter or large biscuit cutter.

Cream the guava paste and cream cheese in a mixing bowl. Add the sugar as needed for the desired sweetness. Place a heaping teaspoon of the filling in the center of each circle, taking care that the filling does not touch the edge. Fold each circle in half and seal the edges together using wet fingertips. Press the edges together with a fork.

Preheat the oven to 325 degrees. Place the empanadas on a baking sheet and brush lightly with the beaten eggs. Bake for 15 minutes and roll while hot in cinnamon-sugar.

Note: You may use forty frozen empanada wrappers instead of making your own. To fry the empanadas, do not brush with the beaten eggs. Pour vegetable oil to a depth of 1 inch in a heavy skillet and heat until small bubbles begin to rise. Add the empanadas and fry for 1 minute on each side or until golden brown, turning with a slotted spoon.

Makes 40

Guavas, the Abundant Fruit

Guava trees are prolific in South Florida. The luscious fruit of the guava tastes similar to strawberries. Unfortunately, guava fruit has many small, hard black seeds and is messy to eat. Rather than attempting to eat the raw fruit, most South Floridians make or buy products made from guava such as guava paste, nectar, marmalade, jelly, and guava shells.

Guava paste is a thick red jelly which is sold in cardboard boxes and in flat tin cans. It is sold in Hispanic markets and in all South Florida supermarkets. The paste in the tin cans has a better flavor and should be used in all recipes.

Stuffed guava shells are a popular traditional Hispanic dessert, particularly for Cubans. To make Stuffed Guava Shells, drain and chill a 16-ounce can of guava shells. Fill the shells with a creamed mixture of 10 ounces cream cheese, softened, 1 tablespoon sugar, and 3 ounces of your favorite citrus juice.

Fabulous Fig Cake with Buttermilk Topping

CAKE

- 2 cups all-purpose flour
- 1 teaspoon baking soda
- 1 teaspoon salt
- 1/2 teaspoon cloves
- 1 teaspoon cinnamon
- 3 eggs, lightly beaten
- 1 1/2 cups sugar
- 1 1/2 cups vegetable oil
- 1 cup buttermilk
- 1 cup fig preserves
- 1 cup chopped pecans
- 1 tablespoon vanilla extract

TOPPING

- 1/2 cup (1 stick) butter
- 1 cup sugar
- 1/2 cup buttermilk
- 1 teaspoon vanilla extract
- 1 tablespoon cornstarch
- 1/2 teaspoon baking soda

To prepare the cake, preheat the oven to 350 degrees. Sift the flour, baking soda, salt, cloves and cinnamon together. Combine the eggs and sugar in a large bowl and mix well. Stir in the oil. Add the flour mixture and buttermilk alternately, mixing well after each addition and beginning and ending with the flour mixture. Stir in the fig preserves, pecans and vanilla. Spoon into a greased and floured tube pan. Bake for 1 hour.

To prepare the topping, combine the butter, sugar, buttermilk, vanilla, cornstarch and baking soda in a heavy saucepan and mix well. Bring to a boil and boil for 3 minutes, stirring constantly.

To assemble, remove the cake from the oven and immediately pour the topping over the top to seep through the cake. After the topping has seeped through the cake and while the cake is still warm, remove from the pan.

Serves 14

During 2007 over 30,000 elementary school students in South Florida saw performances of the children's opera, *Rumpelstiltskin*, which was produced by The Young Patronesses of the Opera. A hugely popular program, the In-School Opera combines classic children's stories, slapstick, and fine operatic singing to give thousands of children their first experience of opera. The In-School Opera program was started in 1975 by President Loraine Kayal, and past President Louise Todaro has served as director of the program since its inception. Louise and her committee produce a new children's opera every two years. South Florida schoolchildren have enjoyed performances of *Cinderella*, *The Pied Piper*, *The Ransom of Red Chief* and many other children's operas.

Kiwifruit Breakfast Cake

The sweet topping is a great contrast to the slightly tart kiwifruit.

2 cups all-purpose flour
1 teaspoon baking soda
1/8 teaspoon salt
1/2 cup (1 stick) butter, softened
1 1/2 cups granulated sugar
2 eggs, lightly beaten
1 teaspoon vanilla extract
1/2 cup sour cream
1 1/2 cups chopped peeled kiwifruit (about 7 kiwifruit)
2 tablespoons granulated sugar
2 tablespoons brown sugar
1 tablespoon butter, softened

Preheat the oven to 325 degrees. Sift the flour, baking soda and salt in a medium bowl. Cream 1/2 cup butter and 1 1/2 cups granulated sugar in a mixing bowl until light and fluffy. Beat in the eggs and vanilla. Add the flour mixture and sour cream alternately, mixing well after each addition and beginning and ending with the flour mixture. Stir in the kiwifruit. Pour into a greased and floured 7×12-inch baking pan. Combine 2 tablespoons granulated sugar, the brown sugar and 1 tablespoon butter in a bowl and mix until crumbly. Sprinkle over the top of the batter. Bake for 40 to 50 minutes or until a wooden pick inserted in the center comes out clean.

Serves 12

Measuring Flour

Since flour tends to compact, it is important to stir your flour with a fork or whisk before measuring it. Use a spoon or small scoop to spoon your flour into the measuring cup. Don't use the measuring cup as a scoop, because you will end up with too much flour. If possible, level the top of the flour with a straight edge to get an even cup. If you only have a glass or plastic liquid measuring cup to measure flour and the cup is larger than the quantity of flour required, gently tap the bottom of the cup to distribute the mounded flour. Hold the measuring cup up to eye level to make sure you have accurately measured the flour.

Mango Madness

During the 1930s and 1940s, groves of luscious mangoes flourished in Miami. Many new varieties of mangoes were cultivated in Miami groves, including the popular varieties we see in today's markets— Tommy Atkins, Kent, Keitt, and Haden. Today many of the groves have been lost to development, but yards, parks, and public grounds still have mango trees which bear wonderful fruit. Locals trade or give away fruit to neighbors and friends, so recipes using mangoes are widely sought after.

When buying a mango, make sure it has a fruity aroma since unripe mangoes have no scent. A ripe mango should be very slightly soft. Some mangoes ripen to a golden yellow or green; others ripen to a combination of pink, orange, and green shades. Like many fruits, mangoes will ripen when stored in a paper bag for a few days.

Mango Bread with Citrus Glaze

The combination of butter and sour cream keeps this bread moist.

BREAD
   1 1/2 cups all-purpose flour
   1 teaspoon baking soda
   1/2 teaspoon salt
   1 teaspoon cinnamon
   1/2 cup (1 stick) butter, softened
   1 cup sugar
   2 eggs
   1/2 cup sour cream
   1 teaspoon vanilla extract
   1 cup mashed mango

CITRUS GLAZE
   1 1/2 tablespoons fresh lemon juice
   3 tablespoons fresh orange juice
   3/4 teaspoon vanilla extract
   1 1/2 cups plus 2 tablespoons confectioners' sugar
   1/2 cup chopped pecans, toasted (optional)

To prepare the bread, preheat the oven to 350 degrees. Sift the flour, baking soda, salt and cinnamon together. Cream the butter and sugar in a large mixing bowl until light and fluffy. Stir in the eggs one at a time. Stir in the flour mixture. Add the sour cream and vanilla and mix well. Stir in the mango. Pour into a greased and floured 9-inch loaf pan. Bake for 1 hour or until a wooden pick inserted in the center comes out clean. Remove from the oven and cool in the pan for 20 minutes.

To prepare the glaze, mix the lemon juice, orange juice and vanilla in a small bowl. Sift in the confectioners' sugar and whisk until dissolved and smooth.

To assemble, place paper towels under a wire rack. Invert the warm loaf onto the rack. Drizzle the glaze over the top and sides of the loaf. Sprinkle with the pecans. (For a thicker layer of glaze, drizzle with additional glaze after the initial layer of glaze cools.)

Note: You may bake in several smaller loaf pans or one 9×9-inch baking pan, but reduce the amount of baking time.

Serves 10

Poppy Seed Muffins

If you wish to make amends with a friend or a co-worker, consider baking and giving them these delicious muffins. As soaking the poppy seeds washes away their bitterness, presenting a gift of these muffins or this cake will do the same.

1/4 cup fresh poppy seeds
1 cup buttermilk
2 1/2 cups all-purpose flour
1 teaspoon baking soda
1/2 teaspoon salt
1 cup (2 sticks) butter, softened
1 1/2 cups sugar
4 eggs
1 teaspoon vanilla extract
1/2 cup sugar
1 1/2 tablespoons cinnamon

Soak the poppy seeds in the buttermilk in a bowl in the refrigerator for 6 to 8 hours. Preheat the oven to 350 degrees. Mix the flour, baking soda and salt together. Cream the butter in a large mixing bowl. Stir in 1 1/2 cups sugar gradually. Beat until the mixture is light and fluffy. Add the eggs one at a time, beating well after each addition. Stir in the vanilla. Add the flour mixture alternately with the buttermilk mixture, beating well after each addition and beginning and ending with the flour mixture.

Mix 1/2 cup sugar and the cinnamon together. Pour the batter into paper-lined miniature muffin cups or into greased and floured miniature muffin cups, filling each no more than three-fourths full. Sprinkle with the cinnamon-sugar mixture and bake for 15 to 20 minutes or until the muffins test done. Cool on a wire rack.

Variation: For **Poppy Seed Bundt Cake**, sprinkle one-third of the cinnamon-sugar in the bottom of a greased and floured bundt pan. Pour one-half of the batter into the prepared pan. Sprinkle with one-half of the remaining cinnamon-sugar. Add the remaining batter and sprinkle the remaining cinnamon-sugar over the top. Bake for 50 minutes. Cool in the pan on a wire rack for 1 hour. Remove to a cake platter.

Makes 2 dozen miniature muffins

Photograph on page 108.

Mango Madness (continued)

Ripe mangoes make delicious smoothies and are a great way to use slightly overripe mangoes. For a Mango Smoothie, combine 1 cup chopped mango with 1 cup low-fat or nonfat plain or vanilla yogurt in a blender. Add 1/2 cup ice, preferably crushed. Add milk if desired. Blend and serve.

Sectioning Citrus

With a sharp knife, cut off both ends of the citrus. Stand up on one end and carefully cut in an arc from top to bottom, removing all the peel and bitter white pith. Repeat this process until you have removed all the peel and pith. Carefully cut into the membranes of each section. Cut away one section at a time until all the sections have been removed.

For drinks and desserts, use a canella knife to make citrus peel spirals. Hold the knife against the top of the fruit and steadily drag it around the fruit to get a spiral of peel. Wrap the spiral around a pencil and secure it with a pin, then freeze it for five minutes. Citrus peels are pretty both inside clear drinks and dangling over the side of drinks made with citrus or citrus-flavored alcohol.

Summer Vegetable Frittata

Tempt your guests at lunch or brunch with this flavorful frittata.

3 tablespoons olive oil
1 large sweet onion, thinly sliced
3 garlic cloves, minced
3 summer squash, sliced 1/4 inch thick
3 zucchini, sliced 1/4 inch thick
1 red bell pepper, cut into 1/4-inch strips
1 green bell pepper, cut into 1/4-inch strips
1 yellow bell pepper, cut into 1/4-inch strips
8 ounces fresh mushrooms, sliced
6 eggs
1/4 cup heavy whipping cream
2 teaspoons salt
2 teaspoons freshly ground pepper
Pinch of nutmeg
2 cups (1/2-inch) cubed day-old French bread
8 ounces cream cheese, chopped into small pieces
2 cups (8 ounces) shredded Swiss cheese

Preheat the oven to 350 degrees. Grease the bottom and side of a 10-inch springform pan. Heat the olive oil in a large saucepan over medium-high heat. Add the onion, garlic, squash, zucchini, bell peppers and mushrooms and sauté until the vegetables are evenly cooked and tender-crisp. Drain the vegetables in a colander or sieve.

Whisk the eggs in a large mixing bowl. Stir in the cream. Add the salt, pepper and nutmeg and stir well. Stir in the bread, cream cheese and Swiss cheese. Stir in the vegetables. Pour into the prepared pan and pack tightly. Place the pan in an 10×15-inch baking pan to catch any leaks. Bake for 1 hour or until firm to the touch, puffed and golden brown, covering with foil if needed to prevent overbrowning. Serve hot or at room temperature.

Note: The frittata can be reheated in a 350-degree oven for 15 minutes or until warm.

Serves 10

Tortilla de Papas y Cebollas (Spanish Omelet)

This large omelet can be served with or without the delicious sauce.

SAUCE

6 tomatoes
1 cup chopped onion
1 garlic clove, pressed
3 yellow bell peppers, cut into strips 1/2 inch wide
3 tablespoons olive oil
2 teaspoons fresh basil
Salt and freshly ground pepper to taste

OMELET

1/2 cup extra-virgin olive oil
2 garlic cloves, pressed
4 large potatoes, peeled and cut into 1/8-inch half-moon shapes
1 large onion, thinly sliced into half-moon shapes
6 eggs
Salt and pepper to taste

To prepare the sauce, fill a medium saucepan half full of water and bring to boil. Fill a bowl with cold water. Cut the cores from the tomatoes and score an "x" on the base of each with the tip of a small sharp knife. Immerse the tomatoes with a slotted spoon into the boiling water for 8 to 15 seconds, depending on the ripeness of the tomatoes. Remove the tomatoes and place in the cold water. Peel the tomatoes with a sharp knife when cool enough to handle. Cut each tomato into four pieces. Remove the seeds and drain the tomatoes. Sauté the onion, garlic and bell peppers in the olive oil in a saucepan until the onion is golden brown. Stir in the tomatoes, basil, salt and pepper. (To make the sauce ahead, prepare as directed but do not stir in the basil until just before serving.)

To prepare the omelet, heat the olive oil in a 9-inch omelet pan. Add the garlic and sauté until golden brown. Remove the garlic and discard. Add the potatoes to the pan and cook over medium heat for 5 minutes. Add the onion and cook until tender, stirring constantly. Beat the eggs with a fork in a large bowl until slightly foamy. Add salt and pepper. Spoon the potato mixture with a slotted spoon into the eggs and mix well, leaving the drippings in the pan. Pour the egg mixture into the drippings in the omelet pan, adding additional oil if needed to prevent the eggs from sticking. Spread the egg mixture evenly in the pan and cook over medium heat, shaking the pan. Gently run a spatula around the edge of the omelet to loosen as the eggs begin to cook. Continue to cook until the eggs leave the side of the pan. Invert a plate over the pan and flip the omelet onto the plate. Slide the omelet back into the pan to brown the other side. Serve hot or at room temperature with the sauce.

Serves 4

Oven-Dried Tomatoes or Packaged?

Although time consuming, oven-dried tomatoes are easy to make and you are able to remove the tomatoes from the oven while they still have juice in them. They have a richer and fresher taste than packaged sun-dried tomatoes. When roasting oven-dried tomatoes, consider the recipe in which you are planning to use them and pour herb-infused oil which will complement the dish, such as oil infused with rosemary or thyme, on the tomatoes after they have baked. Do not pour oil on any oven-dried tomatoes which will be baked in a cheese dish. Oven-dried tomatoes are a wonderful addition to many sandwiches.

Crustless Egg Quiche

This is similar to a soufflé and is very popular with those who want a lighter cheese dish. One cup of chopped ham added to this dish is a nice addition.

1/2 cup (1 stick) butter
1/2 cup all-purpose flour
6 eggs
1 cup milk
1 pound Monterey Jack cheese, cut into cubes
3 ounces cream cheese, softened
2 cups small-curd cottage cheese
1 teaspoon baking powder
1 teaspoon salt
1 teaspoon sugar

Preheat the oven to 350 degrees. Melt the butter in a small saucepan. Add the flour and stir until smooth; remove from the heat. Beat the eggs and milk in a large bowl. Add the Monterey Jack cheese, cream cheese, cottage cheese, baking powder, salt and sugar and stir to mix. Stir in the flour mixture. Pour into a well-greased 9×13-inch glass baking dish. Bake for 45 minutes. Serve immediately.

Serves 6

Cheese Strata with Oven-Dried Tomatoes

Since the tomatoes take several hours to bake, plan to make this creamy and rich strata the morning or afternoon before you plan to serve it.

2 pounds ripe red plum tomatoes
1 1/2 teaspoons kosher salt
1 teaspoon unsalted butter
12 eggs
1 1/2 cups milk
1/2 cup heavy cream
1 teaspoon kosher salt
Pepper to taste
Pinch of nutmeg
2 cups (8 ounces) shredded extra-sharp Cheddar cheese
1 loaf French bread, cut into 1 1/2-inch cubes
1 1/2 teaspoons thinly sliced chives
1 tablespoon butter, melted

Preheat the oven to 250 degrees. Cut off the stem ends of the tomatoes. Cut the tomatoes into halves. Scrape out the seeds and pulp. Line a 10×15-inch baking pan with foil and lightly spray with nonstick cooking spray. Place the tomatoes cut side up in a single layer in the prepared pan. Sprinkle with 1 1/2 teaspoons kosher salt. Bake for 2 to 3 hours or until slightly soft, being careful not to burn the edges. (The tomatoes can be prepared ahead and stored in the refrigerator for 3 days.)

Grease a 3-quart baking dish with 1 teaspoon unsalted butter. Whisk the eggs, milk, cream, 1 teaspoon kosher salt, the pepper and nutmeg together in a bowl. Scatter 1/2 cup of the cheese in the prepared baking dish. Cover with one-third of the bread cubes and one-half of the tomatoes. Sprinkle with the one-half of the chives. Repeat the layers. Top with the remaining bread cubes and remaining cheese. Pour the egg mixture over the layers, pushing down with a knife or spoon to make sure all of the layers are covered. Cover with plastic wrap and chill for 8 to 10 hours.

Preheat the oven to 350 degrees. Remove the plastic wrap from the strata. Bake for 45 to 55 minutes or until golden brown and puffy. Remove from the oven and cool for 10 minutes before serving.

Serves 8

Oven-Dried Tomatoes or Packaged? *(continued)*

When a recipe calls for sun-dried tomatoes, try to determine if the recipe calls for sun-dried tomatoes with oil or without oil. If the recipe calls for sun-dried tomatoes without oil, you will need to rehydrate the tomatoes. To rehydrate, place the contents of the package of dry tomatoes in 2 cups simmering water. Remove the water from the heat and allow the tomatoes to rehydrate for 3 minutes or until they are no longer tough. Drain the tomatoes and then chop them to your preferred size.

Yachting on Biscayne Bay

As the sun is setting, dinner is ready on the aft deck. A lacquered tray works to hold our centerpiece filled with objects from the sea. Ralph Lauren Regatta Stripe China and Waterford Kilbarry stainless flatware grace the teak dinner table. Grilled Pork Tenderloin with Red Pepper and Pineapple Chutney, Gioconda's White Beans and Tomatoes, Asparagus and Green Papaya Salad with Mango Vinaigrette, and a French Baguette comprise our wonderful dinner.

Boating in Miami! Think of relaxing days filled with sunshine and miles of sparkling water. The Miami skyline is stunning from Biscayne Bay, and brilliant coral reefs fringe the nearby keys. Miami boasts some of the finest boat shows, fishing waters, and oceanside resorts. Whether it is deep sea or shallow water fishing, snorkeling, diving, or just leisurely cruising, Miami is a haven for boating enthusiasts.

Welcome aboard our one hundred-foot Azimut yacht, definitely a place where dreams come true! We cast off as our guests are enjoying seaside breezes on the flying bridge. This afternoon we are cruising through Indian Creek as we make our way out to Biscayne Bay to enjoy the sunset. We toast the captain as we sip our Millionaire Martinis and munch on vegetables and crackers with Curried Vegetable Dip. Fresh grouper caught earlier is now part of the Grouper Ceviche with Mango and Chiles served in martini glasses.

The hostess keeps the tablescape simple with natural elements. Bright lemons and limes harmonize with the deep blue of the sky. Bisque sea urchins hold tufts of fresh green moss and a piece of driftwood is a striking contrast against the clean, shiny chrome of the yacht.

Six bells! Dinner is served. Although there is a formal dining room on the main deck, we head down to the aft deck. Grilled Pork Tenderloin with Red Pepper and Pineapple Chutney, Gioconda's White Beans and Tomatoes, Asparagus and Green Papaya Salad with Mango Vinaigrette and a freshly baked French Baguette form our simple and delicious meal, accompanied by White Zinfandel, a favorite of the hostess. A centerpiece of natural starfish, cats paw coral, and sea fans is reflected on the gleaming teak table.

As the setting sun streaks the sky a rosy orange, our dessert is served. Fresh mangoes grown locally were brought on board to make a luscious Fresh Mango Tart which is served with Date-Filled Cookies, a rich shortbread cookie (a favorite of our host). Glasses of Sauternes, which are perfect with the tart, are poured for everyone.

Restored and replete, we catch up on family news, trade tales of travels, and share future plans. Life just doesn't get any better!

Vegetables and Side Dishes

Menu

A beautiful Fresh Mango Tart, Date-Filled Cookies, and fruit are our delectable desserts.

Work Plan ∼∼∼∼

ON THE DAY BEFORE THE DINNER

Blend ingredients for Curried Vegetable
Dip and refrigerate until needed.

Prepare marinade for Grilled Pork and
refrigerate pork in the marinade.

Slice pineapple and red peppers. Combine
with the other ingredients to make
Red Pepper and Pineapple Chutney
and refrigerate until needed.

Assemble the crust, prepare the filling, and
bake Fresh Mango Tart. Wrap tightly
and refrigerate until needed.

Assemble and bake Date-Filled Cookies.
Store in an airtight container
until needed.

*Docked with other yachts along Indian Creek,
the flying bridge of our yacht is ready for the
cocktail hour. Simple and portable decorations,
such as the bisque sand dollars with moss and
coral, enhance the tablescape. Grouper Ceviche
with Mango and Chiles sits in martini glasses.*

THE MORNING OF THE PARTY

Make Asparagus and Green Papaya Salad
and refrigerate until needed.

Make French Baguette.

JUST BEFORE SERVING

Prepare Gioconda's White Beans and
Tomatoes.

Grill Pork Tenderloins and serve with Chutney.

Make Grouper Ceviche with Mango and Chiles.

Mix Millionaire Martinis.

Steaming vegetables is the best way to preserve their flavor and vitamins.

For stovetop steamers, 100 percent bamboo steamers are the best since the bamboo inhibits water condensation. Metal steamers allow condensation, which makes the vegetables soggy. If you don't have a steamer, use foil to make balls to line the bottom of your saucepan. Pour water below the level of the foil balls and place the vegetables on top of the balls. Simmer the water, so that only steam, not water, reaches the vegetables. Vegetables can be overcooked by steaming so watch them carefully.

Green Beans with Chiles, Sprouts and Water Chestnuts in Ginger Sauce

Your guests will enjoy this intriguing combination of flavors.

3 tablespoons unseasoned rice wine vinegar
2 tablespoons tamari soy sauce
1 1/2 teaspoons cornstarch
1 tablespoon brown sugar
2/3 tablespoon rice wine (Sake)
8 cups water
1 1/2 pounds fresh green beans,
   chopped into 1-inch pieces (3 to 3 1/2 cups)
3 tablespoons olive oil
1/2 cup scallions, chopped
4 garlic cloves, minced or pressed
2 fresh Anaheim chiles, poblano chiles or other mild chiles, chopped
1 teaspoon ginger, minced
4 ounces fresh bean sprouts
1/4 cup thinly sliced water chestnuts

Combine the vinegar, soy sauce, cornstarch, brown sugar and wine in a bowl and mix well. Bring the water to a boil in a large saucepan. Add the beans and boil for 2 minutes. Drain the beans in a sieve. Heat the olive oil in a heavy skillet or wok. Add the scallions and cook for 30 seconds. Add the garlic, chiles and ginger and stir-fry for 1 minute. Add the beans and bean sprouts and stir-fry for 5 minutes. Stir in the water chestnuts. Add the vinegar mixture and toss to coat the vegetables. Serve immediately.

Serves 6

Every two years thirty young opera performers are selected to participate in the Young Patronesses of the Opera-Florida Grand Opera National Voice Competition. Former opera diva Irene Patti Hammond and her committee coordinate the competition, which is judged by a team of professionals from the most important opera programs and recording companies in the country. More than $45,000 is awarded to aid these promising young singers. Many award recipients have gone on to earn international acclaim in such places as the New York Metropolitan Opera and the Paris Opera.

Festive Green Beans

A pretty and tasty dish which is perfect with pork or beef.

1 pound green beans, trimmed	1 garlic clove, minced
3 slices bacon	1 tablespoon red wine vinegar
3 tablespoons olive oil	1 ripe tomato, cut into chunks
1 sweet yellow onion, chopped	Salt and freshly ground pepper to taste

Snap the beans into halves. Steam the beans in a steamer until tender-crisp. Drain and rinse with cool water. Cook the bacon in a large skillet until crisp. Remove the bacon to paper towels to drain. Drain the skillet, reserving 1 tablespoon of the bacon drippings in the skillet. Add the olive oil, onion and garlic and sauté for 5 minutes. Add the beans, stirring to coat. Crumble the bacon. Add the bacon, vinegar, tomato, salt and pepper to the bean mixture and toss to coat. (The tomatoes should be warmed but not cooked.)

Serves 4

Gioconda's White Beans and Tomatoes

Sometimes the simplest things taste best.

5 cups cooked white beans	6 ribs celery, deveined and thinly sliced
5 tomatoes	2 garlic cloves, minced
Juice of 1 lemon	1 onion, minced
2 tablespoons extra-virgin olive oil	Salt and pepper to taste
1 tablespoon fresh basil or mint, chopped	

Drain the beans well. Cut the tomatoes into halves and remove the seeds. Chop the tomatoes into 1/4-inch pieces. Combine the lemon juice, olive oil and basil in a large bowl. Gently stir in the tomatoes, celery, garlic, onion, salt and pepper. Gently stir in the beans using a wooden spoon. Best served at room temperature, but can also be served chilled.

Note: You may use 2 cups dried beans for the cooked beans. Sort, rinse and cook the beans using the package directions before proceeding with the recipe.

Serves 6

Photograph on page 84.

Steaming Vegetables

(continued)

Electric steamers with timers are now available in most stores that carry kitchen equipment. Electric steamers usually heat the water more rapidly than stovetop steamers so they steam vegetables more quickly. Once you are familiar with the cooking times of different vegetables in your electric steamer, the timer allows you to steam vegetables without the necessity of checking on their doneness. Vegetables are placed in the steaming basket before the steamer is turned on, so electric steamers are safer than stovetop steamers, because you are not required to drop vegetables into a basket above steaming water.

Portobellos Stuffed with Creamy Baby Bellas, Red Bell Pepper and Corn

These pretty portobellos can also be served as a main course for a lighter meal.

5 tablespoons corn oil
10 garlic cloves, pressed
2 tablespoons white balsamic vinegar
1 tablespoon chopped fresh thyme
2 teaspoons chopped fresh oregano
Salt and pepper to taste
8 (5-inch-diameter) portobello mushroom caps
3 tablespoons corn oil
12 ounces baby bella mushrooms
1/2 cup chopped red bell pepper
1/4 cup chopped red onion
1 1/2 cups fresh or thawed frozen corn kernels, well drained
3/4 cup whipping cream
1 cup finely crumbled feta cheese
2 teaspoons chopped fresh thyme
1 tablespoon chopped fresh oregano

Whisk 5 tablespoons corn oil, the garlic, vinegar, 1 tablespoon thyme and 2 teaspoons oregano in a medium bowl until well mixed. Season generously with salt and pepper. Reserve 1/3 cup of the garlic-herb oil in a small bowl.

Remove most of the remaining stem from each portobello cap, being careful not to tear the cap. Lightly coat the portobello caps in the remaining garlic-herb oil, reserving any garlic-herb oil that is not used. Cook the portobello caps in 3 tablespoons corn oil in a large skillet for 2 minutes on each side, turning once. Place the caps rounded side down to drain.

Trim and thinly slice the baby bella mushrooms. Heat the reserved 1/3 cup garlic-herb oil in a skillet over medium-high heat. Stir in the baby bella mushrooms, bell pepper and onion. Sauté for 5 minutes or until the vegetables are tender. Add the corn and sauté for 1 minute or until tender. Add the cream and simmer for 4 to 5 minutes or until the cream is almost absorbed. Stir in the cheese. Season with salt and pepper. Spoon into the portobello caps, mounding in the center. (The stuffed mushrooms can be covered and chilled for up to 6 hours at this point. Remove the portobellos from the refrigerator 45 minutes before baking.)

Preheat the broiler. Place the portobellos on a 10×15-inch baking pan, being careful not to allow any extra oil on the pan as it will burn during broiling. Broil for 4 to 5 minutes or until heated through. Place on a serving platter and sprinkle evenly with 2 teaspoons thyme and 1 tablespoon oregano. Serve immediately.

Serves 8

Garlic and Parmesan Mashed Boniato

Since boniato is sweet, this recipe calls for a lot of garlic to temper the sweetness. It is a delicious combination! This dish refrigerates well. Just add a little extra liquid to moisten if serving after it has been cooked and refrigerated.

12 garlic cloves
2 tablespoons olive oil
2 pounds boniato
3/4 cup (3 ounces) grated Parmesan cheese
3 tablespoons butter, melted
3/4 cup whipping cream
1 teaspoon salt
3 tablespoons chopped fresh parsley

Mince the garlic in a food processor by adding one clove at a time, processing constantly. Cook the garlic in the olive oil in a skillet over medium heat until lightly toasted; drain and set aside.

Fill a large saucepan half full with water. Peel the boniato under running water and add to the saucepan. (The boniato will quickly turn gray in color if exposed to air before being cooked.) Bring to a boil and boil for 20 to 25 minutes or until tender. Drain the boniato and mash. Stir in the cheese, butter, cream and salt. Stir in the garlic. Warm the mixture in a microwave or oven before serving if needed. Sprinkle the top with the parsley.

Serves 4

Boniato

If you have never tried boniato, do not be put off by its appearance. Those who cook it for the first time are surprised to find such an ugly vegetable tastes so sweet and delicate!

The boniato is a tropical sweet potato also known as batatas or camote. It has a pink- to purple-colored skin and its flesh is white or cream colored. Many people believe the boniato to be less sweet than the sweet potato, but it is a different type of sweetness; it lacks the muskiness of a sweet potato. It is also drier than the sweet potato.

Boniato is only fresh when it is rock hard. It turns grey immediately when exposed to air, so it is best to peel it under water and to eat it after it is boiled. Many sweet potato recipes will work well for boniato, but you will need to add extra liquid.

Red Potato Pancakes

This flavorful traditional favorite is a little easier to make since you use red potatoes. Serve hot with sour cream or applesauce.

2 eggs
1/4 cup minced onion
2 tablespoons all-purpose flour
1 tablespoon salt
3/4 teaspoon freshly ground black pepper
1/4 teaspoon finely ground white pepper
6 red potatoes
Vegetable oil for frying

Combine the eggs, onion, flour, salt, black pepper and white pepper in a bowl and mix well. Shred the potatoes to yield 3 cups. Drain the potatoes well by gently squeezing out the excess liquid and patting dry. Add to the egg mixture and mix well.

Fill a large heavy skillet with 1/2 to 1 inch of oil. Heat over medium-high heat until a small bit of batter sizzles on the surface of the oil. Drop the potato mixture by slightly rounded tablespoons into the hot oil. Fry until golden brown, turning once. Do not crowd the skillet. Remove to paper towels to drain.

Note: You may use Idaho potatoes instead of the red potatoes in this recipe. Three Idaho potatoes should yield 3 cups of shredded potatoes. These pancakes can be frozen and reheated. Do not thaw, but reheat from the frozen state.

Serves 6

Wasabi Garlic Mashed Potatoes

2 pounds russet potatoes, peeled and grated
1 cup heavy cream
3 tablespoons butter
2 teaspoons minced garlic
4 teaspoons wasabi paste
Salt and pepper to taste

Boil the potatoes in water to cover in a saucepan until soft; drain. Add the cream, butter, garlic, wasabi paste, salt and pepper and mash with a potato masher. Serve very hot.

Serves 4

Spinach Madeleine

The jalapeño cheese gives zip to this pretty cheese casserole.

2 (10-ounce) packages frozen
 chopped spinach
1/4 cup (1/2 stick) butter
2 tablespoons chopped onion
2 tablespoons all-purpose flour
1/2 cup evaporated milk
1 (6-ounce) roll jalapeño chile
 cheese, grated

1/2 teaspoon pepper
3/4 teaspoon celery salt
3/4 teaspoon garlic salt
Salt to taste
1 teaspoon Worcestershire sauce
1/2 cup plain bread crumbs
1 teaspoon butter

Cook the spinach using the package directions. Drain the spinach, reserving 1/2 cup of the liquid. Melt 1/4 cup butter in a saucepan. Add the onion and cook until translucent. Add the flour and cook until blended and smooth but not brown, stirring constantly. Add the reserved spinach liquid and evaporated milk gradually, stirring constantly to prevent lumps. Cook until smooth and thickened, stirring constantly. Add the cheese, pepper, celery salt, garlic salt, salt and Worcestershire sauce and cook until the cheese melts, stirring constantly. Stir into the cooked spinach. (You may serve immediately at this point.)

Preheat the oven to 350 degrees. Mix the bread crumbs with 1 teaspoon butter in a bowl. Pour the spinach mixture into six ramekins or a large baking dish and top with the bread crumbs. Bake for 20 minutes.

Note: This dish can be cooked a day ahead and chilled until ready to bake.
 It also freezes well.

Serves 6

Jalapeño and Spinach Pesto

This pesto will make your taste buds zing. Serve with fish, veal, or chicken.

2 teaspoons cumin
2 tablespoons extra-virgin olive oil
1 cup chopped fresh spinach leaves
1 large jalapeño chile, seeded and
 finely chopped

4 garlic cloves, pressed
1/2 teaspoon kosher salt
3 green onions, chopped
6 tablespoons extra-virgin olive oil
1 tablespoon Spanish sherry vinegar

Heat a large saucepan over medium heat. Add the cumin and sauté for 30 seconds or until lightly toasted. Add 2 tablespoons olive oil, the spinach, chile, garlic and kosher salt and sauté for 2 to 3 minutes or until the spinach is wilted. Process in a food processor for 1 minute. Add 6 tablespoons olive oil and the vinegar gradually, processing constantly for 1 minute.

Makes 1 cup

Yuca

Yuca (pronounced you-cah) is also known as cassava or manioc. It is a starchy root vegetable found in traditional Cuban meals. Yuca is used in a great variety of dishes from Central and South America and Africa. It can be found fresh and frozen in most South Florida groceries.

To buy fresh yuca, make sure the yuca is firm and the skin is unblemished. Smell the yuca to be sure it is not giving off an unpleasant odor. The flesh of the yuca should only be white; discard if the flesh is gray, blue, or brown.

Oven-Dried Tomatoes with Corn and Queso Blanco

The mild and chewy queso blanco complements the rich taste and texture of the tomatoes.

2 pounds ripe plum tomatoes, cored and
   cut into halves lengthwise
1 1/2 teaspoons kosher salt
4 ears of corn
1 tablespoon butter
4 shallots, coarsely chopped
2 garlic cloves, minced
1 green bell pepper, chopped
1/4 cup chopped fresh basil
1 tablespoon sherry vinegar
4 ounces queso blanco, cut into small chunks

Preheat the oven to 250 degrees. Remove the seeds and inner pulp from the tomatoes. Place the tomatoes in a single layer in a 10×15-inch baking pan and sprinkle with the kosher salt. Bake for 3 to 4 hours or until shriveled but still plump, being careful to not burn. (You may store in the refrigerator for 3 to 4 days at this point.)

Remove the husks and silks from the corn cobbs. Cut the corn kernels from the cobbs into a bowl. Melt the butter in a saucepan over medium heat. Add the corn kernels, shallots, garlic and bell pepper and sauté for 2 minutes or until very slightly cooked. Cool to room temperature. Chop the tomatoes into small pieces. Combine the corn mixture, tomatoes, basil, vinegar and cheese in a bowl and stir gently to mix. Serve with Crab Cakes (page 185).

Serves 6

Our Educator of Note Award was created in 1993 by President Karyn Herterich to honor her mother, Ethel Malcomb Kennedy, an early founder and advocate of children's educational opera programs in Miami. This award, $2,000 and a crystal apple, is presented every May to an elementary school teacher who has done an outstanding job teaching students about the opera. Many recipients have written and directed miniature operas starring students in their elementary schools.

Nochebuena Yuca

4 pounds fresh or frozen yuca
1 tablespoon salt
6 large garlic cloves
1 teaspoon salt

1 cup sour orange juice, or $^1/_2$ cup lime
   juice and $^1/_2$ cup orange juice
$^1/_2$ cup vegetable oil

Cut the yuca crosswise into 3-inch sections. Pare away the brown skin and the pink layer underneath. Remove the fibers in the center. (Frozen yuca also works very well and is already peeled.) Fill a large heavy saucepan with water and bring to a boil. Add 1 tablespoon salt. Cut the yuca into chunks and add to the boiling water. Boil for 20 minutes or until fork-tender; drain. Mash the garlic in a small bowl. Add 1 teaspoon salt and the orange juice and mix well.

To serve, heat the oil in a medium saucepan. Add to the orange juice mixture and mix well. Pour over the yuca and serve.

Note: Potatoes can be substituted for the yuca. Like potatoes, yuca is delicious when cut into $^1/_2$-inch slices and deep fried. It is recommended that yuca never be eaten raw.

Serves 8

Golden and Delicious Zucchini Pancakes

Serve these pancakes with mango chutney as a tasty side dish for grilled fish or chicken.

3 zucchini
$^1/_2$ teaspoon salt
1 tablespoon butter
$^1/_2$ cup finely chopped onion
2 eggs, lightly beaten

$^1/_4$ cup all-purpose flour
$^1/_8$ teaspoon pepper
$^1/_2$ cup vegetable oil
Salt to taste

Peel and seed the zucchini. Shred the zucchini to measure 4 cups. Place in a colander and sprinkle with $^1/_2$ teaspoon salt. Let stand to drain for 30 minutes.

Gently squeeze as much liquid as possible from the zucchini. Melt the butter in a skillet over low heat. Add the onion and cook for 3 minutes, being careful to not brown. Combine the onion and zucchini in a large mixing bowl. Stir in the eggs, flour and pepper.

Heat 2 tablespoons of the oil in a large skillet over medium-high heat. Drop the zucchini mixture by slightly rounded tablespoonfuls into the hot oil. Cook for 2 minutes or until golden on the bottom. Flip the pancakes and cook until golden on the other side, adding the remaining oil as needed. Drain the pancakes on paper towels and season with salt to taste. Serve immediately with sour cream or mango chutney.

Serves 6

Grilled Vegetable Terrine

This is one gorgeous and elegant dish.

TERRINE
- 1 large eggplant
- 2 large zucchini
- 2 red bell peppers
- 2 yellow bell peppers
- 1 red onion
- 1/4 cup olive oil
- 2 tablespoons unflavored gelatin
- 1 1/2 cups tomato juice

- 1 tablespoon olive oil
- 1 tablespoon tomato purée
- 1 tablespoon red wine vinegar

BASIL VINAIGRETTE
- 2/3 cup olive oil or vegetable oil
- 1/3 cup red wine vinegar
- 1/4 cup chopped fresh basil

To prepare the terrine, preheat the grill. Cut the eggplant and zucchini into 1-inch slices. Cut the bell peppers into large pieces. Chop the onion into small pieces. Cook the bell peppers over an open flame on the grill until the skins are slightly charred and the bell peppers are firm but easy to cut. (If needed you may bake in a 350-degree oven after charring.) Brush the eggplant and zucchini with 1/4 cup olive oil. Place on a grill rack and grill until tender. (You may bake in a 350-degree oven for 10 minutes or until tender.) Cool the vegetables.

Soften the gelatin in the tomato juice in a bowl. Heat 1 tablespoon olive oil in a sauté pan. Add the onion and sauté until the onion begins to soften. Add the tomato purée and vinegar and cook until the onion is golden brown. Reduce the heat to low and add the tomato juice mixture. Heat until the gelatin is completely dissolved, stirring constantly.

Line a loaf pan or terrine pan with plastic wrap, leaving an overhang on all sides. Oil the plastic wrap. Place a layer of yellow bell peppers in the prepared pan and add a small amount of the tomato juice mixture to completely cover. Continue alternating the layers of the different vegetables, ending with the red bell peppers and covering each vegetable layer with the tomato juice mixture. Tap the terrine to eliminate any bubbles and cover with the plastic wrap. Chill for 3 hours or until set.

To prepare the vinaigrette, combine the olive oil, vinegar and basil in a bowl and mix well.

To assemble, remove the terrine to a serving platter, discarding the plastic wrap. Serve on individual plates with fresh greens and the vinaigrette on the side.

Serves 8

Photograph on page 145.

Vegetable Tajine

Serve this full-flavored dish on a bed of rice or couscous.

1 (14-ounce) can artichoke hearts
$1/3$ cup olive oil
$1 1/2$ cups chopped onions
3 garlic cloves, pressed
3 cups chopped potatoes
1 cup (1-inch) pieces green beans
1 red bell pepper, sliced
2 cups sliced fresh tomatoes
1 teaspoon dried thyme
3 cups vegetable stock
   (can be made from vegetable bouillon cubes)
Pinch of crushed saffron
$1/4$ cup fresh lemon juice
$1/2$ cup parsley, chopped
Salt and freshly ground pepper to taste
Chopped almonds for garnish

Drain the artichoke hearts, reserving the liquid. Cut the artichoke hearts into halves. Heat the olive oil in a skillet over medium-low heat. Add the onions and garlic and sauté until the onions are translucent. Add the potatoes, green beans, bell pepper, tomatoes and thyme and cook over medium-high heat for 3 minutes, stirring occasionally. Reduce the heat to low. Add the stock and reserved artichoke liquid. Simmer, covered, for 15 to 20 minutes or until the vegetables are tender. Stir in the artichokes and saffron. Simmer for 5 to 10 minutes or until the saffron dissolves, stirring constantly. Stir in the lemon juice, parsley, salt and pepper. Garnish with chopped almonds.

Serves 8

Spinach Sauté

This versatile side dish is easy and appetizing. To prepare, mash 1 garlic clove, pressed, into $1/2$ cup (1 stick) butter, softened, in a large saucepan. Cook over low heat until the butter melts, stirring constantly. Add 1 shallot, chopped, and 8 ounces fresh spinach leaves, trimmed. Sauté over medium-high heat for 1 minute or until the spinach is wilted and slightly cooked. Sprinkle with salt and pepper to taste. Place in a small baking dish and sprinkle with 3 tablespoons freshly grated Parmesan cheese. Preheat the broiler. Broil for a few seconds until the Parmesan cheese is melted. Serve immediately. This recipe will serve 2.

Elegant Vegetable Casserole

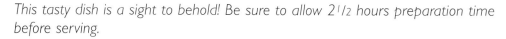

This tasty dish is a sight to behold! Be sure to allow 2 1/2 hours preparation time before serving.

2 pounds red potatoes	1/2 teaspoon salt
1 1/4 pounds parsnips	2 (10-ounce) packages frozen chopped
1 cup light sour cream	spinach, thawed and drained
1/4 cup milk	2 cups (8 ounces) shredded Swiss cheese
1 teaspoon salt	1 small onion, grated
3 pounds butternut squash	1/4 teaspoon salt
1/4 teaspoon nutmeg	3 tablespoons sliced almonds, lightly toasted

Peel the potatoes and parsnips and cut into 1-inch pieces. Place in a large saucepan and fill with water to cover. Bring to a boil and reduce the heat to low. Cover and simmer for 15 to 20 minutes or until the vegetables are tender; drain. Mash in a large bowl with a potato masher. Stir in the sour cream, milk and 1 teaspoon salt.

Cut the squash into halves lengthwise and discard the seeds. Cut the halves into 1 1/4-inch slices. Place in a large saucepan and fill with water to cover. Bring to a boil and reduce the heat to low. Cover and simmer for 10 to 15 minutes or until tender; drain. Place the squash in a large bowl. Add the nutmeg and 1/2 teaspoon salt and mash well. Mix the spinach, cheese, onion and 1/4 teaspoon salt in a bowl.

Preheat the oven to 350 degrees. Spoon half the potato mixture, all the spinach mixture, all the squash mixture and the remaining potato mixture in four parallel rolls in a greased shallow 3-quart baking dish. Bake, loosely covered, for 40 minutes. Sprinkle with the almonds.

Serves 12

Vegetable Medley

1 pound baby vegetables	2 tablespoons chopped fresh parsley
(carrots, zucchini or squash)	1 teaspoon Dijon mustard
8 ounces sugar snap peas	1 garlic clove, minced
10 to 15 grape tomatoes	1/2 cup olive oil
1 lemon	Salt and pepper to taste
2 tablespoons chopped fresh basil	1 tablespoon water

Steam the baby vegetables and sugar snap peas in a steamer for 5 minutes or until tender-crisp. Drain and rinse with cold water. Place in a serving bowl and add the tomatoes. Grate the lemon zest and squeeze 2 tablespoons lemon juice from the lemon into a bowl. Add the basil, parsley, mustard, garlic, olive oil, salt, pepper and water in a bowl and mix well. Pour over the vegetables and serve.

Serves 6

Moros y Cristianos (Black Beans and Rice)

A staple that is the perfect accompaniment for many Hispanic dishes.

8 ounces dried black beans
3 cups water
2 tablespoons vegetable oil
1 1/2 cups chopped onions
3 garlic cloves, finely chopped
1 green bell pepper, thinly sliced
1 red bell pepper, thinly sliced
2 large tomatoes, chopped
1/2 teaspoon cumin
1/2 teaspoon cayenne pepper
1 cup long grain white rice
Salt and freshly ground black pepper to taste
1 tablespoon red wine vinegar (optional)
1 tomato, chopped for garnish
1/4 onion, chopped for garnish
1/2 cup chopped parsley for garnish

Sort and rinse the beans. Cook the beans in 3 cups boiling water for 1 hour or until barely tender, skimming off the foam that rises to the surface. Drain the beans, reserving 2 1/2 cups of the cooking liquid. Heat the oil in a skillet over medium heat. Add 1 1/2 cups onions and the garlic and sauté for 2 minutes. Add the bell peppers and sauté for 3 minutes. Add two tomatoes, the cumin and cayenne pepper. Stir in the rice. Add the beans and the reserved cooking liquid. Simmer for 20 to 30 minutes or until the rice is tender and the water is absorbed, adding the salt and pepper during the last 10 minutes of cooking and adding additional water if needed. Stir in the vinegar. Strain any remaining liquid from the mixture before serving. Garnish with one tomato, one-fourth onion and/or parsley.

Serves 4

Sublime Sofrito

If you find that many dishes you prepare have a combination of garlic, onion and some kind of chile cooked in oil, you are making sofrito. Sofrito is the basis for many dishes from the Caribbean and Central and South America. Puerto Ricans believe that a true sofrito must include chopped tomatoes and be infused with annatto seeds, and Jamaicans feel that fiery hot chiles like Scotch Bonnet should be substituted for the mild chiles. Cubans prefer Cubanelle or mild bell peppers, and Guatemalans enjoy adding peeled, chopped chayote and chopped cilantro. Whatever your preference, this vegetable sauté works to enhance the flavor of many dishes. Seafood Paella (page 183), Arroz con Pollo (page 165), and Moros y Christianos (at left) all contain a sofrito.

Take a tip from many busy Latin households and prepare a large quantity of sofrito and freeze in ice cube trays or small sealable bags for use later. A small amount of sofrito enhances the flavor of many soups and chowders and serves as the basis for many entrées.

Congri

Congri (pronounced con-gree) is similar to Moros y Cristianos (page 99). It is a Cuban red beans and rice dish with the addition of ham and bacon. This is a substantial dish which works well as a main course.

4 ounces bacon, chopped
2 tablespoons olive oil
3 garlic cloves, finely chopped
1 1/2 cups chopped onions
1 green bell pepper, thinly sliced
1 red bell pepper, thinly sliced
1 tablespoon fresh thyme
1 teaspoon cumin
1/2 teaspoon cayenne pepper
3 cups chicken stock or chicken broth
2 cups long grain rice
1 cup chopped smoked ham
4 cups cooked kidney beans, well drained
Salt and black pepper to taste

Sauté the bacon in 2 tablespoons olive oil in a large saucepan until slighty crispy. Add the garlic, onions, bell peppers, thyme, cumin and cayenne pepper and stir to mix well. Add the stock, rice and ham. Bring to a simmer and reduce the heat to low. Cook for 15 minutes. Stir in the beans. Cook for 5 to 10 minutes or until the stock is absorbed. Season with salt and black pepper. Serve immediately.

Serves 8

Wine Recommendations: Riesling, Beaujolais, or Sauvignon Blanc

Every October the Young Patronesses of the Opera coordinate a teacher's workshop for around one hundred elementary school teachers to help them learn to present opera in the classroom. These workshops show how opera can be taught through lessons in history, literature, and creative writing as well as music appreciation. During the workshop teachers are treated to performances by Florida Grand Opera Young Artists. The teachers are supplied with YPO Opera Funtime workbooks for their classrooms as well.

Grilled Polenta with Sweet Corn

Polenta is so versatile! These wedges serve as a delicious accompaniment for any spicy dish

3¹/2 cups water
1 teaspoon salt
1 cup cornmeal
1 cup fresh corn kernels

¹/2 cup (2 ounces) grated
   Parmesan cheese
Olive oil for brushing

Bring the water and salt to a boil in a large saucepan. Add the cornmeal gradually, stirring constantly. Stir in the corn and cheese. Cook until bubbly and thick enough for a wooden spoon to stand upright in the saucepan. Pour into a 9×13-inch baking dish. Let stand to cool.

Preheat the grill or broiler. Cut the polenta into wedges and place on a grill rack or baking sheet. Brush with olive oil. Grill or broil until golden on each side.

Serves 8

Polenta with Sun-Dried Tomatoes

Creamy polenta should always be served hot, so it is best to prepare any sauces or vegetables ahead of time.

¹/4 cup sun-dried tomatoes or
   oil-pack sun-dried tomatoes
5 sprigs of fresh thyme
3¹/2 cups water

1 teaspoon salt
1 cup cornmeal
Salt and pepper to taste

Reconstitute the sun-dried tomatoes by soaking in boiling water until tender; drain. (If you are using oil-pack sun-dried tomatoes, just drain well.) Chop the sun-dried tomatoes. Remove the thyme leaves from the stems, discarding the stems.

Bring the water and 1 teaspoon salt to a boil in a large saucepan. Add the cornmeal gradually, stirring constantly. Stir in the thyme and sun-dried tomatoes. Cook until bubbly and thick enough for a wooden spoon to stand upright in the saucepan. Season with salt and pepper to taste. Serve immediately.

Note: To serve as an appetizer, spread the cooked polenta in a lightly greased 10×15-inch baking pan and bake in a 350-degree oven until light golden brown. Use a biscuit cutter to cut the polenta into circles or cut into squares. Place on a baking sheet. Top each with sautéed mushrooms and blue cheese such as Cabrales. Bake in a 425-degree oven for 5 minutes or until the cheese melts.

Serves 4

What is the sauce on your dish? Does some herb, spice, or a particular flavor dominate its taste? In selecting a wine for a dish, the main ingredient, whether it is poultry, beef, fish, pork, or anything else, may need to take a backseat in the selection of wine for the dish. Here are some recommendations for pairings with sauces:

Savory fruit sauce, relish, chutney, or a fruit salsa pairs with Merlot or Chardonnay.

Citrus-flavored sauce pairs with Sauvignon Blanc or Pinot Noir.

Basil-flavored sauce pairs with Chardonnay, Chianti, or Sangiovese.

Sauces with pungent flavors from olives, capers, or anchovies pair with Sauvignon Blanc or Sangiovese.

Cilantro-flavored sauce pairs with Sauvignon Blanc.

Sauces dominated by oregano, thyme, marjoram, or sage pair with Pinot Noir or Merlot.

Risotto with Wild Mushrooms

Your guests will beg for seconds when you serve this creamy risotto dish.

1 cup dried porcini mushrooms
1 cup boiling water
1/2 cup finely chopped onion
1 1/2 cups arborio rice
2 tablespoons olive oil
5 cups homemade beef broth, heated
2 tablespoons butter
1/2 cup (2 ounces) freshly grated Parmigiano-Reggiano
1/2 cup chopped fresh basil
Salt and freshly ground pepper to taste

Soak the mushrooms in the water in a heatproof bowl to reconstitute. Drain and chop the mushrooms. Cook the onion in a large saucepan until translucent. Add the mushrooms, rice and olive oil. Cook until the rice is translucent but not brown. Add 1/2 cup of the broth and cook until the broth is absorbed, stirring constantly. Repeat the process until almost all of the broth is absorbed and the rice is tender and firm to the bite. Turn off the heat. Stir in the butter, cheese and basil. (The rice should be creamy and soupy.) Season with salt and pepper.

Note: You may use two bouillon cubes dissolved in 5 cups water instead of the homemade broth.

Serves 6

Golden Risotto with Creamy Wine Sauce

A rich combination of flavors which pleases everyone.

3 tablespoons olive oil
1 onion, finely chopped
2 1/3 cups arborio rice
6 cups chicken broth, heated
1/2 teaspoon powdered saffron

3/4 cup dry white wine
3 tablespoons butter
1 cup (4 ounces) freshly
   grated Parmigiano-Reggiano

Heat the olive oil in a large heavy saucepan. Add the onion and cook until translucent; do not brown. Add the rice and cook over low heat until the rice glistens with oil and becomes translucent. Add 1/2 cup of the broth and cook until the liquid is absorbed, stirring constantly. Stir in the saffron. Continue adding the broth 1/2 cup at a time until almost all of the broth is absorbed and the rice is tender and firm to the bite. Add the wine, stirring constantly. Stir in the butter and 1/2 cup of the cheese. Serve immediately with the remaining 1/2 cup cheese on the side.

Note: If you use saffron threads, distill in 1/4 cup very hot water before using.

Serves 8 to 10

Orzo with Broccoli, Feta Cheese and Olives

Easy and light, this dish is perfect served with chicken or lamb.

1 1/2 cups orzo
1 bunch broccoli, cut into
   bite-size florets
1/4 cup olive oil
3 tablespoons pine nuts
3/4 cup kalamata olives, pitted
   and cut into halves

1/4 cup chopped fresh basil
3/4 cup crumbled feta cheese
1/2 cup (2 ounces) freshly
   grated Parmesan cheese
Salt and freshly ground
   pepper to taste

Cook the orzo in a saucepan for 8 minutes using the package directions. Add the broccoli and cook for 2 to 3 minutes or until the broccoli is tender-crisp. Drain and place in a large serving bowl.

Heat the olive oil in a saucepan. Add the pine nuts and sauté for 3 minutes or until brown. Pour over the orzo mixture and toss to coat. Add the olives and basil and toss to coat. Add the feta cheese and Parmesan cheese and toss to mix well. Season with salt and pepper.

Serves 4

Wine Pairings— Consider the Sauce

(continued)

Pesto sauce and vinaigrette both pair with Chardonnay or Sauvignon Blanc.

Soy sauce-based sauce or marinade pairs with Riesling or Gewürztraminer.

Saffron-flavored sauce pairs with Chardonnay or Pinot Noir.

Hot-and-spicy barbecue sauce pairs with Riesling; sweet barbecue sauce pairs with chilled White Zinfandel.

Southeast Asian or Indian curry sauce pairs with Riesling or a well chilled dry rosé.

Spicy or meaty tomato-based sauces pair with Zinfandel or Barbera.

Spicy sauce or marinade pairs with Riesling or Chardonnay.

Cheesy sauces or dressings pair with Chardonnay or Pinot Noir.

For wine reduction sauce or marinade, use the wine you have used for the sauce.

For close girlfriends, special occasions should be celebrated with special parties. It may be a bridal or baby shower, a decade birthday party, or even a party honoring a good friend leaving or moving to your community. Whatever the reason, it is an opportunity to invite friends over for a ladies' luncheon.

This bridal shower is being held in a lovely garden on a large and gracious estate in Gables Estates, a neighborhood which is part of the City of Coral Gables. All the homes in this neighborhood have splendid water views. The owners of this home enjoy a view of nearby Matheson Hammock Park and the downtown skyline of Miami.

Friends have been enlisted to design and make a special shower album for the bride. As each guest arrives, a Polaroid photo is taken of her, and she is asked to write on a small card "words of wisdom" about marriage. Each picture and its corresponding card are then taped onto part of a page in a beautifully bound album. These albums, with their serious and witty advice, are always cherished.

The hostess chose feminine and cheerful pink and green as the colors of the day. The buffet table is covered with a pink chintz cloth with a matching striped topper. The large French crystal decanter holds pink lemonade, perfect for a bright and breezy day.

The striped cloths on the round tables are perfectly set off by Limoges Artois china and are complemented by delicate and flowery Towle Old Master silver and Waterford Lismore crystal. The centerpieces are a charming mixture of hydrangea, Gerber daisies, spray roses, tulips, and hypericum. This hostess has an eye for details! Even the party favors, in boxes wrapped in slick white paper, have tiny matching larkspur florettes tied on with green grosgrain ribbon.

In the dappled sunlight, everyone enjoys Biscayne Bay Chicken Salad and Scrumptious Shrimp Salad with Cilantro Dressing. Poached Pears in Pomegranate Glaze and Chocolate Chip Pound Cake with Chocolate Drip Icing are the luscious and elegant dessert choices.

Toasts are given and gifts are unwrapped and admired. The bride, her mother, and her future mother-in-law are warmly embraced and wished the very best by everyone. After the guests have left, the bride and her mother share a last bite of dessert and discuss the wedding plans and the bride's hopes for the future as they sit and enjoy the view of Biscayne Bay.

Salads

Spread out in the garden, this ladies' luncheon will be a very special day. White cheveré chairs for the round tables have been selected to match the lawn furniture. The elegant and feminine buffet table has a beautiful centerpiece of hydrangea, ranunculus, viburnum, and pink roses and a French crystal decanter with pink lemonade.

Menu

Biscayne Bay Chicken Salad *page 109*

Scrumptious Shrimp Salad with Cilantro
    Dressing *page 116*

Poppy Seed Muffins *page 79*

Potato Crescent Knot Dinner Rolls
    page 71

Roasted Pears with Pomegranate
    Glaze and Rum and Raisin Ice Cream
    page 220

Chocolate Chip Pound Cake with
    Chocolate Drip Icing *page 229*

Pink Lemonade

Riesling

*Place cards with names in calligraphy
in matching green ink are attached to the
wrapped party favors for everyone.*

*Pink lemonade and Roasted Pears with Pomegranate
Glaze are enjoyed by the bay. Matheson Hammock Park
and the skyline of downtown Miami are in the distance.*

Work Plan

SEVERAL DAYS AHEAD

Purchase Rum and Raisin Ice Cream and place in the freezer to harden.

THE DAY BEFORE

Cook chicken and dressing for Biscayne Bay Chicken Salad and refrigerate until final prep time.

Bake Poppy Seed Muffins and Chocolate Chip Pound Cake, which can be stored out of the refrigerator if tightly wrapped or placed in airtight containers.

Prepare Cilantro Dressing, but omit cilantro until right before serving,

Chill Riesling.

ON THE DAY

Biscayne Bay Chicken Salad can be assembled without avocado and pecans.

Clean and cook shrimp. Assemble the Shrimp Salad without the Cilantro Mayonnaise and refrigerate until serving time.

Prepare Chocolate Drip Icing and Chocolate Curls and apply to Chocolate Chip Pound Cake at serving time.

Bake Potato Crescent Knot Dinner Rolls.

JUST BEFORE SERVING

Add the pecans and avocado to the Biscayne Bay Chicken Salad.

Roast Pears with Pomegranate Glaze.

Add cilantro to dressing and serve on or with Scrumptious Shrimp Salad.

*Clockwise: Poppy Seed Muffins, Potato Crescent Knot Dinner Rolls, Scrumptious
Shrimp Salad with Cilantro Dressing, and Biscayne Bay Chicken Salad*

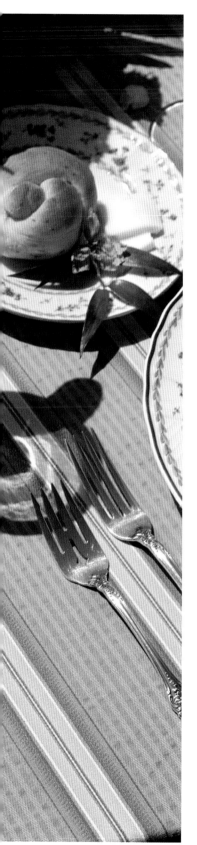

Biscayne Bay Chicken Salad

This is the perfect salad for a picnic or a day on the boat. It tastes delicious chilled or slightly warm. Your guests will always want seconds!

GARLIC DIJON
MUSTARD DRESSING
- 6 large garlic cloves, minced
- 3 tablespoons Dijon mustard
- 1 1/2 teaspoons salt
- 3/4 teaspoon sugar
- 3/4 teaspoon freshly ground pepper
- 3/4 cup rice wine vinegar
- 2/3 cup vegetable oil

SALAD
- 4 whole boneless chicken breasts
- 2 (14-ounce) cans chicken broth
- 12 cups cooked wild and brown rice, rinsed
- Juice of 1 1/2 lemons
- 6 ounces snow peas, trimmed and cut diagonally into 1-inch pieces
- 2 red bell peppers, chopped
- 9 scallions, diagonally sliced
- 2 cups toasted pecan halves
- Lettuce leaves
- 2 avocados

To prepare the dressing, process the garlic, mustard, salt, sugar, pepper, vinegar and oil in a food processor until thoroughly blended.

To prepare the salad, preheat the oven to 350 degrees. Place the chicken in a single layer in a large rectangular baking pan. Pour the broth over the chicken. Bake for 15 minutes and turn. Bake until the chicken is cooked through. Remove from the oven to cool slightly; drain. Chop the chicken into small pieces. Combine the rice with the lemon juice in a bowl and toss to mix. Let stand to cool. Steam the snow peas and bell peppers in a steamer until tender-crisp; drain. Combine the rice, chicken, steamed vegetables and scallions in a large bowl and toss to mix well. Reserve 1/4 cup of the dressing. Stir the remaining dressing into the chicken mixture. (The salad may be chilled for several hours at this point until ready to serve.)

To serve, stir the pecans into the chicken mixture. Mound the chicken salad on a lettuce-lined serving platter. Cut the avocados into halves and remove the pits. Cut each avocado diagonally into slices 1/2 inch wide with a paring knife, being careful not to pierce the skin. Gently scoop out the avocado slices. (You may peel the avocado first and cut into 1×3-inch slices.) Lay the avocado slices decoratively on the mounded salad and drizzle with the reserved salad dressing.

Serves 12

M.O.B. Parties

*With weddings now costing
a fortune and requiring many
months of planning, a new
type of party has evolved—
a party given by friends to
honor and show appreciation
to the mother of the bride.
This type of party provides a
great opportunity to honor
valued friends in a more
intimate setting.*

*Mother-of-the-bride parties
are best enjoyed with only
the closest girlfriends of the
mother-of-the bride and with
plenty of either Champagne
or special party drinks. Here
are suggestions:*

- *Decorate using the theme
colors of the wedding or
the M.O.B.'s favorite colors.*

- *Buy or make inexpensive
veils of chiffon, taking care
that each veil has a comb
secured at the top. Drape
a veil over the back of each
dining chair for decoration.*

- *Before sitting down to eat,
take a group photo of
everyone wearing their veil
for the M.O.B.*

- *Gifts are not always
expected, but a joint gift
of a spa day is always
appreciated by the M.O.B.*

110

Chicken Salad with Cellophane Noodles and Spicy Ginger Dressing

This intriguing combination of flavors is delicious!

SPICY GINGER DRESSING	SALAD
1/2 cup coarsely chopped fresh ginger	3 pounds boneless skinless chicken breasts
1/4 cup red wine vinegar	5 tablespoons fresh lime juice
2 tablespoons unseasoned rice wine vinegar	1 1/2 teaspoons crushed hot pepper
2 tablespoons Mirin (sweet Sake)	4 navel oranges
2 tablespoons honey	8 cups water
2 tablespoons low-sodium soy sauce	8 ounces Chinese cellophane noodles
2 tablespoons fresh basil, minced	2 tablespoons peanut oil
1/2 teaspoon crushed hot pepper	1/4 cup fresh cilantro, chopped
1/2 teaspoon sesame oil	3 scallions, chopped
1/4 cup water	1 red bell pepper, chopped
1 cup peanut oil	8 ounces snow peas
	1 head romaine
	1 bunch radishes, trimmed and sliced for garnish

To prepare the dressing, process the ginger, red wine vinegar, rice wine vinegar, Mirin, honey, soy sauce, basil, hot pepper, sesame oil and water in a food processor. Add the peanut oil gradually, processing constantly until smooth.

To prepare the salad, combine the chicken, lime juice and hot pepper in a nonreactive bowl, turning the chicken to coat. Marinate, covered, in the refrigerator for 8 to 10 hours. Peel the oranges with a sharp knife, being careful to remove the white pith. Cut between the membranes to release the orange slices. Bring the water to a boil in a large saucepan. Add the noodles and cook for 4 minutes or until tender. Drain the noodles and rinse under cold water. Place in a large bowl. Add 3/4 cup of the dressing and toss to coat, adding more dressing if the noodles seem too dry. Heat the peanut oil in a large heavy skillet over medium-high heat. Add the chicken. Cook for 4 minutes on each side or until cooked through, turning once. Remove the chicken to a cutting board and slice against the grain into bite-size pieces. Combine the chicken and remaining dressing in a large bowl and mix well. Add the oranges, cilantro, scallions, bell pepper and snow peas and mix well. Arrange the romaine on a serving platter. Place the noodles on the lettuce and mound the chicken mixture on top of the noodles. Garnish with the radish slices.

Serves 12

Apollo's Chicken Salad

The basil sauce with feta cheese, olives, and vegetables makes this a crowd pleaser.

CHICKEN

    6 chicken breasts with ribs
    Salt and pepper to taste
    Juice of 2 lemons
    2 (14-ounce) cans low-sodium
       chicken broth

BASIL SAUCE

    2 large garlic cloves, minced
    4 eggs
    1 teaspoon dry mustard
    1/4 cup lemon juice
    1 teaspoon salt
    1 1/2 cups olive oil
    6 tablespoons chopped fresh basil

SALAD

    2 bunches broccoli, cut into florets
    8 scallions, chopped
    2 cups sliced mushrooms
    Boston or curly lettuce leaves
    2 (6-ounce) cans kalamata olives,
       pitted and cut into halves
    Tomato wedges or grape tomatoes
    8 ounces feta cheese, crumbled

To prepare the chicken, preheat the oven to 325 degrees. Place the chicken in a single layer in a large roasting pan and sprinkle with the salt, pepper and lemon juice. Pour the broth into the pan so the chicken is partially covered. Cover with foil and bake for 15 minutes. Turn the chicken and bake for 30 minutes longer or until cooked through. Cool in the pan for 15 minutes, drain. Cut the chicken into bite-size pieces, discarding the bones.

To prepare the sauce, process the garlic, eggs, dry mustard, lemon juice and salt in a food processor. Add the olive oil gradually, processing constantly until the sauce is thick and well combined. Stir in the basil.

To prepare the salad, steam the broccoli in a steamer for 4 to 6 minutes or until tender-crisp. Let stand until cool. Combine the chicken, scallions and mushrooms in a bowl and toss to mix. Add enough of the sauce to bind the chicken mixture together. Arrange the lettuce on a serving platter. Mound the chicken salad in the center and surround with the steamed broccoli, olives and tomatoes. Sprinkle with the feta cheese. Serve the remaining sauce on the side.

Note: If you are concerned about using raw eggs, use eggs pasteurized in their shells, which are sold at some specialty food stores, or use an equivalent amount of pasteurized egg substitute.

Serves 12

Stone Crab

Until you have tried stone crab for the first time, you can't understand the attraction of this slightly sweet and succulent crustacean. Not only is it a joy to the taste buds, but compared to lobster and other crab, it is simple to eat. Freezing or icing raw stone crab claws causes the meat to stick to the shell, so stone crab claws are always immediately cooked. The shells on the large claws are easily cracked and removed to show snowy-white meat edged with red and yellow. Stone crabs are delicious with no condiment, but if you prefer, try them with drawn butter or a sweet honey mustard sauce. As you are enjoying a stone crab claw, you can be happily aware that the crab from which the claw was harvested is most likely still residing in the ocean. Fisherman are only allowed to harvest one claw and must return the stone crab to the water so the crab will grow a new claw.

Crunchy Cabbage and Chicken Salad

This is an inexpensive and delicious salad for a crowd when served on a platter with Bibb lettuce and garnished with citrus slices.

1/2 cup sliced almonds
1 tablespoon sesame seeds
1 (3-ounce) package Top Ramen chicken-flavored ramen noodles
2 whole chicken breasts, cooked and cut into bite-size pieces
1 (16-ounce) package shredded cabbage coleslaw, or 1/2 head cabbage, shredded
4 scallions, chopped
1/2 cup canola oil
2 tablespoons sugar
2 tablespoons unseasoned rice wine vinegar
1 teaspoon salt
1/2 teaspoon freshly ground pepper

Preheat the oven to 400 degrees. Spread the almonds and sesame seeds in a baking pan. Bake for 4 to 6 minutes or until toasted, watching carefully to prevent burning. Place the ramen noodles in a small sealable plastic bag, reserving the seasoning packet for the dressing. Break the noodles into small pieces. Combine the chicken, cabbage, scallions, almonds, sesame seeds and crumbled noodles in a salad bowl and toss to mix.

Combine the oil, sugar, vinegar, salt, pepper and reserved seasoning packet in a bowl and mix well. Pour over the salad just before serving and toss to coat.

Serves 8 to 10

Stone Crab Salad with Lime and Orange Vinaigrette

Stone crab and avocado! The premier South Florida shellfish with its match in fruit.

¹/4 cup fresh lime juice
2 tablespoons fresh orange juice
¹/2 cup vegetable oil
¹/4 teaspoon salt
3 pounds cracked fresh stone crab claws
¹/2 cup parsley, chopped
2 tablespoons fresh thyme leaves
2 small ripe avocados, chopped
8 ounces field greens, rinsed and patted dry

Combine the lime juice, orange juice, oil and salt in a bowl and mix well. Reserve four of the crab claws for garnish. Remove the crab meat from the remaining claws. Combine the crab meat, parsley and thyme leaves in a bowl and stir gently to mix. Add one-half of the vinaigrette and toss to coat. Stir in the avocados gently, being careful not to mash. Divide the salad greens among four individual salad plates. Mound the stone crab mixture in the center of each plate. Garnish with a crab claw on the side of each plate. Serve the remaining dressing on the side.

Note: You may also layer this salad in a clear serving bowl with the crab claws decoratively around the edge of the bowl.

Serves 4

Stone Crab (continued)

Stone crabs are only available from October 15th until May 15th, so many Miami residents have made serving stone crabs a holiday tradition, especially at New Year's. If you want stone crabs shipped to you, try Joe's Stone Crab in Miami Beach (1-800-780-2722 or joesstonecrab.com) or Fresh Choice Seafood in Key West (1-305-498-8500 or fresh choiceseafood.stores.yahoo.net /florstonclaw.) As a main course, allow three crab claws per person, which should yield approximately one pound of crab meat per person. Stone crabs will last for up to two days in the coldest part of your refrigerator.

113

Sea Scallops on a Bed of Bibb Lettuce with Warm Vinaigrette

An elegant and special choice for a first course.

2 heads Bibb lettuce
4 ounces bacon, cut into small pieces
1/2 red onion, finely chopped
1/4 cup dried cranberries
1/4 cup golden raisins
1 teaspoon fresh thyme, finely chopped
1 teaspoon fresh rosemary, finely chopped
12 large sea scallops
6 tablespoons olive oil
1 teaspoon garlic, minced
1/2 cup olive oil
2 tablespoons Champagne vinegar
1 teaspoon Dijon mustard
Salt and freshly ground pepper to taste

Rinse the lettuce well. Drain and pat dry. Arrange the lettuce leaves decoratively on four salad plates. Sauté the bacon in a small sauté pan until almost crisp. Add the onion, cranberries, raisins, thyme and rosemary. Cook until the onion is transparent and the bacon is crisp.

Sauté the scallops a few at a time in a small amount of 6 tablespoons olive oil in a skillet until light golden brown and opaque in the middle, draining the skillet of the water which will leak from the scallops and adding additional olive oil as needed.

Whisk the garlic, 1/2 cup olive oil, the vinegar, mustard, salt and pepper in a bowl until well combined. Add to the bacon mixture and heat slightly, stirring constantly.

Place three scallops on each prepared salad plate. Ladle the warm vinaigrette over the scallops and lettuce. Serve immediately.

Serves 4

Wine Recommendations: Chardonnay or Sauvignon Blanc

Scrumptious Shrimp Salad with Cilantro Dressing

Serve this beautiful salad on a bed of salad greens.

CILANTRO DRESSING
- I cup chopped cilantro
- I egg yolk
- I tablespoon Dijon mustard
- I shallot, chopped
- I garlic clove, chopped
- I mild chile, chopped
- I 1/2 cups peanut oil
- 1/2 teaspoon salt
- I tablespoon lime juice

SALAD
- 1/2 zucchini
- 1/2 teaspoon salt
- 1/2 cup baby carrots
- I red bell pepper
- 1/2 green bell pepper
- 1/2 yellow bell pepper
- I pound shrimp, grilled, peeled and deveined
- 1/2 cup black beans, rinsed and drained
- 1/2 cup corn kernels, drained
- Salad greens

To prepare the dressing, process the cilantro in a food processor. Add the egg yolk, mustard, shallot, garlic and chile. Add the oil in a thin stream, processing constantly. Add the salt and lime juice and mix well.

To prepare the salad, peel the zucchini and remove the seeds. Cut the zucchini into julienne pieces. Place in a colander and sprinkle with the salt. Let stand in the sink to drain for 30 minutes. Remove any green tops from the baby carrots. Cut the carrots into julienne pieces. Cut the bell peppers into julienne pieces. Steam the bell peppers in a steamer for 5 minutes or until tender-crisp. Cool the bell peppers. Combine the zucchini, bell peppers, carrots, shrimp, beans and corn in a bowl. Add the dressing and toss to mix well. Spoon into a serving bowl lined with salad greens.

Note: If you are concerned about using raw egg yolks, use yolks from eggs pasteurized in their shells, which are sold at some specialty food stores, or use an equivalent amount of pasteurized egg substitute.

Serves 4

Left to right: Chocolate Chip Pound Cake with Chocolate Drip Icing, Roasted Pears with Pomegranate Glaze, Scrumptuous Shrimp Salad with Cilantro Dressing, Biscayne Bay Chicken Salad, Potato Crescent Knot Dinner Rolls, and Poppy Seed Muffins

Clean all patio surfaces the day before the party, including not only furniture but also fans, doors, windows, and ceilings. On the day of the party, clean glass tabletops and patio decking.

The day before the party, watch the play of the sun and place furniture to allow for your preference of sun and shade.

Position the table near the kitchen to allow for ease in serving.

If you are serving guests buffet-style, select a table or counter in your home which can be used as an alternate buffet table if the weather is inclement.

Baby Greens Salad with Lime and Honey Vinaigrette

Delicious, light, and easy to prepare, this salad is a wonderful first course for many rich and spicy main courses.

LIME AND HONEY VINAIGRETTE
6 tablespoons extra-virgin olive oil
3 tablespoons lime juice
2 teaspoons honey
1/4 teaspoon kosher salt
Freshly ground pepper to taste

SALAD
2 small heads baby romaine
20 ounces baby greens
10 ounces baby spinach
1/2 red onion, sliced and separated into rings
1 pint grape tomatoes

To prepare the vinaigrette, combine the olive oil, lime juice, honey, kosher salt and pepper in a bowl and mix well.

To prepare the salad, tear the romaine into bite-size pieces. Rinse the romaine, baby greens and spinach and spin dry or pat dry. Combine the romaine, baby greens and spinach in a large salad bowl. Add the onion, tomatoes and one-half of the vinaigrette and toss to mix. Serve with the remaining dressing on the side.

Serves 12

Badi's Caesar Salad

This classic recipe is a family favorite that has been passed down through the generations. Serving the salad with frozen salad forks will ensure this salad stays cold and crisp.

2 heads romaine
1 garlic clove
$^1/_4$ cup ($^1/_2$ stick) butter, melted
3 slices day-old bread
1 (2-ounce) can flat anchovies
3 or 4 garlic cloves
$^1/_2$ teaspoon McCormick's seasoned salt, or to taste
Seasoned pepper to taste

1 tablespoon olive oil
1 tablespoon tarragon vinegar
1 teaspoon dry mustard
2 egg yolks
Juice of $^1/_2$ lemon
2 dashes of Worcestershire sauce
$^1/_4$ to $^1/_2$ cup (1 to 2 ounces) freshly grated Parmesan cheese or Romano cheese

Rinse the lettuce in cool water. Tear the leaves into pieces, removing most of the vein from the pieces and any brown spots. Wrap the pieces in a towel and chill until crisp and dry.

Preheat the oven to 250 degrees. Press one garlic clove and stir into the butter. Lightly brush the top and bottom of the bread slices with the butter mixture. Place on a baking sheet and bake until lightly brown on each side, turning once. Remove from the oven to cool. Cut the bread into $^3/_4 \times ^3/_4$-inch pieces.

Drain the anchovies, reserving 1 tablespoon of the oil. (If there is less than 1 tablespoon of oil available, add enough additional olive oil to measure 1 tablespoon.) Crush three or four garlic cloves and the seasoned salt in the bottom of an unfinished wooden salad bowl to flavor the bowl. Remove one-third to one-half of the garlic, depending upon your taste preference. Add the seasoned pepper, reserved anchovy oil and olive oil to the garlic in the bowl. Stir in the vinegar and dry mustard. Add the egg yolks and stir to mix well. Stir in the lemon juice and Worcestershire sauce. Add the anchovies and mash to a mushy consistency.

Add the romaine to the dressing. Top with the croutons and cheese and toss to coat. Add additional croutons or cheese if desired. Serve immediately.

Note: If you are concerned about using raw egg yolks, use yolks from eggs pasteurized in their shells, which are sold at some specialty food stores, or use an equivalent amount of pasteurized egg substitute.

Serves 4 to 6

Outdoor Dining Tips

(continued)

Place the buffet table, the drinks table, and any dining tables or other furniture apart from each other to ease traffic congestion.

If guests will be holding dishes on their laps, serve food that does not need to be cut with a knife.

Choose food which can be served at room temperature and will not be affected by additional humidity or wind.

Wait to light any decorative candles until the sun is setting. Since most candles can be snuffed out easily by wind, have someone watching and ready to relight candles after it is dark.

Fattoush

Miami has several long-established Middle Eastern food markets.
This healthful, light salad is perfect for Miami's hot weather.

2 (3- to 4-day old) pita bread rounds
1 seedless cucumber, cut into $1/2$-inch pieces
1 teaspoon kosher salt
3 cups chopped romaine
3 ripe tomatoes, cut into $1/2$-inch pieces (about $1 1/4$ pounds)
6 scallions, thinly sliced
1 green bell pepper, cut into $1/2$-inch pieces
$1/4$ cup fresh flat-leaf parsley, chopped
$1/3$ cup fresh mint, chopped
$1/4$ cup fresh cilantro, chopped
Salt and freshly ground pepper to taste
2 garlic cloves, minced
$1/4$ cup fresh lemon juice
$1/3$ cup extra-virgin olive oil

Preheat the oven to 375 degrees. Split each pita bread round horizontally into halves and tear into 1-inch pieces. Spread on a baking sheet and bake for 10 to 12 minutes or until dry and golden brown.

Place the cucumber in a single layer on several layers of paper towels. Sprinkle with the kosher salt and let stand for 20 minutes. Place in a colander and rinse under cold running water to remove the kosher salt. Pat dry with paper towels.

Combine the cucumber, lettuce, tomatoes, scallions, bell pepper, parsley, mint and cilantro in a large bowl. Season with salt and pepper to taste and toss gently. Cover and chill for 1 hour.

Whisk the garlic, lemon juice and olive oil together in a small bowl. Season with salt and pepper to taste. Add the dressing and pita crisps to the salad and toss together. Place on a serving platter and serve immediately.

Serves 6

Summer Pear and Parmesan Salad with Lemon Dijon Vinaigrette

A tangy vinaigrette complements this appetizing salad.

LEMON DIJON VINAIGRETTE

1 tablespoon lemon juice
1 tablespoon white wine vinegar
1 garlic clove, minced
1 tablespoon Dijon mustard
1/2 cup extra-virgin olive oil
Salt and freshly ground pepper to taste

SALAD

3 tablespoons pine nuts
10 ounces mixed salad greens
2 Bartlett pears, cored
3 ounces Parmesan cheese, thinly shaved
1 bunch fresh basil, chopped

To prepare the vinaigrette, combine the lemon juice and vinegar in a bowl and mix well. Stir in the garlic, mustard, olive oil, salt and pepper.

To prepare the salad, heat a small skillet over high heat. Add the pine nuts and toast until light brown. Remove from the skillet and let stand until cool. Toss the salad greens with the vinaigrette in a large bowl to coat. Arrange on a large platter. Thinly slice the pears and lay decoratively over the salad greens. Sprinkle the cheese over the top, reserving any extra for another purpose. Sprinkle with the basil and toasted pine nuts.

Serves 4 to 6

Papaya, Fruit of the Angels

During Columbus's explorations of the New World, the Caribbean Indians introduced him to one of the sweetest tropical fruits, the papaya. Columbus adored papaya and called it "the fruit of the angels." Columbus and other explorers brought papayas to subtropical lands throughout the world when they traveled to India, the Philippines, and parts of Africa.

For cooks using papaya for the first time, they come as a very pleasant surprise. For a fruit, papaya has a long shelf life, so usually the papaya purchased in markets is ripe and juicy. Papayas, also called paw-paw, are shaped like pears and can be as large as twenty inches and as short as six inches.

Asparagus and Green Papaya Salad with Mango Vinaigrette

The mango vinaigrette is the perfect sweet and tart accompaniment for the asparagus and green papaya.

Mango Vinaigrette
1/2 cup fresh orange juice
5 tablespoons olive oil
1 1/2 tablespoons white balsamic vinegar, or to taste
Kosher salt and freshly ground pepper to taste
1 cup (1/4-inch) chopped mango

Salad
24 thin stalks asparagus, or 20 thick stalks asparagus
4 cups mixed baby greens
2 cups chopped green papaya, or 1 large cucumber, peeled and cut into circles 1/4 inch thick
1/4 cup chopped chives for garnish

To prepare the vinaigrette, combine the orange juice, olive oil, vinegar, kosher salt and pepper in a bowl and blend well. Stir in the mango. Chill in the refrigerator.

To prepare the salad, snap off the thick woody ends of the asparagus stem so the asparagus will lie on a salad plate. Steam the asparagus in a steamer until tender-crisp. Chill in the refrigerator. Arrange the baby greens on four individual salad plates. Lay five or six asparagus stalks in the center of each plate. Surround the asparagus with the papaya. Spoon the vinaigrette over the top and garnish with the chives.

Serves 4

Photograph on page 150.

Black Bean Salad with Chipotle Vinaigrette

Serve this salad with Plantain Chips (page 63) or Mojitos (page 26) on a sunny day or on a balmy evening.

2 teaspoons cumin seeds
1 tablespoon adobo sauce
    (from a can of chipotle chiles in adobo sauce)
1/4 cup red wine vinegar
1/4 cup extra-virgin olive oil
1 (28-ounce) can Italian-style chopped tomatoes, drained
1/4 teaspoon sugar
5 (15-ounce) cans black beans, drained and rinsed,
    or 8 cups cooked dried black beans
2/3 cup finely chopped red or sweet yellow onion
2 tablespoons thinly sliced tender scallions, green parts only
1/4 cup finely chopped cilantro
3 tablespoons finely chopped parsley
Kosher salt and freshly ground pepper to taste
Lettuce leaves
5 ounces goat cheese, crumbled
1 tablespoon finely chopped parsley

Toast the cumin seeds in a small heavy skillet over medium heat for 1 to 2 minutes or until the seeds darken and become fragrant, shaking the skillet constantly. Let the seeds stand to cool slightly. Grind the seeds to a fine powder in a mortar with a pestle or in a spice mill or coffee grinder.

Whisk the adobo sauce and cumin together in a medium bowl. Whisk in the vinegar and olive oil. Cover and set aside. (The vinaigrette can be prepared ahead to this point and left at room temperature for up to 8 hours before serving.)

Two hours before serving time, stir the tomatoes and sugar in a small bowl. Let stand for 15 minutes. Combine the beans, onion, scallions, cilantro and 3 tablespoons parsley in a large serving bowl. Fold in the tomato mixture. Whisk the vinaigrette and add to the salad, tossing gently but thoroughly. Season with kosher salt and pepper and toss again. Cover and let stand in a cool place for 1 3/4 hours, stirring occasionally.

To serve, spoon the salad on a lettuce-lined platter. Scatter the goat cheese over the salad and sprinkle with 1 tablespoon parsley.

Serves 12 to 14

Photograph on page 36.

Papaya, Fruit of the Angels *(continued)*

Be sure to peel away the bitter skin of the papaya. Most papaya have some green unripe flesh which is pleasant but bland, and the apricot-colored flesh in the heart of the papaya is sweet and fragrant. The black seeds in the center are edible with a sharp, peppery taste. Choose papaya with unblemished skin and no soft patches. Papaya ripens easily on its own.

The sweetness of ripe papaya is offset nicely by the tartness of lime juice, which makes it perfect for salsas. Salt also complements its sweetness, so serve it as an appetizer wrapped with proscuitto as you would melon.

Crispy Green Bean Salad

This is a colorful and flavorful side dish for roast pork.

1/2 cup honey
Pinch of cayenne pepper
1 1/2 cups pecans
3 tablespoons sherry vinegar
2 teaspoons Dijon mustard
1/4 teaspoon kosher salt
1/2 cup walnut oil

2 pounds string green beans, trimmed
    and cut into bite-size pieces
3/4 cup dried cranberries
2 heads Belgian endive, trimmed and
    sliced lengthwise
Freshly ground black pepper to taste

Preheat the oven to 350 degrees. Heat the honey and cayenne pepper in a small saucepan over low heat until warm. Remove from the heat and stir in the pecans. Line a baking pan with foil and spray with nonstick cooking spray. Spread the pecans in a single layer in the prepared pan and bake for 10 minutes or until golden brown. Remove the pecans to waxed paper to cool, being careful that the pecans do not touch each other.

Whisk the vinegar, mustard and kosher salt together in a small bowl. Drizzle in the walnut oil gradually, whisking constantly until well combined.

Fill a large bowl with ice water and set aside. Fill a medium saucepan with water and bring to a boil. Add the beans and cook for 2 minutes or until just tender. Drain immediately and immerse in the ice water. Remove the beans from the water and pat dry. Place in a large bowl and toss with the vinaigrette. Add the pecans, cranberries, endive and black pepper and toss gently. Serve immediately.

Serves 8

Beet Salad with Cilantro, Lemon and Cumin Dressing

8 cups water
3 large beets, peeled and
    cut into 1/2-inch pieces
2 tablespoons chopped fresh cilantro
1 tablespoon chopped fresh chives

3 garlic cloves, finely chopped
3 tablespoons lemon juice
1 teaspoon cumin
3 tablespoons virgin olive oil
Salt to taste

Bring the water to a boil in a large saucepan. Add the beets and reduce the heat to low. Cover and simmer for 10 minutes or until tender. Drain well and let stand until cool.

Combine the cilantro, chives, garlic, lemon juice, cumin, olive oil and salt in a large bowl. Add the beets and toss to coat. Chill, covered, for 40 minutes or longer before serving.

Serves 6

Sweet and Salty Broccoli Salad

This sweet and salty salad reflects the cook's preference for a sweeter or more salty dish.

1 cup mayonnaise
1/4 cup sugar, or to taste
1/2 teaspoon curry powder, or to taste
3 1/2 tablespoons white vinegar
1 large head broccoli, cut into bite-size florets
5 scallions, chopped, or 1/2 cup chopped red onion
1/2 to 1 cup dried cranberries or mandarin orange or tangerine slices
1 to 2 cups cashews

Combine the mayonnaise, sugar, curry powder and vinegar in a bowl and mix well. Chill, covered, in the refrigerator. Combine the broccoli, scallions and cranberries in a bowl and toss to mix. Chill, covered, for 3 to 10 hours.

To serve, add the cashews and dressing to the broccoli mixture and toss to coat.

Serves 8

Yogurt Cucumber Salad

Light and flavorful.

1 teaspoon salt
2 garlic cloves, pressed
2 cups plain yogurt
1 seedless cucumber, thinly sliced
Dash of paprika
1 tablespoon parsley, chopped
1 tablespoon fresh mint, chopped
    or 1/2 tablespoon dried mint
Salt and freshly ground black pepper to taste

Mash 1 teaspoon salt and the garlic together in a salad bowl. Blend in the yogurt. Add the cucumber, paprika, parsley, one-half of the mint and salt and black pepper to taste and mix gently. Sprinkle with the remaining mint. Chill, covered, until ready to serve. Serve cold.

Serves 6

Yogurt Tahini Dressing

This tantalizing dressing with a sharp edge works well as a dip for vegetables or pita chips. To prepare, combine 3/4 cup plain yogurt, 1/3 cup tahini, 1/4 cup water, 3 tablespoons (or more) lemon juice, 2 garlic cloves, pressed, 1/2 teaspoon salt, 1 pinch of cumin and 1 tablespoon parsley, chopped in a jar with a tight-fitting lid. Seal the jar and shake well. This recipe makes about 1 1/3 cups.

Jicama

Like the boniato, many people are surprised at the delicate, delicious flavor of peeled jicama, which unpeeled looks like a turnip or large radish. Its raw taste and texture is similar to that of apples or pears. Because it does not discolor quickly when exposed to open air, it works beautifully in salads. Cooked jicama takes on the flavors of whatever it is cooked with.

Jicama belongs to the bean family and is a staple in Latin America and China. It is also known as the Mexican potato, Mexican yam bean, Chinese potato, Chinese turnip, and lo bok. When purchasing, select only jicama that are firm, dry, and have no blemishes.

Mango and Jicama Salad

If you have never eaten jicama, try this salad. You will love it.

1 pound jicama
4 small mangoes, coarsely chopped
2 cups best-quality frozen corn kernels, thawed and drained
1/2 cup chopped red onion
1/4 cup fresh lime juice
2 tablespoons olive oil
1 or 2 jalapeño chiles, chopped (optional)
1 small avocado, chopped
Salt and pepper to taste
1/2 cup chopped fresh cilantro

Peel the jicama and cut into matchstick slices 1/4 inch wide and 1 inch long. Combine the jicama, mangoes, corn, onion, lime juice, olive oil, jalapeño chiles and avocado in a bowl and toss to mix. Season with salt and pepper. Cover and chill for 3 hours to allow the flavors to blend. Add the cilantro and toss to mix. Serve cold.

Note: Chop the cilantro, measure and add to the salad just before serving.

Serves 12

Picnic Potato Salad with Mustard Vinaigrette

This light and tasty potato salad is perfect for a picnic as it has no dairy products.

MUSTARD VINAIGRETTE

$1/3$ cup safflower oil

3 tablespoons olive oil

2 to 4 tablespoons white or red wine vinegar

Juice of 1 lemon

2 garlic cloves, minced

2 tablespoons grainy mustard

$1/4$ teaspoon dried basil

$1/4$ teaspoon dried thyme

$1/4$ teaspoon dried summer savory

Salt and freshly ground pepper to taste

SALAD

$1 1/2$ pounds red potatoes

$1/2$ cup finely chopped celery

$1/2$ cup minced green bell peppers

1 scallion, chopped

$1/3$ cup black olives, chopped

2 tablespoons fresh parsley, chopped

Salt and freshly ground pepper to taste

To prepare the vinaigrette, combine the safflower oil, olive oil, vinegar, lemon juice, garlic, mustard, basil, thyme, savory, salt and pepper in a cruet or a jar with a tight-fitting lid. Cover and shake well. (The flavor is enhanced if made in advance.)

To prepare the salad, boil the potatoes in water to cover in a saucepan for 20 minutes or until soft. Drain the potatoes and cool to room temperature. Place in a bowl and chill in the refrigerator. Chop the potatoes. Add the celery, bell peppers, scallion, olives, parsley, salt and pepper and mix well. Stir in $1/2$ cup of the vinaigrette, reserving the remaining vinaigrette for another purpose. Cover and chill until ready to serve.

Serves 6

Jamaican Pigeon Peas, Wild Rice and Pepper Salad with Apple Cider Vinaigrette

Jamaican pigeon peas and rice have long been staples in the Caribbean. Here we have turned it into a refreshing salad. Add a fiery chile if you prefer heat with your dishes.

3/4 cup long grain and wild rice blend
2 1/2 cups chicken broth
1 (15-ounce) can high-quality pigeon peas,
   or 2 cups cooked dried pigeon peas
1 red bell pepper, chopped
1 cup chopped red onion
1/2 cup olive oil
1/4 cup apple cider vinegar
1 small bunch of fresh cilantro
8 sprigs of thyme
1 teaspoon salt
Salt and pepper to taste
Lettuce leaves
4 small tomatoes, sliced
1/2 (8-ounce) jar hearts of palm,
   chopped into 1/4-inch pieces

Cook the rice in the simmering broth in a medium saucepan until al dente; drain and rinse. Drain and rinse the peas. Combine the rice, peas, bell pepper and onion in a large bowl. (You may make ahead up to this point and chill until ready to serve.) To serve, combine the olive oil and vinegar in a bowl and blend well. Chop the cilantro coarsely. Remove the thyme leaves from the stems. Stir 2 tablespoons of the cilantro, 3 tablespoons of the thyme and 1 teaspoon salt into the olive oil mixture. Stir into the rice mixture. Season with salt and pepper to taste. Line a serving platter with the lettuce leaves. Mound the rice salad in the middle and arrange the tomatoes around the edge. Sprinkle the top of the salad with the remaining cilantro and thyme. Sprinkle the hearts of palm on the tomato slices.

Note: Do not chop the cilantro or remove the thyme leaves from the stems for the dressing until you are ready to serve the salad. Both the thyme and cilantro lose their flavor quickly, and the cilantro will turn brown.

Serves 8

Pasta Salad with Baked Salmon and Fresh Vegetables

A delectable combination of flavors.

1 (1-pound) fresh salmon fillet
2 tablespoons soy sauce
12 ounces bow tie pasta
1 tablespoon olive oil
2 cups sour cream
1/4 cup fresh dill weed, finely chopped
1 bunch scallions, finely chopped (about 4)
1 (14-ounce) can artichoke hearts, finely chopped
20 small green olives
1 large seedless cucumber, finely chopped
1 cup walnut pieces, lightly toasted
Salt and freshly ground pepper to taste

Preheat the oven to 350 degrees. Coat the fish with the soy sauce. Wrap the fish in foil and bake for 30 minutes or until cooked through. Remove from the oven and unwrap. Let stand until cool. Remove the skin and cut the fish into bite-size pieces along the grain.

Cook the pasta using the package directions and drain. Rinse with cold water and drain again. Place in a large bowl and lightly toss with the olive oil. Stir in the sour cream and dill weed. Add the salmon, scallions, artichoke hearts and olives and toss to mix. Chill, covered, for several hours. Stir in the cucumber and walnuts just before serving. Season with salt and pepper.

Serves 6

Basil, Tomato and Pine Nut Pasta Salad

A tasty combination of flavors and textures your friends and family will enjoy.

3 cups chopped tomatoes
8 ounces cream cheese or Brie cheese
3/4 cup olive oil
1 tablespoon red wine vinegar
1/3 cup chopped fresh basil
2 garlic cloves, minced
Salt and freshly ground pepper to taste
1 pound linguini
1/2 cup pine nuts, toasted
3/4 cup (3 ounces) freshly shaved Parmesan cheese

Combine the tomatoes, cream cheese, olive oil, vinegar, basil, garlic, salt and pepper in a large serving bowl and mix lightly. Cover and marinate at room temperature for 2 hours.

Prepare the pasta using the package directions; drain well. Rinse with cool running water and drain well again. Add to the tomato mixture and toss lightly. Sprinkle with the pine nuts and Parmesan cheese.

Serves 8

Versatile Grain Salad

Use your choice of grains and vegetables in this salad. The tangy dressing works well with all combinations.

3 cups cooked grain (such as white or brown rice, couscous, millet or barley)
1/2 to 1 cup chopped vegetables (such as chopped tomatoes,
    cucumber, celery, carrots, parsley, green, red or yellow
    bell peppers, scallions, cooked corn and/or cooked peas)
1/4 cup lemon juice
1/2 cup olive oil
3 garlic cloves, pressed
Salt and freshly ground pepper to taste

Combine the grain and vegetables in a large bowl and stir with a fork to mix. Whisk the lemon juice, olive oil, garlic, salt and pepper in a bowl until well mixed. Pour over the salad just before serving and mix well with a fork.

Serves 4 to 6

Curried Rice Salad with Carrots, Coconut and Raisins

This flavorful salad serves well as a main course when combined with chopped cooked chicken or shrimp.

4 (6-ounce) packages chicken-flavored Rice-A-Roni
6 tablespoons butter or margarine, melted
2 1/4 teaspoons curry powder
10 cups water
3/4 cup olive oil
1/3 cup white wine vinegar
1 tablespoon lemon juice
1/3 cup chopped parsley
3 garlic cloves, pressed
6 tablespoons mango chutney
3/4 cup dark raisins
3/4 cup golden raisins
6 tablespoons sliced scallions
1 1/2 cups grated coconut
2 1/4 cups shredded carrots
3 tablespoons mango chutney

Remove the seasoning packets from each package of the Rice-A-Roni and set aside. Brown the contents of each package of Rice-A-Roni separately with 1 1/2 tablespoons of the butter and a little over 1/2 teaspoon of the curry powder in a large skillet. Place in a large saucepan. Add the water and the contents of the reserved seasoning packets. Bring to a boil and then reduce the heat to low. Simmer for 15 minutes. Drain the rice, stirring while the rice drains and cools. Cover and chill for 30 minutes.

Combine the olive oil, vinegar, lemon juice, parsley and garlic in a large bowl and mix well. Stir in 6 tablespoons chutney and the raisins. Let stand for 15 minutes. Add the rice, scallions, coconut and carrots and toss to mix. Stir in 3 tablespoons chutney 1 tablespoonful at a time, if desired.

Serves 12

Should I Rent That Tent?

You're planning a large casual outdoor party during a time of the year when the weather is usually beautiful. You are sure it won't rain, but as the day approaches the weather forecast is grim. You are unable to locate a tent to rent because it is the time of year when many people in your area entertain outdoors, and no tents are available on short notice. After weeks of planning the day arrives, and it rains! Everyone crowds in your home to eat all the delicious food you've prepared. The money you saved on a tent rental will now be used to recover your living room sofa because someone spilled barbecue sauce.

Plan ahead and rent that tent! Find out the last possible time and date that you can cancel and keep an eye on the weather forecast. If you are entertaining at a time of year when it may rain but is very rarely windy, try ordering a decorative tent which may not have sides such as a tent with a pagoda top.

Tabouli

This classic dish takes little time when you use a food processor for the parsley and scallions. Serve with fresh pita bread.

DRESSING
3 garlic cloves
1/2 teaspoon salt
1 cup fresh lemon juice
1 cup extra-virgin olive oil
Salt and freshly ground pepper to taste

SALAD
1/2 cup fine- to medium-grade bulgur wheat
2 cups water
1 1/2 cups finely chopped parsley
1/2 cup finely chopped seeded tomato
1/2 cup finely chopped cucumber
1/4 cup finely chopped scallions
1/2 cup finely chopped fresh mint (optional)
Lettuce leaves
Tomato wedges and mint leaves for garnish

To prepare the dressing, mash the garlic cloves with 1/2 teaspoon salt in a small bowl. Stir in the lemon juice and olive oil. Season with salt and pepper to taste.

To prepare the salad, place the bulgur in a large bowl and cover with 2 cups water. Let stand for 2 hours. Drain in a colander and press down on the bulgur with the back of a spoon to squeeze out the excess moisture. Combine the bulgur, parsley, chopped tomato, cucumber, scallions and chopped mint in a large bowl and toss to mix. Add enough of the dressing to moisten but not soak the bulgur mixture. Serve in a lettuce-lined salad bowl or on a lettuce-lined platter. Garnish with tomato wedges and mint leaves.

Note: You may also squeeze the bulgur dry with your hands. Alternatively, you may bring 3 cups of water to a boil in a large saucepan. Add the bulgur and boil for 1 minute. Cover and turn off the heat. Let stand for 6 minutes. Uncover and drain the bulgur. Let stand until cool. Squeeze out any excess moisture.

Serves 6

The Unicorn's Miso Dressing

Miso is a salty condiment that is a combination of soy, some type of grain, salt, and a mold culture which are combined and fermented for one to three years. Miso can be found in Asian markets and should be refrigerated.

2 tablespoons mellow white miso
¹/4 cup soy oil or canola oil
¹/2 teaspoon minced onion
1 tablespoon cider vinegar
1 teaspoon tamari
1 tablespoon minced parsley
5 tablespoons water

Process the miso, soy oil, onion, vinegar, tamari, parsley and water in a blender until smooth and creamy. Chill until ready to serve.

Makes about 1 cup

My Girlfriend's Salad Dressing

This popular recipe has been passed from friend to friend.

¹/2 cup balsamic vinegar
2 tablespoons minced garlic
¹/4 cup sugar
¹/4 cup minced cilantro
¹/2 teaspoon salt
¹/2 teaspoon pepper
1 cup olive oil

Combine the vinegar, garlic, sugar, cilantro, salt and pepper in a bowl and mix well. Add the olive oil in a steady stream, stirring constantly until well combined. (You can also mix with a handheld mixer.)

Makes about 2 cups

Picture a place of elegance, beauty, and calm. In all directions—over an expanse of 150 acres—is eye-pleasing green: palms, banyan trees, tropical gardens, and classic fairways. Pools and fountains, small lakes, and waterways sparkle in the sun. The location for our intimate dinner for ten is the historic Biltmore Hotel in Coral Gables. With its eighteen-hole golf course, ten tennis courts, world-class spa and fitness center, and its famous swimming pool flanked by handsomely furnished private cabanas, the Biltmore Hotel also has sumptuously decorated interiors, including the opulent dining room where our dinner will be held.

Hundreds of world leaders have enjoyed the charms of the Biltmore, including presidents Clinton, Bush, and Carter and the Dalai Lama and countless celebrities, including Johnny Depp, Oprah Winfrey, Andy Garcia, and Jamie Foxx. The Biltmore's magnificent tropical setting and iconic towering architecture have been the setting for many Hollywood films.

As the sun is setting, our guests arrive, and we gather on a large balcony overlooking the sparkling pool and the swaying palm trees. Cucumber Flowers Filled with Crab and Salmon Roe and Sunset Bisque serve as our enticing appetizers. When we move inside, we find our banquet table for ten has been set with lovely antique china and crystal and Tiffany's Richelieu silver. Elegant antique silver candelabras flank our colorful and gorgeously exuberant floral arrangement of hybrid delphinium, millet, fragrant stock, deep blue hydrangeas, and a palette of roses, including Orange Unique, Raphaella, and Ilse spray roses.

The vivid blues, oranges, and reds of our flowers set off the pale greens and deep reds of our delicious first course, Sea Scallops on a Bed of Bibb Lettuce with Warm Vinaigrette. Charmed by the sumptuous meal and setting, conversation is happy and lively this evening. Toasts and laughter are shared as our guests enjoy the main course, which features tropical vegetables, Garlic and Parmesan Mashed Boniato, and Grilled Vegetable Terrine paired with Roasted Leg of Lamb with Wine and Garlic Herb Sauce.

Every fabulous dinner should have a fabulous dessert. Ours is an exquisite tower of cream, raspberries, and ginger-flavored cookies, Raspberry Rosinas with Passion Fruit Coulis, lovely in its presentation and sinfully satisfying with its sweet tartness.

As the evening draws to a close, our guests linger. Everyone has completely enjoyed our luxurious and intimate party, and everyone wishes to prolong the magic of a perfect evening.

Meat and Poultry

Sumptuous Banquet

Menu

Sunset Bisque *page 18*

Cucumber Flowers Filled
with Crab and Salmon
Roe *page 38*

Sea Scallops on a Bed of
Bibb Lettuce with Warm
Vinaigrette *page 114*

Roasted Leg of Lamb with
Wine and Garlic Herb
Sauce *page 144*

Garlic and Parmesan
Mashed Boniato
page 91

Grilled Vegetable Terrine
page 96

Potato Crescent Knot
Dinner Rolls *page 71*

Pinot Noir, Syrah or Red
Zinfandel

Raspberry Rosinas with
Passion Fruit Coulis
page 222

*Toasts and laughter are shared as our guests enjoy the main course which features
tropical vegetables, Garlic and Parmesan Mashed Boniato and Grilled Vegetable
Terrine paired with Roasted Leg of Lamb with Wine and Garlic Herb Sauce.*

As the sun is setting, our guests arrive and we gather on a large balcony overlooking the sparkling pool and the swaying palm trees. Cucumber Flowers Filled with Crab and Salmon Roe and Sunset Bisque serve as our enticing appetizers.

Work Plan

SEVERAL DAYS AHEAD

Cookies for Raspberry Rosinas can be made several days ahead and stored in airtight containers until assembly time.

Passion Fruit Coulis can be made up to two days ahead but must be removed from the refrigerator 30 minutes before using.

ON THE DAY

Make Sunset Bisque and place in the refrigerator to chill. Serve cold.

Roast peppers, eggplant, and zucchini. Assemble terrine and refrigerate until set.

Clean, pat dry, and refrigerate greens for terrine.

Make the Cucumber Flowers and the crab topping. Store the topping in a bowl and refrigerate. Wrap the flowers and refrigerate.

Make Garlic and Parmesan Mashed Boniato and warm in the microwave before serving.

JUST BEFORE SERVING

Lay Cucumber Flowers on a platter and top with the filling. Dollop the top with the caviar. Serve as a passing appetizer with the Sunset Bisque.

Add chilled cream to Sunset Bisque before serving.

Prepare lettuce for scallop bed. Cook the bacon until crisp. Sauté the scallops. Whisk the vinaigrette. Assemble on a lettuce bed and serve immediately.

Roast the leg of lamb. While lamb is resting make Garlic Herb Sauce from drippings.

Make dressing for Vegetable Terrine. Remove Vegetable Terrine from the pan. Serve on bed of fresh greens with dressing on the side.

Make whipped cream for the Raspberry Rosinas. Assemble the dessert. Top with mint and add extra dollops of Coulis if desired.

Boliche Relleno (Roasted Eye of Round Beef Stuffed with Chorizo and Ham)

This delicious Cuban classic should be marinated for 8 to 10 hours.
The stuffing could also include chopped carrots and chiles.

1 teaspoon salt
2 teaspoons freshly ground pepper
2 tablespoons dried oregano, or 6 tablespoons finely chopped fresh oregano
1/4 cup paprika
1 (4- to 5-pound) boliche (eye of round beef), pierced about 1 inch in diameter
    through the center and the entire length (The butcher can do this for you.)
3 small whole chorizos, or 1 (6-inch) chorizo
8 ounces smoked ham (optional)
1/4 cup olive oil
3 large onions, cut into thin crescent-shaped pieces
1 large green bell pepper, cut into strips
6 garlic cloves, minced
4 bay leaves
1 cup red wine
3 cups beef broth
1 tablespoon all-purpose flour
1/4 cup water

Mix the salt, pepper, oregano and paprika together and rub on the outside of the boliche until well covered. Marinate in the refrigerator for 8 to 10 hours. Preheat the oven to 300 degrees. Cut the ends from the chorizos and discard. Chop the chorizos and ham into small pieces and mix together. (If you are using only the chorizos, then leave whole.) Stuff all the way through the boliche. Heat the olive oil in a Dutch oven over medium heat. Add the onions, bell pepper and garlic and stir to coat with the olive oil. Add the boliche and brown on all sides. Add the bay leaves, wine and broth. Remove the Dutch oven from the heat source and cover. Bake for 3 hours, turning in the sauce and basting every 30 minutes. Remove the boliche from the Dutch oven and set aside.

To prepare the gravy, process the remaining drippings and contents of the Dutch oven in a food processor until smooth. Let stand for 10 minutes to allow the fat to rise to the top. Skim off the fat, reserving 1 tablespoon. Place the remaining mixture in a saucepan and heat over low heat until warm. Mix the reserved fat and flour in a small bowl. Add the water and mix well. Stir into the heated mixture. Cook until thickened, stirring constantly.

Cut the boliche into slices 1/2 inch thick and serve with the gravy. Serve with white rice, black beans and Fried Ripe Plantains (see page 63).

Serves 8

Wine Recommendations: Syrah, Cabernet Franc, Pinot Noir, Malbec, Cabernet Sauvignon, or Chianti Classico

Ropa Vieja (Shredded Beef in a Rich Savory Sauce)

Since the beef required is shredded, this Cuban dish has come to be called Ropa Vieja, which translates to "old clothes" in Spanish. There is nothing shabby about this dish, however; the beef is tender and the sauce is flavorful and rich. You may substitute skirt steak or brisket for the flank steak. Plan to serve it with white rice and Fried Ripe Plantains (see page 63). This dish is wonderful reheated the next day.

1 1/2 pounds flank steak, cut into large pieces	2 tablespoons olive oil
8 cups water	4 garlic cloves, minced
2 Spanish onions, chopped	1 bay leaf
1 green bell pepper, cut into strips	1 teaspoon dried oregano
4 garlic cloves	1/4 teaspoon cumin
2 ripe tomatoes, peeled and seeded	1/2 cup red wine
2 bay leaves, crushed	1 (15-ounce) can tomato sauce
1 teaspoon salt, or to taste	Pinch of sugar
2 large Spanish onions, chopped	1 tablespoon white vinegar
1 green bell pepper, cut into narrow strips	Salt and pepper to taste

Bring the steak and water to a boil in a large stockpot over high heat, skimming and discarding the foam from the top. Add two onions, one bell pepper, four garlic cloves, the tomatoes, crushed bay leaves and 1 teaspoon salt. Reduce the heat to low and simmer, covered, for 1 1/2 hours or until the steak is tender and the strands of beef begin to separate, skimming the surface to eliminate any foam as needed. Remove from the heat to cool. Remove the beef, reserving the broth in the stockpot. Shred the beef by pounding with a mallet to separate the strands and then separating along the grain with your fingers. Set the beef aside.

Strain the broth, discarding the solids. Reserve 1 cup of the broth and store the remaining broth for another purpose. (The broth may be frozen.) Sauté two onions and one bell pepper in the olive oil in a large skillet over medium heat for 5 minutes or until tender. Add four minced garlic cloves, the whole bay leaf, oregano and cumin and cook for 10 minutes. Mix the reserved broth, wine, tomato sauce, sugar and vinegar in a bowl and stir into the sautéed vegetables. Add the shredded beef and salt and pepper to taste and mix well. Reduce the heat and cook for 10 minutes. Discard the bay leaf. Serve immediately or keep warm over low heat for up to 30 minutes.

Serves 4

Wine Recommendations: Cabernet Sauvignon, Cabernet Franc, Pinot Noir, Rioja, Dão, Barolo, or Montepulciano

Flavorful Grilling

Marinate grilled meat, fish, or poultry to enhance the flavor. A marinade is a combination of liquid and dry ingredients such as herbs, fruit juice, garlic, soy sauce, vinegar, wine, beer, fruits, or vegetables. Marinades that are more acidic will shorten grilling times. Marinades are usually acidic, so marinating foods should be placed in nonreactive containers such as resealable plastic bags or glass dishes. If part of the marinade is to be used as a sauce with the dish, then reserve some of the marinade before marinating uncooked meat, fish, or poultry to prevent contamination.

Grilled Fillet of Beef with Peppercorns

Prepare this recipe earlier in the day and warm up the sauce for an elegant buffet.

2 garlic cloves, minced
1 bay leaf, crushed
1 cup good-quality Cabernet
1 tablespoon olive oil
1 tablespoon balsamic vinegar
1 1/2 pounds center-cut fillet of beef
2 tablespoons cracked black pepper
Salt to taste
1 tablespoon tomato paste
1/4 cup (1/2 stick) butter
Freshly ground black pepper to taste

Combine the garlic, bay leaf, wine, olive oil and vinegar in a bowl and mix well. Rub the beef with the cracked pepper and place in a glass container. Pour the wine mixture over the beef to cover. Marinate in the refrigerator for 1 hour or longer. (The marinade strongly affects the flavor of the beef, so if you want a stronger taste of the marinade, especially the flavor of the wine, then marinate for 4 to 10 hours.) Drain the beef, reserving the marinade. Sprinkle the beef with salt.

Preheat the grill. Place the beef on a grill rack and grill over high heat until seared on both sides. Move the beef to a grill rack set over indirect heat. Close the lid and grill for 6 to 8 minutes for a fillet that is 1 1/2 inches thick for rare or for 8 to 10 minutes for medium. Remove the beef to a warm platter and let stand for 10 minutes.

Bring the reserved marinade and tomato paste to a boil in a saucepan. Whisk in the butter a little at a time until the sauce is a creamy consistency. Discard the bay leaf. Season the sauce with salt and pepper. Serve over the beef.

Serves 4

Wine Recommendation: Cabernet

Grilled Flank Steak with Chimichurri Sauce

This Argentinean dish has been adopted by Nicaraguan restaurants throughout Miami. The marinated grilled flank steak is commonly known as churrasco. Chimichurri sauce is a type of pesto and is also delicious with chicken and fish. Many Miamians have created their own special chimichurri sauce; this is our favorite.

CHIMICHURRI SAUCE

1/4 cup fresh cilantro leaves
1 cup fresh Italian parsley leaves
1/4 cup extra-virgin olive oil
2 very large garlic cloves
1/2 teaspoon cumin
1/2 teaspoon salt

STEAK

3 tablespoons olive oil
1 tablespoon onion powder
1 tablespoon chili powder (optional)
1/2 teaspoon cumin
Juice from 1 bitter orange, or juice from 1/2 lemon and 1/2 orange
2 1/2 pounds flank steak or skirt steak

To prepare the sauce, pulse the cilantro, parsley, olive oil, garlic, cumin and salt in a food processor until puréed. (The sauce is best made the day before serving. If you plan to serve the sauce with pork, add an additional 2 tablespoons cilantro leaves.)

To prepare the beef, combine the olive oil, onion powder, chili powder, cumin and orange juice in a bowl and mix well. Place the beef in a sealable plastic bag and add the marinade. Seal the bag and marinate in the refrigerator for 1 to 10 hours.

Preheat the grill. Drain the beef, discarding the marinade. Place the beef on a grill rack and grill over high heat for 4 minutes for medium-rare, turning once. Cut the steak into strips 1 inch wide and serve with the sauce. Black beans, rice and Fried Ripe Plantains (see page 63) are the perfect accompaniment.

Serves 6

Wine Recommendations: Malbec, Zinfandel, Syrah, Merlot, or Rioja

Photograph on page 36.

Flavorful Grilling
(continued)

Try this Caribbean Marinade for Chicken. Place 6 chicken breasts in a sealable plastic bag. Mix 1 1/3 cups light rum, the juice of 4 limes, 2 tablespoons vegetable oil, 1/4 cup grated onion, and 1 teaspoon salt in a bowl. Reserve one-half of the marinade to serve with the chicken. Pour the remaining marinade over the chicken breasts and seal the bag. Marinate in the refrigerator for 2 hours, turning every 30 minutes. Drain the chicken discarding the marinade. Place on a grill rack and grill until the chicken is cooked through. Serve with the reserved marinade.

Grilling Kabobs

When you are preparing kabobs, always soak wooden skewers for at least thirty minutes so the skewers won't burn on the grill. Metal kabobs work best for all meat and chicken kabobs, because these have to grill longer. If you are using a metal skewer for the first time, be careful of any plastic that may be part of the handle of the metal skewer; this plastic may melt.

Because chicken must be cooked all the way through, it helps to pound it before cutting it for skewers. If you have marinated the kabobs ahead of time, either remove some of the marinade with a paper towel or cook the kabobs over high heat, so the kabobs won't have a mushy texture.

Sweet and Savory Brisket with Vegetables

The addition of ale, sugar, and cinnamon gives this recipe a delicious new twist.

1 (4-pound) corned beef brisket
3 sweet onions, chopped
1 large package baby carrots
1 package red or new yellow golden potatoes
1 head cabbage, cut into quarters
1 cinnamon stick
12 whole allspice berries
6 garlic peppercorns
12 Melange peppercorns
4 bay leaves
6 whole cloves
1/2 teaspoon dill weed, or 1/4 teaspoon dill weed and
   1/4 teaspoon dill seeds
2 tablespoons brown sugar
1 (12-ounce) bottle Killian red ale
1 tablespoon garlic salt
1 cup heavy whipping cream
2 tablespoons potato starch
1 tablespoon dill weed

Place the brisket, onions, carrots, potatoes, cabbage, cinnamon, allspice, peppercorns, bay leaves, cloves, 1/2 teaspoon dill weed and the brown sugar in a Dutch oven or any pan large enough to hold all of the ingredients in a single layer. Pour the ale over the top. Add enough water to barely cover the layers. Bring to a boil, skimming any fat from the surface. Reduce the heat to low and cook for 4 hours. Let stand for 15 minutes or longer. Remove the beef to a cutting board and cut into slices. Place the beef slices on a serving platter and surround with the vegetables. Strain the broth from the brisket, reserving 3 cups.

Combine the reserved broth, 1 tablespoon garlic salt, the cream, potato starch and 1 tablespoon dill weed in a saucepan and mix well. Cook over low heat until thickened, stirring constantly. Pour into a gravy boat and serve with the brisket and vegetables.

Note: The brisket can also be served with yellow or spicy mustard or white sauce.

Serves 8

Wine Recommendation: Gewürztraminer

Lamb Kabobs with Cilantro, Cucumber and Yogurt Sauce

Although it seems unusual, the cucumber with cilantro and mint makes a delightful sauce for these kabobs.

CILANTRO, CUCUMBER AND YOGURT SAUCE
2/3 cup plain yogurt
1 tablespoon chopped fresh cilantro
1 tablespoon chopped fresh mint
2 teaspoons grated onion
1/2 cup chopped seedless cucumber

KABOBS
2 pounds boneless lean lamb
5 sprigs of fresh thyme, minced
5 sprigs of fresh rosemary, minced
Salt and pepper to taste
Sprigs of fresh rosemary and lemon wedges for garnish

To prepare the sauce, combine the yogurt, cilantro, mint, onion and cucumber in a bowl and mix well. Chill, covered, for 8 to 10 hours. Remove from the refrigerator 30 minutes before serving.

To prepare the kabobs, cut the lamb into 1-inch pieces and place in a glass bowl or other nonmetal container. Mix the thyme and minced rosemary together and press onto the lamb. Season with salt and pepper. Cover with plastic wrap and chill for 8 hours or longer.

Preheat the grill. Thread the lamb onto skewers and place on a grill rack. Grill over high heat for 10 minutes, turning the skewers carefully. Serve with the sauce and garnish with sprigs of fresh rosemary and lemon wedges.

Serves 4

Wine Recommendation: Sauvignon Blanc

Grilling Kabobs *(continued)*

Always load your skewers with ingredients that take about the same time to cook. Although it is a temptation to pack food tightly on a skewer, leave a small space between the kabob pieces so the pieces will cook evenly.

Sear the meat and chicken kabobs to lock in the flavor and then cook the kabobs over medium heat to finish cooking. Chicken kabobs should grill for 12 to 16 minutes or to 170 degrees on a meat thermometer. Lamb or beef kabobs should grill for 6 to 9 minutes on a charcoal grill and 7 to 10 minutes on a gas grill. For medium-rare lamb or beef, the internal temperature should be 145 degrees.

Roasted Leg of Lamb with Wine and Garlic Herb Sauce

This delicious and satisfying roasted leg of lamb has an elegant presentation.

2 sprigs of fresh thyme
2 sprigs of fresh rosemary
1 (6-pound) leg of lamb
1 tablespoon olive oil
Salt and pepper to taste
2 large garlic cloves, cut into small slivers
3/4 cup white wine
3/4 cup water
2 small white onions, cut into quarters
2 large garlic cloves, cut into small slivers
1 to 2 tablespoons all-purpose flour

Preheat the oven to 400 degrees. Remove the leaves from the thyme and rosemary sprigs and set aside. Trim the lamb, leaving only a thin layer of fat. Cut small slits in the lamb with a sharp knife all the way to the bone. Rub the lamb with the olive oil and sprinkle with salt and pepper. Cover with the thyme and rosemary leaves. Slide two slivered garlic cloves into the slits.

Reserve 1 tablespoon of the wine. Combine the remaining wine with the water, onions and two slivered garlic cloves in a bowl. Pour into a roasting pan and place the lamb in the mixture. Place the pan on the bottom oven rack and roast for 20 minutes. Reduce the oven temperature to 350 degrees. Roast for 50 minutes longer or until a meat thermometer registers 145 degrees for medium-rare. (The juices should be pink and not red when pierced with a fork.) Remove from the oven and let stand for 15 minutes. Remove the lamb to a carving board. Skim the fat from the pan drippings and deglaze the pan by stirring to remove the drippings, garlic and onion from the bottom of the pan. Stir the flour into the reserved wine in a small cup. Add to the pan drippings. Cook over low heat until thickened, stirring constantly. Carve the lamb and serve with the gravy.

Serves 4

Wine Recommendations: Pinot Noir, Merlot, Syrah, Zinfandel, or Malbec

Clockwise: Grilled Vegetable Terrine, Garlic and Parmesan Mashed Boniato, and Roasted Leg of Lamb with Wine and Garlic Herb Sauce

Delicious Pork Tenderloin

Pork tenderloin is easy to cook and because it has a milder taste than other cuts of pork, it works well with many marinades and sauces.

To prepare a pork tenderloin you will need to use a sharp knife to trim away the glossy white outer membrane called the silver skin. Cutting away this layer of sinew allows the meat to absorb marinades and rubs more easily and allows the meat to cook more evenly.

At one end of the tenderloin, cut into the edge of the silver skin. Lift this skin up and away from the tenderloin, keeping the silver skin taut as you cut it away from the tenderloin. Trim away any extra fat from the tenderloin.

Oriental Glazed Rack of Lamb

Serve this easy and elegant recipe with Wasabi Garlic Mashed Potatoes (page 92).

1/2 cup hoisin sauce
2 tablespoons honey
1/2 tablespoon soy sauce
1 tablespoon vegetable oil
1 rack of lamb, trimmed
Salt and pepper to taste
Parsley for garnish

Preheat the grill. Combine the hoisin sauce, honey, soy sauce and oil in a bowl and mix well. Season the lamb with salt and pepper and place on a grill rack. Grill over low to medium heat for 20 minutes, brushing with some of the glaze during the last few minutes of grilling. (The lamb should be pink in the middle.) Cut the lamb into slices and place on a serving platter. Pour the remaining glaze over the top.

Serves 4

Wine Recommendations: Gewürztraminer or Riesling

Pork Tenderloin with Guava and Ginger Marinade

1 cup guava jelly
1/4 cup light rum
1/4 cup tomato paste
1/4 cup fresh lime juice
1 tablespoon soy sauce
2 tablespoons ketchup
1 tablespoon Worcestershire sauce
2 tablespoons minced sweet yellow onion
1 1/2 tablespoons fresh ginger
2 garlic cloves, pressed
1/4 teaspoon salt
Freshly ground pepper to taste
1 (3-pound) pork tenderloin

Cook the jelly, rum, tomato paste, lime juice, soy sauce, ketchup and Worcestershire sauce in a medium saucepan over low heat until the jelly melts. Add the onion, ginger, garlic, salt and pepper. Simmer until the mixture is slightly thickened, stirring constantly.

Place the pork in a nonreactive pan. Pour one-half of the marinade over the pork, reserving the remaining marinade in the refrigerator for basting. Marinate, covered, in the refrigerator for 4 to 10 hours. Bring the pork to room temperature.

Preheat the oven to 325 degrees. Drain the pork, discarding the marinade. Place the pork in a roasting pan and baste with the reserved marinade. Roast for 30 minutes, basting every 15 minutes. Remove from the oven and let stand for 5 minutes. Cut the pork diagonally into slices.

Serves 4

Wine Recommendations: Merlot or Chardonnay

Delicious Pork Tenderloin *(continued)*

Pork tenderloin cooks quickly and is far less fatty than traditional pork roasts and chops. Since it is less fatty, it is important to carefully watch it while roasting or grilling so it does not overcook. Tenderloin should be ready when it is between 160 and 170 degrees. Like most roasts, it will continue to cook after it is removed from the oven.

Roasted Pork with Mojo Marinade

Mojo (pronounced mo-ho) is a staple of Cuban cuisine loved by many Miami residents. This marinade also works well as a sauce for grilling and is delicious with chicken, turkey, fish, and yuca. Bottled mojo is no substitute for fresh. The basic ingredients are citrus juice or some other acidic juice, olive oil, and garlic. Vegetable oil may be substituted for olive oil, and lime, grapefruit, or even pomegranate juice may be substituted for the sour orange juice. Thyme, oregano, bay leaves, or parsley are also welcome additions. A traditional Cuban Thanksgiving features turkey marinated (under the skin) in mojo sauce and either roasted or grilled. Serve with Moros y Cristianos (page 99) or with boiled yuca with extra mojo sauce.

6 garlic cloves
1/4 cup olive oil
1 cup sour orange juice, or 1/2 cup lime juice and 1/2 cup orange juice
1 teaspoon cumin, or to taste
Salt and freshly ground pepper to taste
1 (3-pound) pork tenderloin

Process the garlic cloves one a time in a food processor until chopped. Heat the olive oil in a saucepan. Add the garlic, scraping the side of the bowl of the food processor with a spatula. Sauté until lightly toasted, being careful not to overcook or the garlic will become bitter. Add the orange juice and cumin and bring to a boil. Season with salt and pepper. Add additional cumin if desired. Remove from the heat to cool.

Place the pork in a nonreactive roasting pan or baking dish. Pour one-half of the sauce over the pork. Store the remaining sauce in the refrigerator until serving time. Cover the pork and marinate in the refrigerator for 4 to 10 hours.

Preheat the oven to 350 degrees. Roast the pork for 25 minutes or until 160 degrees on a meat thermometer. Let stand for 10 minutes. (If the pork has not had time to marinate long, wrap in foil and roast for 30 to 35 minutes. Remove from the foil.)

Heat the remaining sauce in a saucepan. Cut the pork across the grain into slices. Serve with the warm sauce.

Serves 4

Wine Recommendations: Chardonnay, Fumé Blanc, Cabernet Franc, or Barbera

Cuban Sandwich

This is Miami's favorite sandwich. Cuban sandwiches are similar to sub sandwiches. They are always made with pork roasted in mojo sauce and never have mayonnaise, lettuce, or tomato. They are grilled in a sandwich griller called a plancha, which leaves grill marks. If you don't have a plancha, try grilling on top of a small kitchen grill with a heavy object wrapped in foil pressing down on top of the sandwich. This will allow the cheese to melt, the meat to warm, and will give the sandwich its distinctive grill marks. Be sure to spray the surface of the grill or plancha with nonstick butter spray. In a pinch, a sandwich press may also be used or a waffle iron which has the sides inverted to the flat side.

1 loaf Cuban bread
Mustard to taste
8 ounces Roast Pork with Mojo Marinade (at left)
8 ounces baked ham
8 ounces Swiss cheese
8 thin slices dill pickle

Cut the bread into halves horizontally. Spread the cut sides of the bread with mustard. Layer the pork, ham, cheese and dill pickle on the bottom half of the bread. Top with the remaining half. Grill in a plancha coated with nonstick butter spray until the sandwich is heated through and the cheese melts.

Makes 1 large sandwich

Medianoche Sandwich

These small sandwiches have the same ingredients as a Cuban sandwich except pan suave, or Cuban sweet rolls, is used. Why the difference? These sandwiches were created to be eaten in the middle of the night, or "medianoche," after a night of dancing and partying. Pan suave is very similar to challah bread, which could be substituted. There is no substitution, however, for the Roasted Mojo Pork with Mojo Marinade.

*Clockwise: Asparagus and Green Papaya Salad with
Mango Vinaigrette, Gioconda's White Beans and Tomatoes, and
Grilled Pork Tenderloin with Red Pepper and Pineapple Curry*

Grilled Pork Tenderloin with Red Pepper and Pineapple Chutney

An outstanding dish for elegant grilling. You will love the chutney!

RED PEPPER AND
PINEAPPLE CHUTNEY

- 1 pineapple, cored
  and chopped
- 1/2 red bell pepper, chopped
- 3 tablespoons golden raisins
- 1/2 lemon, thinly sliced
- 1/2 teaspoon salt
- 1 teaspoon cinnamon
- 1 cup light brown sugar
- 1 cup granulated sugar
- 1/4 teaspoon allspice
- 1/4 teaspoon cumin seeds
- 2 tablespoons white vinegar
- 1 to 3 tablespoons chopped
  jalapeño chiles
- 1 tablespoon white vinegar

PORK

- 1 (3-pound) boneless
  pork roast
- 1/2 cup peanut oil
- 1/2 cup soy sauce
- 1/4 cup red wine vinegar
- 3 tablespoons lemon juice
- 3 tablespoons Worcestershire
  sauce
- 1 garlic clove, pressed
- 1 tablespoon chopped
  fresh parsley
- 1 tablespoon dry mustard
- 1 1/2 teaspoons pepper

To prepare the chutney, bring the pineapple, bell pepper, raisins, lemon, salt, cinnamon, brown sugar, granulated sugar, allspice, cumin, 2 tablespoons vinegar and the jalapeño chiles to a boil in a saucepan. Reduce the heat and simmer until the pineapple and bell pepper are cooked through and the liquid has nearly evaporated. Add enough of the 1 tablespoon vinegar to taste to adjust the sweet-and-sour balance. Remove from the heat to cool. (The chutney may be poured into hot sterilized jars and sealed with two-piece lids to store for 1 year.)

To prepare the pork, place the pork in a glass container. Mix the peanut oil, soy sauce, vinegar, lemon juice, Worcestershire sauce, garlic, parsley, dry mustard and pepper in a bowl. Pour over the pork and cover with plastic wrap. Marinate in the refrigerator for 8 to 10 hours. Preheat the grill. Drain the pork, discarding the marinade. Place the pork on a grill rack and grill over direct high heat for 1 to 2 minutes on each side to sear. Grill over indirect medium-high heat with the lid down for 20 to 25 minutes or to 160 degrees on a meat thermometer for medium. Serve with the chutney.

Serves 4

Wine Recommendation: Riesling

Roasted Stuffed Pork with Mango Papaya Sauce

Start this savory roasted pork the day before serving.

2 cups dry Sherry	6 whole cloves
1 tablespoon cider vinegar	1 (3 1/2-pound) boneless pork loin,
1 cinnamon stick, broken into halves	trimmed
2 tablespoons fresh lemon juice	1 onion, finely chopped
1 1/2 teaspoons grated lemon zest	1/3 cup chopped mango
1/2 cup golden raisins	1/3 cup chopped papaya
1/2 cup chopped dried apricots	1 tablespoon light brown sugar
2 cups dry Sherry	Salt and pepper to taste
1/2 teaspoon pepper	1 tablespoon vegetable oil

Combine 2 cups Sherry, the vinegar, cinnamon stick, lemon juice and lemon zest in a medium saucepan and simmer over medium-high heat for 2 minutes. Add the raisins and apricots and simmer for 20 minutes or until the fruit is tender and the mixture thickens slightly. Pour into a dish and chill, covered, for 8 to 10 hours.

Combine 2 cups Sherry, 1/2 teaspoon pepper and the cloves in a small saucepan and simmer for 2 minutes. Remove from the heat and cool to room temperature. Cut the pork lengthwise three-fourths of the way down the center and open as for a book. Sprinkle the cut side with some of the onion. Fold the pork to close and place in a 9×13-inch glass baking dish. Sprinkle with the remaining onion. Pour the marinade over the pork and marinate in the refrigerator for 8 to 10 hours.

Preheat the oven to 375 degrees. Drain any liquid from the apricot mixture, reserving the liquid and discarding the cinnamon stick. Stir the mango, papaya and brown sugar into the apricot mixture. Drain the pork and pat dry, discarding the marinade. Open the pork as for a book and season with salt and pepper to taste. Spoon two-thirds of the fruit mixture down the center of the pork, reserving the remaining fruit mixture. Fold the pork over to enclose the filling and tie in several places with kitchen string. Season with salt and pepper.

Heat the oil in a large heavy Dutch oven over medium-high heat. Add the pork and cook for 5 minutes on both sides until brown. Place in a large roasting pan and roast for 1 1/4 hours or to 160 degrees on a meat thermometer. Place the pork on a platter, reserving the pan juices. Tent with foil and let stand for 20 minutes.

Mix the reserved liquid from the apricot mixture, remaining fruit mixture and the reserved pan juices in a small heavy saucepan and bring to a simmer. Cut the pork into slices and serve with the sauce.

Serves 6

Wine Recommendations: Merlot or Chardonnay

Nochebuena Pork

This delicious dish is traditionally served on Christmas Eve in many Hispanic households. Many families will cook a whole pig in their backyards. This recipe, calling for a leg of pork, has been adopted by many families as an easier alternative.

1 (6-pound) leg of pork
1/4 cup dry white wine
2 cups sour orange juice,
   or 1 cup lemon juice and
   1 cup orange juice
4 bay leaves, finely chopped
2 teaspoons dried oregano,
   or 2 tablespoons finely
   chopped fresh oregano
1 1/2 teaspoons cumin
1 teaspoon paprika

1 teaspoon salt, or to taste
1 teaspoon freshly
   ground pepper
6 garlic cloves, pressed
3 tablespoons all-purpose flour
1 cup finely chopped onion
1/2 cup dry Sherry
Dash of hot red pepper sauce
1/2 teaspoon dry mustard
1/4 teaspoon sugar

Rinse the pork and pat dry. Trim off any excess fat. Place the pork in a roasting pan and make incisions or gashes with a knife all over the pork. Mix the wine and orange juice together and pour over the pork. Add the bay leaves to the mixture in the bottom of the pan. Crush the oregano, cumin, paprika, salt, pepper and garlic in a mortar with a pestle to form a paste. Rub in the incisions and over the surface of the pork. Cover and chill for 8 to 10 hours.

Preheat the oven to 325 degrees. Remove the pork to a platter and pour the marinade into a bowl. Line the bottom of the roasting pan with foil and return the pork to the pan. Cover and roast for 45 minutes. Uncover and roast for 30 minutes per pound, basting every 15 minutes with the reserved marinade until all of the marinade is used. Remove from the oven and let stand at room temperature for 20 to 30 minutes.

Pour the pan drippings into a fat separator. Separate the fat from the remainder of the drippings, reserving about 3 tablespoons fat. Mix the reserved fat and flour in a bowl. Place the drippings in a saucepan and add the onion. Cook over low heat until the onion is cooked through, stirring constantly. Stir in the Sherry, hot sauce, mustard and sugar. Add the flour mixture 1 tablespoon at a time, cooking until the mixture is thickened, stirring constantly. Carve the pork into slices. Serve with the gravy and Nochebuena Yuca (page 95).

Serves 6

Wine Recommendations: Riesling, Beaujolais, or Syrah

Adobo

Adobo is a wonderfully versatile marinade popular with many South Floridians. The basic ingredients include garlic, salt, cumin, oregano, and some type of citrus juice. Sour orange juice makes this a quintessential Cuban marinade. If sour oranges aren't available, combine equal amounts of orange juice and lime juice.

Varieties of adobo are popular throughout the country, particularly with chipotle (smoked jalapeño) chiles added for a fiery taste. To modify the recipe at left, add three tablespoons chopped chipotle chiles to the paste. Two tablespoons of vinegar can also be substituted for the wine for a tangier taste.

Slow-Cooked Pork with Zesty Mustard Barbecue Sauce

This tasty shredded pork also makes great sandwiches.

PORK

- 1 whole pork ham
- 1 cup (or more) vinegar
- 1 teaspoon freshly ground pepper
- 2 tablespoons onion powder
- 2 tablespoons garlic powder
- 2 tablespoons dry mustard
- 1 tablespoon paprika

ZESTY MUSTARD BARBECUE SAUCE

- 2 cups ketchup
- 2 cups mustard
- 2 cups white vinegar
- 2 tablespoons Worcestershire sauce
- 1 tablespoon lemon juice
- 1/4 cup packed light brown sugar or honey
- 1/2 cup (1 stick) butter
- 1/2 teaspoon cayenne pepper
- 1/4 teaspoon black pepper
- 1 teaspoon Tabasco sauce (optional)

To prepare the pork, preheat the oven to 350 degrees. Trim the pork, removing all of the fat and skin. Rub the pork liberally with the vinegar, adding more if needed. Mix the pepper, onion powder, garlic powder, dry mustard and paprika together and rub over the pork to coat. Place in a roasting pan lined with heavy-duty foil. Cover tightly with foil. Place in the oven and reduce the oven temperature to 200 degrees. Bake for 10 to 12 hours.

To prepare the sauce, combine the ketchup, mustard, vinegar, Worcestershire sauce, lemon juice, brown sugar, butter, cayenne pepper and black pepper in a saucepan and mix well. Cook until the butter melts, stirring constantly. Divide the sauce between two separate serving bowls. Stir the Tabasco sauce into one of the bowls for an extra-hot sauce.

To serve, cut the pork into slices; it will shred. Serve au jus or with either of the two sauces. The pork can also be served with the Barbecue Sauce (see page 163).

Serves 8

Wine Recommendations: Gewürztraminer, Riesling, Merlot, Malbec, Burgundy, or Pinot Noir

Slow-Cooked Pork with Achiote Marinade

If you buy garlic already peeled at the supermarket, this rich and tasty pork dish will be simple to prepare.

4 ounces achiote paste
20 garlic cloves, pressed
3 cups orange juice
1 1/2 cups chicken stock
4 teaspoons olive oil
4 teaspoons shortening
1 bay leaf
1 (6-pound) pork picnic (leg of pork)
6 banana leaves (optional)

Preheat the oven to 325 degrees. Process the achiote paste, garlic, orange juice, stock and olive oil in a food processor until smooth. Heat the shortening in a large skillet. Add the achiote mixture and bay leaf and simmer for 10 minutes. Place the pork in a large Dutch oven. Pour the achiote mixture over the pork. Cover with the banana leaves. Bake, covered, for 3 hours. Shred the pork and serve the sauce on the side.

Serves 6

Wine Recommendations: Bordeaux (Saint-Emilion), Fleurie, Merlot, Chianti, Malbec, or Beaujolais

During the fall of each year, over six hundred Girl Scouts participate in our Girl Scout Workshop program. The scouts earn their opera badge through lessons in dance, music, makeup, crafts, and staging centered on one of the Florida Grand Opera's planned performances for the season. All interested parents and leaders should contact their Girl Scout Council headquarters in early fall.

Roast Loin of Veal with Rosemary Mustard Gravy

The herb wine sauce enhances the deliciously spicy roasted veal.

1 (2- to 2¹/2-pound) boned veal loin, trimmed and tied together
Salt and pepper to taste
¹/3 cup Dijon mustard
6 garlic cloves, pressed
10 shallots, minced
1 tablespoon rosemary, finely chopped
1¹/2 cups dry white wine
4 ounces bacon
¹/2 cup water

Preheat the oven to 325 degrees. Season the veal with salt and pepper. Cover the top and side with the mustard. Place in a small roasting pan and add the garlic, shallots, rosemary and wine. Cover the portion of the veal not covered in wine with the bacon. Roast for 1 hour, basting every 15 minutes with the pan juices. Remove the bacon and set aside. Continue to roast the veal for 15 to 20 minutes or to 145 degrees on a meat thermometer. Remove to a cutting board with a well for the pan juices and let stand, covered with foil, for 15 minutes. Strain the pan drippings in a colander, returning the liquid drippings to the roasting pan and placing the solids in a bowl. Continue to cook the bacon in a skillet until crisp; drain and crumble.

Let the liquid pan drippings stand for 3 minutes to allow any fat to rise to the top. Skim off the fat and discard. Return any drippings from the veal to the pan. Add the water and bring to a simmer, stirring to deglaze the pan. Strain the gravy through a fine mesh strainer or two layers of cheesecloth into a bowl. Stir in the reserved solids. Season with salt and pepper and add the crumbled bacon. Cut the veal into slices and spoon the gravy over the top. Serve immediately.

Serves 4

Wine Recommendation: Pinot Noir

Spicy Pork Chops with Pineapple Salsa

Make the salsa a day ahead and rub the spice mixture into the pork chops in the morning before work or a day out. You will have a delicious dinner ready in thirty minutes in the evening.

1 tablespoon cardamom	1 teaspoon salt
3 garlic cloves, pressed	1 teaspoon freshly ground black pepper
1 tablespoon coriander	6 loin pork chops, 1 to 1 1/2 inches thick
1 1/2 teaspoons cayenne pepper	Pineapple Salsa (page 65)
3 tablespoons grated lemon zest	

Mix the cardamom, garlic, coriander, cayenne pepper, lemon zest, salt and black pepper in a bowl. Rub into the pork chops and place in a glass dish. Marinate, covered, in the refrigerator for 3 to 4 hours.

Preheat the grill. Place the pork chops on a grill rack and grill over medium-high heat to sear both sides. Reduce the heat to medium and grill for 10 minutes or until cooked through. Serve with salsa.

Serves 3 to 4

Wine Recommendations: Chardonnay or Merlot

Rigatoni alla Bosciola

1 teaspoon salt	1 cup boxed Pomi chopped tomatoes or
2/3 pound rigatoni, preferably Italian brand	other chopped plum tomatoes
4 Italian sausages, casings removed	2 cups heavy whipping cream
1 onion, chopped	3/4 cup (3 ounces) grated
1 garlic clove, minced	Parmigiano-Reggiano
2 tablespoons plus 2 teaspoons olive oil	1 teaspoon olive oil, or to taste
4 ounces thinly sliced cremini mushrooms	Salt and freshly ground pepper to taste

Fill a large stockpot with water and add 1 teaspoon salt. Bring to a boil and then add the pasta. Cook for 9 minutes, stirring to keep the pasta from sticking together. Drain and rinse with cold water; drain well, Crumble the sausages into small pieces. Sauté the onion and garlic in 2 tablespoons plus 2 teaspoons olive oil in a large skillet until translucent. Add the sausages and mushrooms and sauté until light brown. Add the tomatoes and cook over low heat until the sausages are cooked through. Stir in the cream. Increase the heat to high and add the pasta, tossing well with the sauce. (Do not overcook; the pasta should be al dente.) Remove from the heat. Sprinkle with the cheese and drizzle with 1 teaspoon olive oil. Season with salt and pepper to taste.

Serves 4

Wine Recommendations: Zinfandel or Barbera

Osso Buco

This wonderful dish should be accompanied by Golden Risotto with Creamy Wine Sauce (page 103).

2 tablespoons all-purpose flour
8 pieces veal shank, each piece
   2 inches thick with bone and marrow
   in the center
Salt and freshly ground pepper to taste
1 large onion, finely chopped
3 carrots, finely chopped
2 ribs celery with leaves removed,
   finely chopped
2 garlic cloves, finely chopped
1/4 cup olive oil
1 cup white wine

1/2 cup beef stock or salt-free beef broth
1 (28-ounce) can peeled tomatoes
1 teaspoon dried sage
1 teaspoon dried thyme
2 bay leaves
1/4 cup (1/2 stick) butter, softened
   (optional)
2 tablespoons all-purpose flour (optional)
Grated zest of 1 lemon
1/2 garlic clove, finely chopped
1 teaspoon chopped parsley

Spread 2 tablespoons flour on a plate or sheet of waxed paper. Tie each veal shank with kitchen string to keep their shape and season with salt and pepper. Dredge in the flour and shake off any excess.

Sauté the onion, carrots, celery and two garlic cloves in 2 tablespoons of the olive oil in a large Dutch oven over medium heat for 3 minutes. Remove the vegetables with a slotted spoon and set aside. Place the remaining 2 tablespoons olive oil in the Dutch oven. Add the veal shanks in a single layer and cook until brown on both sides. Remove the veal shanks and keep warm. Discard the excess fat from the pan drippings. Add the wine and stock to the Dutch oven, stirring to deglaze. Return the vegetables and veal shanks to the Dutch oven and add the tomatoes, sage, thyme and bay leaves. Bring to a boil and then reduce the heat. Simmer, covered, for 1 1/4 hours or until the veal shanks are tender. (Do not overcook or the veal shanks will fall apart. The veal shanks may also be baked in a 350-degree oven.) Remove the veal shanks from the sauce and keep warm.

Remove the bay leaves from the sauce and discard. (The sauce should be slightly thick. To thicken the sauce, mix the butter and 2 tablespoons flour together in a bowl. Cook the sauce, adding just enough of the butter mixture a small amount at a time to thicken to the desired consistency, stirring constantly.)

Combine the lemon zest, half garlic clove and the parsley in a bowl to make a cremolata. Serve the veal shanks with the sauce poured over the top. Sprinkle the cremolata on top of the sauce.

Serves 4

Wine Recommendations: Pinot Gris or Sauvignon Blanc

Lemon Parmesan Veal Scaloppine with Artichokes, Mushrooms and Pine Nuts

The addition of Parmesan cheese greatly enhances the flavor of the traditional crust of the scaloppine. The appetizing sauce with artichoke hearts and pine nuts is quick and easy.

2 tablespoons pine nuts
3/4 cup mushrooms
1 egg
1 tablespoon milk
1/4 cup all-purpose flour
1/4 cup finely grated fresh Parmesan cheese
6 veal scallops
6 tablespoons (about) butter
2 to 3 tablespoons lemon juice
1/2 cup chicken broth
1/4 cup whipping cream
1 (6-ounce) jar sliced artichoke hearts, drained (do not use marinated)
Salt and pepper to taste

Preheat the oven to 350 degrees. Spread the pine nuts on a baking sheet and bake for 3 to 4 minutes or until toasted; set aside. Remove the bottoms of the stems from the mushrooms and discard. Chop the mushrooms into pieces. Beat the egg and milk in a bowl until blended. Mix the flour and Parmesan cheese together on a plate or in a shallow dish.

Pound the veal scallops vigorously with a wooden mallet for 1 minute to tenderize. Melt 2 tablespoons of the butter in a large skillet over medium heat. Add the mushrooms and sauté until soft. Remove the mushrooms and set aside. Reduce the heat to low and add 1 tablespoon of the remaining butter. Dip each veal scallop into the egg mixture until well coated and then dredge in the cheese mixture to coat. Increase the heat to medium and place in the melted butter in the skillet. Fry for 1 to 2 minutes or until each veal scallop is cooked through, adding an additional tablespoon of the remaining butter at a time as needed. Remove the veal scallops immediately to a warm serving platter or onto a baking sheet placed in a warm oven.

Add the lemon juice and broth to the drippings in the skillet. Simmer for 2 minutes, stirring and scraping up the bits on the bottom of the skillet. Strain through a sieve into a small saucepan, discarding the solids. Add the cream and simmer until reduced. Add the artichokes and mushrooms and simmer for 1 minute. Remove from the heat and season with salt and pepper.

Place the scaloppine onto serving plates. Spoon the sauce over the top and sprinkle with the pine nuts.

Serves 2

Wine Recommendations: Sauvignon Blanc, Sangiovese, or Pinot Grigio

Stir-Fried Ginger Veal with Snow Peas and Bamboo Shoots

This nutritious stir-fry has a satisfying combination of ginger and jalapeño chiles that will please your guests.

I pound top round veal, cut into slices
   1/4 inch thick
2 teaspoons freshly grated ginger
5 garlic cloves, minced
1/2 cup soy sauce
I tablespoon sesame oil
1/4 cup unseasoned rice wine vinegar
I teaspoon chopped jalapeño chile
2 cups water
I cup jasmine rice
I tablespoon cornstarch

1/4 cup chicken broth
2 tablespoons vegetable oil
3 scallions, thinly sliced diagonally
I pound snow peas, trimmed
I cup tightly packed bamboo shoots
1/4 cup chicken broth
Salt and freshly ground pepper to taste
2 tablespoons soy sauce (optional)
I tablespoon unseasoned rice wine
   vinegar (optional)
Toasted sesame seeds for garnish

Place the veal slices between two sheets of plastic wrap and pound to 1/8-inch thickness. Cut into 1×1-inch pieces. Mix half the ginger, half the garlic, 1/2 cup soy sauce, the sesame oil, 1/4 cup vinegar and the jalapeño chile in a bowl. Stir in the veal pieces and marinate, covered, in the refrigerator for 2 hours.

Bring the water to a boil in a medium saucepan over medium-high heat. Add the rice and then reduce the heat. Simmer for 18 minutes or until tender; drain. Fluff with a fork.

Drain the veal, discarding the marinade. Mix the cornstarch with 1/4 cup broth in a bowl to form a paste; set aside. Stir-fry the veal, remaining garlic and remaining ginger in the vegetable oil in a large skillet or wok for 3 minutes or until the veal is cooked through. Add the scallions, peas and bamboo shoots and stir-fry for 2 minutes. Add 1/4 cup broth and the cornstarch paste and stir-fry over high heat for 1 minute or until thickened. Remove from the heat. Add salt, pepper, 2 tablespoons soy sauce and 1 tablespoon vinegar. Return to the heat and stir-fry for 30 seconds or until heated through. Serve immediately with the rice. Garnish with the toasted sesame seeds.

Serves 4

Wine Recommendation: Riesling or Gewürztraminer

Herb-Roasted Chicken and Vegetables

The herbs under the skin of this chicken pack a punch.

6 tablespoons unsalted butter, softened
1/2 tablespoon chopped fresh parsley
1/2 tablespoon chopped fresh thyme
1/2 tablespoon chopped fresh rosemary
1 teaspoon fennel seeds, crushed,
   or rosemary
1/2 teaspoon kosher salt
1 (3- to 31/2-pound) roasting chicken
Salt and pepper to taste
3 large sprigs of fresh parsley

3 large sprigs of fresh thyme
3 small sprigs of fresh rosemary
7 garlic cloves
2 onions, cut into quarters lengthwise
   without removing the root end
2 cups canned low-sodium chicken broth
12 baby carrots
1/2 cup dry white wine
11/2 to 2 tablespoons all-purpose flour

Combine the butter, chopped fresh herbs, fennel seeds and kosher salt in a bowl and mix well. (This may be prepared a day ahead and stored, covered, in the refrigerator. Bring to room temperature before continuing.)

Position the oven rack in the bottom third of the oven and preheat the oven to 400 degrees. Sprinkle the main cavity of the chicken with salt and pepper. Fill with the sprigs of herbs, two of the garlic cloves and two of the onion quarters. Beginning at the neck, slide your fingers under the skin of the breasts and upper legs to loosen. Spread 3 tablespoons of the herb butter under the skin. Place on a rack in a large roasting pan and tie the legs together loosely with kitchen string to hold shape. Pour 1 cup of the broth in the pan. Brush the chicken with 1 tablespoon of the remaining herb butter. Sprinkle with salt and pepper. Roast for 30 minutes. Remove from the oven and scatter the remaining garlic cloves, remaining onion quarters and carrots around the chicken. Brush the chicken, onions and garlic with 1 tablespoon of the remaining herb butter. Roast for 30 minutes. Reserve 1 tablespoon of the remaining herb butter for the sauce. Brush the remaining herb butter on the chicken and vegetables. Roast for 15 minutes or until golden brown and to 180 degrees on a meat thermometer when inserted into the thickest part of the thigh. Insert a wooden spoon into the main cavity of the chicken and tilt the chicken so that the juices drain into the pan. Remove the chicken to a serving platter and surround with the onions and garlic. Tent with foil.

Add the remaining broth and wine to the pan drippings. Bring to a simmer over medium-high heat, stirring to scrape up the brown bits. Pour into a large glass measuring cup. Skim off the fat and discard. Pour the pan drippings into a medium saucepan. Mix 1 tablespoon reserved herb butter and the flour in a small bowl to form a smooth paste. Bring the pan dripping mixture to a simmer and whisk in the butter paste. Simmer for 4 minutes or until thickened, whisking occasionally. Season with salt and pepper. Serve the chicken with the sauce.

Serves 4

Wine Recommendations: Pinot Noir or Viognier

Rubs and Mops

Rubs and mops often work better than marinades to enhance the flavors of food that taste better when grilled slowly such as ribs and some chicken dishes. A rub is a combination of spices such as paprika, cumin, garlic powder, and cayenne pepper blended together and then rubbed onto the surface of the beef, pork, or chicken. Like a marinade, a rub is applied before the meat or poultry is cooked.

Some people feel it is not necessary to "rub in" a rub; they prefer to sprinkle the rub on the surface and allow time in the refrigerator to marinate. A liquid may be added in small amounts to form a paste. Many people consider rubs to be better than marinades for large pieces of meat such as pork butts or briskets since these are fattier cuts of meat. The fat melts during cooking and the rub helps lock in the flavor. If you take the time to make a rub, allow refrigeration time for the rub to be effective.

Anywhere, Anytime Barbecued Chicken and Ribs

Whether you plan to barbecue on a large, top-of-the-line grill on your patio or you will be barbecuing on a small grill on the campground or on the apartment balcony, this recipe will guarantee tender and tasty ribs and chicken. Eliminate the dry rub if you prefer your ribs and chicken less spicy. Using a leek brush eliminates any concern about bristles from a mopping brush sticking to the grill. If you prefer a mustard-style barbecue sauce, use Zesty Mustard Barbecue Sauce (page 154).

DRY RUB
3 tablespoons garlic powder
3 tablespoons paprika
3 tablespoons dry mustard
3 tablespoons garlic powder
3 tablespoons crumbled bay leaves
3 tablespoons salt
2 tablespoons black pepper
2 tablespoons onion powder

MOPPING SAUCE
1 1/2 cups cider vinegar
1 cup Mazola vegetable oil
3/4 cup Worcestershire sauce
1 teaspoon Tabasco sauce, or hot red pepper sauce
3 tablespoons paprika
3 tablespoons mild chili powder
1 tablespoon dry mustard
1 tablespoon crumbled bay leaves
1 tablespoon garlic powder

To prepare the rub, mix the garlic powder, paprika, dry mustard, garlic powder, bay leaves, salt, black pepper and onion powder in a bowl.

To prepare the mopping sauce, combine the vinegar, oil, Worcestershire sauce, Tabasco sauce, paprika, chili powder, dry mustard, bay leaves and garlic powder in a bowl and mix well.

BARBECUE SAUCE

4 cups cider vinegar

1 1/3 cups ketchup

1 cup packed brown sugar

2 tablespoons chili powder, or to taste

2 tablespoons Worcestershire sauce

2 teaspoons dry mustard

1 teaspoon salt

BARBECUED PORK AND CHICKEN

4 pounds pork spareribs, separated

4 to 6 chicken breasts

3 leeks

To prepare the barbecue sauce, bring the vinegar, ketchup, brown sugar, chili powder, Worcestershire sauce, dry mustard and salt to a boil in a saucepan. Reduce the heat and simmer for 30 minutes. Remove from the heat to cool before using.

To prepare the pork and chicken, rub the pork and chicken with the dry rub. Place in a glass dish and marinate, covered, in the refrigerator for 1 hour. Trim the ends of the leeks. Slit the leeks lengthwise down to the bulb to form brushes.

Preheat the grill. Place the pork and chicken on a grill rack. Grill, covered, over low heat for 30 minutes for the chicken and 40 minutes for the pork or until cooked through, basting frequently with the mopping sauce using the leek brush. Brush with the barbecue sauce during the last 5 to 6 minutes of grilling time. (Any longer than this and the sugar in the sauce will burn.) Serve with the remaining barbecue sauce.

Serves 4 to 6

Wine Recommendation: California Zinfandel

Rubs and Mops *(continued)*

A mop is a liquid with a vinegar base to which other seasonings have been added. Mops are applied during the grilling process to keep the food moist and tender. For slow-cooked ribs and chicken, rub the chicken or ribs at least 30 minutes before grilling. Immerse the chicken or ribs in the mopping sauce and place them immediately on the grill. Continue to mop every 30 minutes. To make a disposable, flavor-enhancing "mop," use a leek! Slit the green stems of the leek into half-inch-wide sections down to the bulb and use the leek as a sloppy brush to mop the ribs or chicken.

163

Roasted Chicken and Vegetables with Papaya Glaze

The sweet, piquant papaya glaze gives this roasted chicken a tropical taste.

Papaya Glaze

2 tablespoons lemon juice
2 teaspoons pressed garlic
1 teaspoon cayenne pepper
1/4 teaspoon nutmeg
1/4 teaspoon cumin
1/2 teaspoon salt
1 1/2 teaspoons cinnamon
7 tablespoons brown sugar
1 teaspoon rice wine vinegar
2 (14-ounce) packages frozen
    papaya purée
Salt and freshly ground black pepper
    to taste

Chicken and Vegetables

1 whole roasting chicken,
    cut into pieces
2 teaspoons salt
2 teaspoons cumin
2 tablespoons extra-virgin olive oil
2 tablespoons pressed garlic
1/4 cup fresh lemon juice
1/2 cup chopped onion
1/2 cup chopped red bell pepper
1/2 cup chopped yellow bell pepper
2 tablespoons butter

To prepare the glaze, combine the lemon juice, garlic, cayenne pepper, nutmeg, cumin, 1/2 teaspoon salt, the cinnamon, brown sugar, vinegar and papaya purée in a saucepan and mix well. Cook over low heat for 10 minutes or until syrupy. Season with salt and black pepper to taste. Remove from the heat to cool. Store in the refrigerator.

To prepare the chicken and vegetables, remove the fat from the chicken, leaving the skin on. Combine the salt, cumin, olive oil and garlic in a mortar and crush with a pestle to form a paste. Rub the paste under the skin of the chicken. Place the chicken in a glass dish and cover the skin with lemon juice. Marinate, covered, for 8 to 10 hours. Preheat the oven to 425 degrees. Cover the bottom of a roasting pan with foil and spray with nonstick cooking spray. Place the chicken in the prepared pan and cover with one-half of the glaze. Roast on the top oven rack for 10 minutes. Reduce the oven temperature to 325 degrees. Roast for 25 to 30 minutes longer or until the chicken is cooked through, basting with the pan drippings during the last 10 minutes of cooking.

Sauté the onion and bell peppers in the butter in a skillet for 5 minutes. Discard any fat from the drippings in the roasting pan and stir the drippings into the vegetable mixture. Stir in the remaining glaze and heat through. Serve with the roasted chicken and white rice.

Serves 4

Wine Recommendation: Chardonnay

Arroz con Pollo (Chicken with Yellow Rice)

*There are many regional and personal variations of this popular dish.
If you are unable to find annatto seeds, substitute ground annatto or
Bijol, which is a commercial blend of annatto, flour, and seasonings.
If you prefer long grained rice, use arborio rice.*

1 (3-pound) whole chicken
2 teaspoons fresh oregano
1 1/2 teaspoons cumin
1/2 teaspoon pepper
3 tablespoons lime juice
3 tablespoons olive oil
2 teaspoons annatto seeds
1 cup chopped onion
1 cup chopped red bell pepper
3 garlic cloves, minced
2 tablespoons cilantro, minced
1 cup chopped seeded tomatoes
1 1/2 cups white wine
1 tablespoon tomato paste
3 1/2 to 4 cups chicken broth or chicken stock
1 1/2 cups Valencia rice
8 ounces frozen baby peas, thawed and drained
1 small container pimento-stuffed green olives
Salt and freshly ground pepper to taste
1 (6-ounce) can red pimentos, chopped

Cut up the chicken and remove the skin. Place the chicken in a glass bowl. Mix the oregano, cumin, 1/2 teaspoon pepper and the lime juice in a bowl and pour over the chicken. Marinate, covered, in the refrigerator for 1 hour.

Heat the olive oil in a Dutch oven. Add the annatto seeds and cook until the seeds begin to crackle. Remove the seeds and discard. Place the undrained chicken in the olive oil and cook until the chicken is evenly cooked on all sides. Add the onion, bell pepper, garlic and cilantro. Cook for 3 minutes, being careful not to burn the garlic. Stir in the tomatoes. Add the wine and tomato paste and bring to a boil. Add 3 cups of the broth and bring to a boil. Stir in the rice and reduce the heat to a low simmer. Simmer for 20 to 25 minutes or until the rice is tender, adding the remaining broth as needed. Stir in the peas and olives and cook for 2 minutes. Season with salt and pepper to taste. Top with the pimentos before serving.

Serves 4 to 6

Wine Recommendations: Sauvignon Blanc, Pinot Grigio, White Zinfandel, or
Beaujolais (Brouilly)

Grilled Lemon Chicken Kabobs

Cut 1¹/4 pounds boneless skinless chicken breasts into bite-size pieces. Combine ¹/4 cup olive oil, 2 tablespoons fresh lemon juice, 3 garlic cloves, pressed, and ¹/2 teaspoon coarsely ground pepper in a small bowl and mix well. Add the chicken and toss to coat. Marinate in the refrigerator for 15 to 60 minutes.

Soak wooden skewers in water for 20 minutes to prevent burning; drain. Preheat the grill. Drain the chicken, reserving the marinade. Thread seven to eight pieces of chicken onto each skewer and place on a grill rack. Grill over medium heat for 6 minutes, basting frequently with the reserved marinade. Turn the chicken and grill for 6 minutes longer or until cooked through, basting frequently with the reserved marinade.

Pollo a L'Espanola

For a different taste try this South Florida favorite with fresh chorizo.

1 whole chicken, cut into pieces
3 tablespoons olive oil
1 onion, sliced
1 garlic clove
2 small packages chorizo, sliced
1 (30-ounce) can tomatoes
1 (3-ounce) bottle baby capers
1 (3-ounce) jar pimento-stuffed green olives
Salt and freshly ground black pepper to taste
1 bay leaf
1 tablespoon paprika or dried pimento
Hot cooked rice
¹/2 cup chopped parsley for garnish

Brown the chicken in the olive oil in a large Dutch oven or heavy skillet. Remove the chicken and keep warm. Add the onion and garlic to the pan drippings and cook for 2 to 3 minutes or until the onion is translucent. Stir in the chorizo, tomatoes, capers and olives. Return the chicken to the Dutch oven and season with salt and pepper. Add the bay leaf and paprika. Cook over low heat for 30 minutes or until the chicken is tender and cooked through and the sauce has a rich taste, stirring frequently. Discard the bay leaf. Spoon over rice and garnish with the parsley.

Serves 4 to 6

Wine Recommendations: Sauvignon Blanc or Sangiovese

Fragrant and Spicy Chicken and Couscous with Onions, Tomatoes and Olives

The delectable smell of this dish will bring your guests right into the kitchen. It can also be mostly prepared a day in advance. This will generously serve six.

3 cups sliced onions
6 large garlic cloves, minced
2 tablespoons olive oil
1 1/2 teaspoons kosher salt
1 tablespoon Hungarian
   sweet paprika
1 teaspoon turmeric
1 teaspoon ground coriander
1 teaspoon ground fennel
   seeds
1/2 teaspoon cumin
1 (28-ounce) can diced
   tomatoes, drained
3 tablespoons fresh lemon juice
1 cup water
2 tablespoons olive oil
4 skinless chicken thighs

4 skinless chicken legs
3 skinless chicken breasts
2 small jars marinated
   artichoke hearts, drained
   and chopped
1 (7-ounce) jar pitted
   Kalamata olives, drained
1 (5-ounce) jar green
   olives, pitted
1 tablespoon fresh marjoram
Salt and freshly ground black
   pepper to taste
1 1/2 cups water
1 1/2 cups uncooked couscous
1/2 cup pine nuts
1/2 cup dark raisins
1/2 cup dried cranberries

Cook the onions and garlic in 2 tablespoon olive oil in a medium saucepan over medium heat for 10 minutes. Add 1 1/2 teaspoons kosher salt, the paprika turmeric, coriander, fennel and cumin and cook for 1 minute, stirring constantly. Add the tomatoes, lemon juice and 1 cup water and bring to a boil. Set aside.

Heat 2 tablespoons olive oil in a large saucepan. Add the chicken and cook until brown on all sides. Remove the chicken and layer in a large stockpot. Spoon the sauce over the chicken. Bring to a boil and reduce the heat to medium-low. Simmer for 1 hour. (You may cover and chill for 3 to 10 hours at this point.) Stir in the artichoke hearts, olives, marjoram and salt and black pepper to taste. Simmer for 30 minutes.

Bring 1 1/2 cups water to a boil in a saucepan. Stir in the couscous quickly. Let stand for 4 to 5 minutes or until the water is absorbed. Fluff with a fork and stir in the pine nuts, raisins and dried cranberries. Serve with the chicken.

Serves 6

Wine Recommendation: Beaujolais, Pinot Grigio, Pinot Noir, Chianti, or Rioja

Grilled Lemon Chicken Kabobs *(continued)*

Note: You may place the chicken kabobs on a rack in a broiler pan and broil for 6 minutes, turning after 3 minutes and basting frequently with the reserved marinade. This recipe serves 3.

Wine Recommendations: Sauvignon Blanc or Pinot Grigio

Chicken Tomato Tagliatelle

Comfort food—cheesy with mushrooms and scallions.

8 ounces tagliatelle
1 green bell pepper, chopped
2 bunches scallions, chopped
1 tablespoon olive oil
2 garlic cloves, pressed
8 ounces sliced mushrooms
1 (16-ounce) container high-quality tomato pasta sauce
1 tablespoon chili powder
3 tablespoons dark brown sugar
4 ounces cream cheese
3 tablespoons Worcestershire sauce
1 teaspoon dry mustard
3 tablespoons medium dry Sherry
1 whole roasted chicken
2 cups (8 ounces) shredded sharp Cheddar cheese
Salt and pepper to taste
1 cup (4 ounces) freshly grated Parmesan cheese

Preheat the oven to 350 degrees. Cook the pasta in a large saucepan using the package directions; drain. Sauté the bell pepper and scallions in the olive oil in a skillet until softened. Add the garlic and mushrooms and sauté until tender. Add the pasta sauce, chili powder, brown sugar, cream cheese, Worcestershire sauce, dry mustard and Sherry and cook for 5 minutes.

Chop the chicken into small pieces, discarding the skin and bones. Add the chicken and Cheddar cheese to the mushroom sauce and mix well. Add to the pasta and toss to coat. Season with salt and pepper. Spoon into a 9×13-inch baking dish or three or four smaller baking dishes and sprinkle with the Parmesan cheese. (You may prepare ahead and freeze at this point. Thaw in the refrigerator for 1 to 10 hours before baking.) Bake for 30 to 40 minutes or until bubbly and heated through.

Serves 10

Wine Recommendations: Pinot Grigio, Chianti Classico, or Bordeaux

Spicy Adobo Braised Chicken

The Scotch Bonnet chile makes this a spicy dish. For less heat, substitute a milder chile.

1 (3 1/2-pound) chicken, cut into serving pieces
1/2 teaspoon kosher salt
1/2 teaspoon cumin
1/2 teaspoon crumbled dried oregano
3 garlic cloves, minced
1/2 cup sour orange juice, or
   1/4 cup lime juice and 1/4 cup orange juice
1 tablespoon Spanish sherry vinegar
1/2 cup chopped red onion
1/4 cup olive oil
1/2 Scotch Bonnet chile, seeded and minced

Remove any excess fat from the chicken. Rinse the chicken and pat dry with paper towels. Place in a large sealable plastic bag. Combine the kosher salt, cumin and oregano in a small bowl and press the spices to release the flavors. Stir in the garlic, orange juice and vinegar. Pour over the chicken. Add the onion and seal the bag. Marinate in the refrigerator for 2 to 24 hours, turning the bag several times to distribute the marinade.

Drain the chicken, reserving the marinade and onion. Pat the chicken dry with paper towels. Heat the olive oil in a large skillet over medium-high heat. Add the chile and sauté until toasted. Remove the chile from the oil with a slotted spoon and set aside. Cook the chicken in the oil for 10 minutes or until brown on all sides. Reduce the heat to medium-low and cook for 10 minutes longer. Remove the chicken to a platter with tongs.

Drain the oil from the skillet. Add the reserved marinade, onion and chile to the skillet. Bring to a boil over high heat and then reduce the heat to a simmer. Return the chicken along with any juices to the skillet. Simmer, covered, for 30 minutes or until the juices from the chicken run clear. Remove the chicken to a serving platter and cover with foil. Increase the heat to high and boil the remaining liquid in the skillet, stirring to scrape up the brown bits from the bottom of the skillet with a wooden spatula. Cook until thickened, stirring constantly. Pour over the chicken and serve.

Serves 4

Wine Recommendations: Sauvignon Blanc or Sangiovese

Coq au Vin

This elegant, classic French dish will taste best when paired with the wine you use for the sauce.

4 ounces lardons or thick-cut bacon
3 pounds chicken pieces
1 small package mushrooms, chopped
1 package frozen baby onions, thawed and drained
1/4 cup Cognac
3 to 4 cups full-bodied red wine,
   such as a Bordeaux, Zinfandel or Cabernet Sauvignon
2 beef bouillon cubes
1 tablespoon tomato paste
3 garlic cloves, chopped
1 bay leaf
2 whole cloves
Salt and freshly ground pepper to taste
1 to 2 tablespoons butter, melted
1 to 2 tablespoons all-purpose flour
2 tablespoons parsley, chopped

Cut the lardons into 1-inch pieces. Brown in a large Dutch oven until crisp. Remove to paper towels to drain. Add the chicken to the pan drippings and cook until brown on all sides. Remove 2 tablespoons of the drippings in the Dutch oven to a skillet. Add the mushrooms and onions to the skillet and sauté over low heat until brown.

Return the lardons to the Dutch oven. Cover and cook over low heat for 10 minutes. Uncover and add the Cognac. Ignite the Cognac carefully with a match, averting your face from the flames. Shake the Dutch oven until the flames subside. Pour enough of the wine over the chicken to cover. Add the bouillon cubes, tomato paste, garlic, bay leaf and cloves. Bring to a simmer and cook for 25 to 30 minutes or until the chicken is tender but not falling off the bones. Remove the chicken and keep warm. Discard the bay leaf and cloves. Season the sauce with salt and pepper. Mix 1 tablespoon butter and 1 tablespoon flour together in a bowl to form a paste. Stir into the sauce and cook until slightly thickened with a nice sheen, stirring constantly. Add a mixture of the remaining butter and flour if needed to thicken the sauce.

Return the chicken to the Dutch oven. Stir in the sautéed vegetables. Cook until heated through. Spoon onto individual serving dishes and sprinkle with the parsley.

Serves 4 to 6

Jamaican Jerk Chicken

Hot and spicy; a true taste of the Caribbean.

1 small onion, chopped

3 large garlic cloves, chopped

2 scallions, chopped

1 to 6 Scotch bonnet chiles,
   seeded and chopped, or to taste

1/4 cup fresh lime juice
   (do not use bottled)

2 tablespoons soy sauce

3 tablespoons vegetable oil

2 tablespoons dark brown sugar

2 teaspoons allspice

1 tablespoon finely chopped fresh thyme

1/2 teaspoon cinnamon

3/4 teaspoon nutmeg

1/2 teaspoon cayenne pepper

1 teaspoon freshly ground black pepper

1 teaspoon kosher salt

3 pounds chicken breasts

2 pounds chicken thighs and legs

Process the onion, garlic, scallions, chiles, lime juice, soy sauce, oil, brown sugar, allspice, thyme, cinnamon, nutmeg, cayenne pepper, black pepper and kosher salt in a food processor or blender until smooth.

Trim any excess fat from the chicken. Rinse the chicken in cold water and pat dry. Place in several sealable plastic storage bags. Pour the marinade in the bags and rub over the chicken. (Be sure to wear plastic or rubber gloves to prevent a reaction from the chiles.) Force the extra air from the bags and seal. Marinate in the refrigerator for 8 to 10 hours. Remove from the refrigerator and let stand at room temperature for 30 minutes before grilling.

Preheat the grill. Drain the chicken, discarding the marinade. Place on a grill rack and grill over high heat for 2 to 3 minutes on each side to sear. Move the chicken to a grill rack over medium-high heat and grill, with the lid down, for 20 to 25 minutes or until the chicken is cooked through. (Begin grilling the wings and legs first, as they will take longer to cook than the breasts.)

Note: To cook indoors, roast the wings and legs in a baking pan in a 375-degree oven for 15 minutes. Add the breasts and bake for 30 minutes or until cooked through. Broil for 1 to 2 minutes for crispness, if desired.

Serves 8

Wine Recommendations: A cool rum drink or a beer would be the best drink to serve; but if you prefer wine, try a Gewürztraminer or a New Zealand Sauvignon Blanc.

Photograph on page 69.

Which Wine to Serve?

In judging the right wine for a meal in your home you have an advantage—you may have already tasted the food, so you can match the taste and richness of the food more easily with the right wine. When you taste wine or consider purchasing wine for specific food, keep in mind four qualities of the wine: its heaviness on the tongue; its intensity; its overall flavor and aroma (what tastes and aromas does it bring to mind—oak, berry, floral, citrus?); and specific flavor qualities, specifically if it is sweet, sour, bitter, or in rare cases, salty.

Some foods and wines taste better when they contrast. Some foods and wines taste better with like to like. This has long been obvious with dessert dishes. A slightly sweet wine will taste terrible with a piece of unfrosted cake, but a dessert wine, such as a Sauterne, will taste delicious. Sauterne is slightly sweeter than most desserts, and as a rule the sweetness of the dessert should be less than the sweetness of the wine.

Goat Cheese-Stuffed Chicken Breasts with Pico de Gallo Verde

Tomatillos, goat cheese, chiles, and cilantro pack a flavorful punch in this dish.

10 tomatillos, chopped
1 red onion, thinly sliced into crescent-shaped pieces
6 dry chipotle chiles, julienned
1 cup fresh lime juice
1/2 cup olive oil
1 bunch cilantro, chopped
1 teaspoon salt
10 ounces goat cheese, thinly sliced
10 chicken breasts
1/4 cup (1/2 stick) butter
1/4 cup olive oil

Combine the tomatillos, red onion, chipotle chiles, lime juice, 1/2 cup olive oil, the cilantro and salt in a large bowl and mix well. Cut the goat cheese into ten equal slices. Cut each slice into halves.

Cut each chicken breast horizontally to form a large pocket, being careful not to completely separate. Insert two halves of the goat cheese into each pocket, being careful that the chicken lies as flat as possible.

Melt 1 tablespoon of the butter with 1 tablespoon of the olive oil in a large skillet over medium heat. Cook the stuffed chicken breasts in batches for 5 to 6 minutes on each side or until cooked through, adding the remaining butter and olive oil 1 tablespoon at a time as needed and keeping the cooked chicken covered until all of the chicken is cooked through. Serve immediately with the sauce.

Serves 5 or 6

Wine Recommendation: Sauvignon Blanc

Chicken Breast with Prosciutto and Fontina Cheese

A quick and easy recipe with a creative combination of tastes and textures.

8 chicken breasts
2 tablespoons canola oil
1 egg
Salt and pepper to taste
2 cups seasoned bread crumbs
8 slices prosciutto
16 fresh sage leaves
8 large slices fontina cheese
2 tablespoons grated Parmesan cheese (optional)

Preheat the oven to 350 degrees. Pound each chicken breast with meat mallet if not thin. Trim off any of the pieces that have separated during pounding so that there are no loose pieces dangling from the edge.

Heat the canola oil in a large skillet. Whisk the egg, salt and pepper in a bowl. Dip the chicken breasts in the egg mixture and then in the bread crumbs, shaking off any excess. Fry in the hot oil until light golden brown and remove to a baking sheet. Place one slice of prosciutto, two sage leaves and one slice of fontina cheese on each chicken breast, making sure the cheese covers all but the edge of each. Sprinkle with the Parmesan cheese and bake for 10 minutes or until bubbly and light brown.

Serves 4

Wine Recommendations: Chardonnay, Chenin Blanc, Chianti Classico, or Cabernet Sauvignon

Which Wine to Serve?

(continued)

Foods with a lot of acid, such as soy sauce, tomatoes, and citrus fruits, pair up better with wines higher in acid such as Sauvignon Blanc and Pinot Grigio. Bitter and astringent foods, such as mixed bitter greens, pair up best with a slightly bitter wine such as a young Cabernet or a Bordeaux.

Some foods taste better when they contrast. Certain spicy, salty, or smoked foods, particularly Chinese and Thai foods, should be paired with a light sweet wine such as a Riesling or a Gewürztraminer.

Most wine experts also stand by another important principle: the heartier the food, the heartier the wine. Roast beef pairs well with Bordeaux, a heavy red wine, while a lighter pasta dish would taste best with a Sauvignon Blanc, a white wine which is not as heavy or as strong as other white wines.

If in doubt, don't be afraid to ask your wine merchant for help and don't be afraid to experiment!

Chicken Stock

Combine I whole chicken, cut into pieces, 2 large carrots, chopped, 3 onions, chopped and 4 ribs celery, chopped in a large stockpot. Add enough water to cover completely. Season with 2 to 3 teaspoons salt or to taste. Bring to a boil and reduce the heat. Simmer until the chicken separates from the bone. Remove from the heat to cool. Strain the stock into a bowl, discarding the skin and bones and reserving the chicken for another purpose. Chill in the refrigerator. Skim the fat from the top. The stock may be frozen and used for up to 3 months. This recipe will make a variable amount.

Grilled Chicken Satay with Peanut Sauce

This favorite with children as well as adults can be served as a main course with rice or as an appetizer. Use only commercial peanut butter since homemade tends to separate.

PEANUT SAUCE
1/4 cup chopped shallots
2 tablespoons canola oil
1/2 cup smooth or crunchy peanut butter
3/4 cup low-salt or low-sodium chicken stock
1 1/2 tablespoons hoisin sauce
1 tablespoon rice wine vinegar
1 1/2 to 2 teaspoons Asian chile oil

CHICKEN
1 pound boneless chicken thighs or breasts
4 garlic cloves, pressed
2 tablespoons minced ginger
1/4 cup less sodium soy sauce
3 tablespoons Sake or dry white wine
1/4 teaspoon Chinese five-spice powder
1 teaspoon Asian chile oil, or to taste
Hot cooked rice

To prepare the peanut sauce, sauté the shallots in the canola oil in a saucepan until translucent. Stir in the peanut butter, stock, hoisin sauce and vinegar and mix well. Stir in the desired amount of chile oil for preferred spiciness.

To prepare the chicken, trim the chicken and cut into 1-inch chunks. Place in a sealable plastic bag. Mix the garlic, ginger, soy sauce, Sake, five-spice powder, and chile oil in a bowl. Pour over the chicken and seal the bag. Marinate in the refrigerator for 3 to 10 hours. Remove from the refrigerator and let stand at room temperature for 30 minutes before grilling.

Preheat the grill. Drain the chicken and pat dry, discarding the marinade. Thread the chicken onto skewers and place on a grill rack. Grill over medium-high heat for 4 to 5 minutes on each side or until cooked through. Serve over rice topped with the warm peanut sauce.

Serves 2 to 3

Wine Recommendation: Gewürztraminer

Chicken Paillards and Shrimp with Baby Bellas and Brandy Cream Sauce

An easy and impressive dish that should be served with linguini or angel hair pasta to absorb the sauce. Do not add additional salt to this dish as the broths in this recipe are salty. The shrimp can be omitted for a lighter meal.

8 ounces baby bella mushrooms
1 red onion
2 whole chicken breasts, skinned and boned
1/2 cup (1 stick) unsalted butter
6 tablespoons brandy
1 cup beef stock or beef broth
1 cup chicken stock or chicken broth
1 cup heavy whipping cream
1/4 teaspoon pepper
1/4 cup all-purpose flour
1 pound medium shrimp, peeled and deveined

Remove the stems from the mushrooms and slice the caps thinly. Cut the onion into thin crescent-shape pieces. Cut the chicken breasts into halves and pound with a wooden meat mallet for 1 minute. Trim the loose pieces from the chicken so that the breasts are an even thickness.

Melt 4 tablespoons of the butter in a large skillet over medium-high heat. Add the onion and mushrooms and sauté until the onion is translucent. Reduce the heat to low and remove the skillet from the heat. Add the brandy and carefully ignite. Let the flames subside. Return the skillet to the heat and simmer for 1 minute. Add the beef stock and chicken stock. Increase the heat to medium-high and cook for 5 minutes. Reduce the heat to low and add the cream. Boil for 12 minutes or until the sauce is slightly thick; set aside.

Melt 2 tablespoons of the remaining butter in a large skillet. Season the chicken with the pepper and dredge in the flour. Add to the skillet and sauté for 3 minutes on each side or until cooked through. Remove to individual serving plates and keep warm. Add the remaining 2 tablespoons butter to the skillet. Add the shrimp and sauté until the shrimp turn pink; do not overcook. Drain the shrimp and add to the sauce. Cook until heated through. Pour over the chicken and serve immediately.

Serves 4

Wine Recommendations: Beaujolais, Gewürztraminer, Muscadet, or Sancerre

Queen's Chicken

*This recipe is similar to a Cordon Bleu recipe first created for
Queen Elizabeth's coronation.*

6 chicken breasts
1 carrot
1 (6-inch) piece of leek
1 bay leaf
1 teaspoon bouquet garni
1 tablespoon vegetable oil
1/4 cup finely chopped onion
1 tablespoon curry powder
1 teaspoon tomato purée
2 tablespoons red wine
2 tablespoons water
2 bay leaves
Juice of 1/2 lemon
1 1/2 cups mayonnaise
2 tablespoons apricot jam
Salt and freshly ground pepper to taste
3 tablespoons heavy whipping cream, whipped

Place the chicken in a large skillet or stockpot and add enough water to cover.
Add the carrot, leek, one bay leaf and the bouquet garni. Cook over medium heat until
the chicken is cooked through. Remove from the heat to cool. Remove the chicken from
the liquid and cut the chicken into long strips, discarding the skin and bones.

Heat the oil over low heat in a skillet. Add the onion and sauté for 3 to 4 minutes or
until translucent. Add the curry powder, tomato purée, wine, water and two bay leaves and
bring to a boil. Add the lemon juice and reduce the heat to low. Simmer for 10 minutes.
Strain the mixture through a sieve and cool, discarding the bay leaves. Combine the
onion mixture with the mayonnaise, jam, salt and pepper in a bowl and mix well. Fold in
the whipped cream. Serve over the chicken.

Serves 6

Wine Recommendations: Chardonnay, Chenin Blanc, or Sauvignon Blanc

Spicy Chicken and Bean Chili

Cumin, oregano, cilantro, and black beans make this a chili with Hispanic flair.

1/4 cup olive oil
1 1/2 cups chopped red onions
1 large red bell pepper, chopped
6 garlic cloves, minced
3 pounds shredded chicken breasts
Salt and pepper to taste
3 1/2 tablespoons chili powder
2 tablespoons tomato paste
1 tablespoon cumin
1 tablespoon crumbled dried oregano
1 (15-ounce) can black beans, drained
1 (15-ounce) can kidney beans, drained
1 1/2 cups chicken broth
30 ounces boxed Pomi chopped tomatoes,
   or 2 (15-ounce) cans high-quality canned diced tomatoes
1/2 cup chopped fresh cilantro, or to taste

Heat the olive oil in a large heavy stockpot over medium high heat. Add the onions, bell pepper and garlic and sauté for 5 minutes or until the vegetables begin to soften. Add the chicken, salt and pepper and sauté for 5 minutes or until the chicken is no longer pink outside. Stir in the chili powder, tomato paste, cumin and oregano. Add the beans, 1 cup of the broth and the tomatoes. Simmer for 25 minutes or until the chicken is cooked through and the chili is thickened. If the chili is too thick, add the remaining broth 1 tablespoon at a time until the desired consistency. Stir in the cilantro or serve with the cilantro on the side.

Serves 6

Wine Recommendations: Zinfandel or Barbera

Chicken with Wine and Capers

This is a scrumptious dish for a crowd that only takes 30 minutes to prepare. To prepare, heat 2 tablespoons olive oil in a large saucepan over medium-low heat. Add 1 onion, finely chopped, and sauté for 10 minutes or until translucent. Add 1 1/2 to 2 pounds boneless skinless chicken thighs and cook until the chicken is cooked through and brown. Reduce the heat and add 1/2 cup chicken broth and 1/2 cup good-quality white wine. Simmer for 10 minutes or until the sauce is reduced. Stir in 1/4 cup capers. Simmer for 10 to 15 minutes or until the sauce is thickened, stirring constantly. This recipe serves 6.

Wine Recommendations: Pinot Grigio, Muscadet, Chianti Classico, or Sauvignon Blanc

Picnic on the Beach

Many think of life in Miami as a "day at the beach." Surrounded by water, Miami offers many beach choices. Today we are visiting Bill Baggs Cape Florida State Park, located at the far end of Key Biscayne. Bill Baggs is known for its mile of pristine Atlantic beach with native vegetation as well as its role in Florida history. Reconstructed in 1846, the Cape Florida lighthouse is the oldest standing structure in Miami-Dade County. The lighthouse and the keeper's cottage can still be visited, and the view from the lighthouse watch room is breathtaking.

Today at the park, friends and families have gathered for a picnic. An old wooden fishing boat has been put to use to hold a wicker tray with glasses and a pitcher of Summer Sangria. Lobster traps prop up a board which serves as a table and is covered with a bright striped towel for a tablecloth. Reflecting the sky and sea, brilliant blues and turquoise are the colors of the day. A hurricane lamp filled with lemons and starfish and topped with yellow gerbera daisies is a simple and festive centerpiece.

As the children swim and play, their parents enjoy their drinks while relaxing in canvas chairs. The hostess has shared the cooking duties with invited friends, and everyone has packed a cooler with one or two dishes for the party. The ingredients for Seafood Paella are set up on a small folding table, and the host and hostess take turns replenishing the Sangria and stirring the Paella, which is cooking in a paellera pan on its own portable burner and stand.

Before the paella is completed, there is plenty to snack on. Everyone sips Gazpacho Andaluz, chilled and refreshing on a sunny day. Chips are perfect with creamy and chunky Haas Avocado Guacamole and Old Florida Caviar.

At the end of the meal, the kids race back to the shore, rebuilding sand castles and competing in a game of Marco Polo. As the afternoon lengthens, they return to pick up a dessert, either a Luscious Lemon Bar or a Butterscotch Blonde Brownie with Chocolate Chunks, both slightly soft and sweet from sitting in the sunshine.

At the end of the day, after packing for home, everyone shares a last leisurely walk along the shore, enjoying conversation and the feel of the sun and salt spray.

Seafood

Who wouldn't enjoy this fun day in the sun? A glass of Summer Sangria is perfect while gazing at the handsome Cape Florida Lighthouse, the coconut palms, and the bright blue sky.

Menu

Butterscotch Blonde Brownies with Chocolate Chunks, a Lemon Tartlet and Luscious Lemon Bars rest on a lobster trap covered with a beach towel.

Starfish, lemons, and gerbera daisies add cheerful bright color to this table. While the Seafood Paella is cooking, everyone snacks on Gazpacho Andaluz, Old Florida Caviar, and Haas Avocado Guacamole.

Work Plan

THE DAY BEFORE THE PARTY

Bake Luscious Lemon Bars and Lemon
   Tarts. Cool, wrap tightly, and refrigerate
   until needed.

Bake Butterscotch Blonde Brownies with
   Chocolate Chunks and wrap tightly.
   They don't need refrigeration.

Prepare Old Florida Caviar and store in
   the refrigerator until needed.

Prepare Gazpacho Andaluz. Keep
   refrigerated and serve chilled.

Make dressing for Baby Green Salad
   with Lime and Honey Vinaigrette.

Make fish stock for Seafood Paella.

THE DAY OF THE PARTY

Mash Haas avocados for Guacamole.
   Assemble and refrigerate.

Clean the salad greens, dry, and chill to crisp.

Assemble and clean seafood ingredients
   for Paella. Prepare vegetables and rice in
   advance if desired (see recipe).

Cut fruit for Summer Sangria. Serve chilled.

Prepare vegetables for Baby Greens Salad,
   but do not combine until right
   before serving.

JUST BEFORE SERVING

Cook rice and other ingredients.
   Add seafood to complete Paella.

Assemble Salad and dressing.

Assemble Summer Sangria.

Seafood Paella

The key to great paella is fresh fish stock. If you are able to make fresh fish stock and prefer an all-fish flavor, omit the chorizo. If you are unable to make fresh fish stock, be sure to add chorizo for outstanding flavor. This recipe calls for spiny Florida lobster. The shells can be kept on, but be sure to provide small forks for removing lobster meat from the shells. Maine lobster without the shell is a delicious alternative.

1 (5-ounce) fresh chorizo, casings
   removed (optional)
2 tablespoons olive oil
1 small red onion, finely chopped
5 garlic cloves, minced
1/3 cup large pieces roasted red
   bell pepper
1 large tomato, chopped
1 cup arborio rice or other
   medium grain white rice
3 cups Fresh Fish Stock (page 184)
1 teaspoon salt
12 thin asparagus spears, ends trimmed

1 1/2 pounds grouper or snapper fillets,
   chopped into 1 1/2-inch pieces, or
   3 fish bouillon tablets
12 mussels, scrubbed and beards removed
12 clams, scrubbed
8 ounces fresh squid, chopped into circles
2 small Florida lobster tails, cut into slices,
   or 1 Maine lobster, cut into 1-inch pieces
1 pound shrimp, peeled and deveined
1 cup frozen baby peas, thawed
   and drained
1 small can sweet red pimentos,
   drained (optional)

Place a 15-inch paellera pan or a very large deep skillet over medium heat. Add the chorizo and cook for 2 minutes, stirring until crumbly. Stir in the olive oil and onion and cook for 5 minutes or until the onion is translucent. Add the garlic, bell pepper and tomato and cook until almost dry. Stir in the rice to coat well. (You may set aside at this point and finish cooking later.)

Add the fish stock and salt and increase the heat to high. Boil for 2 minutes and then reduce the heat. Simmer for 10 minutes. Add the asparagus, grouper, mussels, clams, squid and lobster. Cook over medium-high heat for 5 to 7 minutes or until the lobster is opaque and the mussels and clams open. Add the shrimp. Cover the surface of the paella with foil and add five small ice cubes on top, taking care not to let the water from the cubes melt into the paella. Cover with a lid and reduce the heat to low. (This will allow the rice to absorb the flavors.) Cook for 3 to 5 minutes. Remove the lid, foil and ice cubes and check the rice and seafood for doneness. Stir in the peas and pimentos. Turn off the heat. Cover again with foil and let stand for
10 minutes. Serve immediately.

Serves 10

Wine Recommendation: Rioja

Fresh Fish Stock

This recipe for fish stock, which is used in Seafood Paella (page 183), also works well for the Florida Lobster Tails in Saffron Sauce with Squid Ink Pasta (page 192). Usually fish stock does not have saffron or annatto added. Traditional preparations of fish stock call for using fish bones, but a small fish fillet of an inexpensive fish also works well.

8 cups water
8 ounces grouper or snapper or 4 fish tablets
Shrimp shells
1 small package annatto seasoning, or $3/4$ teaspoon
   pulverized saffron threads

Bring the water, grouper, shrimp shells and annatto seasoning to a boil in a medium saucepan. Boil for 20 minutes. Drain carefully through a sieve into a container, discarding the fish and fish skins.

Note: The stock can be frozen for up to 3 months.

Makes about 2 quarts

Easy Fish Stock

1 cup chopped onion
1 tablespoon unsalted butter
1 large garlic clove, minced
8 cups water
$1/2$ cup white wine
1 (4- to 8-ounce) fish fillet
2 tablespoons parsley

Sauté the onion in the butter in a large stockpot over medium-high heat until the onion is translucent. Stir in the garlic. Add the water, wine, fish and parsley and simmer for 45 minutes. Skim the surface and strain, discarding the solids.

Note: This stock can be refrigerated for one week or frozen for up to three months.

Makes about 2 quarts

Crab Cakes

Make these crab cakes in miniature for a delectable appetizer. Serve with Oven-Dried Tomatoes with Corn and Queso Blanco (page 94).

1 onion, finely chopped
1 green bell pepper, finely chopped
1 cup jumbo lump crab meat, shells removed
1/2 cup crab claw meat, shells removed
1/4 cup parsley, finely chopped
2 tablespoons high-quality mayonnaise
1 teaspoon mustard
1 tablespoon lemon juice
1/4 teaspoon Worcestershire sauce
Dash of hot red pepper sauce
2 tablespoons Old Bay seasoning
Salt and freshly ground pepper to taste
Fresh bread crumbs
Chopped fresh bread
1/4 cup (1/2 stick) butter

Steam the onion and bell pepper in a steamer until tender-crisp; drain and pat dry. Chop the lump crab meat and crab claw meat into small pieces. Combine the steamed vegetables, parsley, mayonnaise, mustard, lemon juice, Worcestershire sauce, hot sauce, Old Bay seasoning, salt and pepper in a bowl and mix well. Gently stir in the crab meat. (The mixture can be chilled for 2 to 3 hours at this point until ready to cook.) Add enough bread crumbs and chopped bread to bind the mixture together. Shape into small crab cakes and dust with bread crumbs if desired. Sauté in the butter in a skillet until cooked through. Serve immediately with Oven-Dried Tomatoes with Corn and Queso Blanco (page 94).

Makes 6 to 8

Wine Recommendations: Sancerre, Muscadet, or Pinot Grigio

Conch (pronounced konk) is a large edible marine snail so popular it is now an endangered species in the United States. Most of the conch we eat is imported from Costa Rica, the Bahamas, and the Turks and Caicos Islands. Conch meat has a mild, sweet taste, but it is extremely tough and must be pounded, ground, and marinated in lime juice to tenderize it for cooking.

For many years conch was an important part of the Key West diet, so much so that residents of Key West now call themselves "Conchs." In 1982, in response to a United States Border Patrol blockade set up at the main highway leading into the Florida Keys from the mainland, Key Westers decided that Key West should secede from the United States. The Conch Republic was formed, and Key West briefly seceded from the United States (the secession was timed at one minute). Many Conchs now claim they have dual citizenship as citizens of the United States and the Conch Republic, whose motto is "We seceded where others failed."

Florida Keys Conch Chowder

There are many versions of this satisfying and hearty chowder; this is our favorite. For a spicier chowder, increase the quantity of Scotch bonnet chile. Serve with crusty bread.

1 pound Grade A conch, cleaned and tenderized
3 tablespoons lime juice
6 slices bacon, cut into 1/2-inch pieces
1 tablespoon vegetable oil
2 garlic cloves, minced
1 yellow onion, finely chopped
2 carrots, peeled and chopped
1 green bell pepper, finely chopped
1/2 Scotch bonnet chile, minced, or 1 jalapeño chile, minced
4 (8-ounce) bottles clam juice
4 cups water

1 (26-ounce) box Pomi tomatoes, or 3 ripe tomatoes, peeled, seeded and chopped, or 1 (14-ounce) can tomatoes, crushed
3 tablespoons tomato paste
1 teaspoon dried thyme
1 teaspoon fresh oregano
2 bay leaves
1 1/2 pounds baking potatoes, peeled and chopped
Hot red pepper sauce to taste
Salt and freshly ground pepper to taste
1 to 3 tablespoons lime juice
3 tablespoons chopped parsley

Cut the conch into small pieces and grind in a food processor or meat grinder until medium fine. Combine the conch and 3 tablespoons lime juice in a bowl and mix well. Marinate in the refrigerator for 1 hour. Brown the bacon in the oil in a large stockpot. Add the garlic, onion, carrots, bell pepper and chile and sauté over medium heat for 3 minutes. Add the clam juice, water, tomatoes, tomato paste, thyme, oregano and bay leaves. Stir in the potatoes and conch. Bring to a boil and then reduce the heat. Simmer for 45 to 60 minutes or until the potatoes and conch are tender. Discard the bay leaves. Correct the seasoning, adding hot sauce, salt, pepper and 1 to 3 tablespoons lime juice. (This should be a spicy chowder.) Sprinkle with the parsley.

Note: Most conch is now sold frozen. Do not purchase conch that has ice crystals or freezer burn. Remove any black or red meat. Conch is very tough, so even if your fish purveyor tenderized it, you may need to pound the conch with a wooden mallet on a chopping block to tenderize it more. For variety, 2 tablespoons dry Sherry can be added during the last 5 minutes of cooking. If you prefer a thicker soup, mix 2 tablespoons melted butter with 2 tablespoons all-purpose flour. Add 1/4 cup of the chowder liquid and stir to form a thick paste. Stir into the chowder and cook until thickened.

Serves 8

Wine Recommendations: Chenin Blanc, Chardonnay, Riesling, or Muscadet

Conch Fritters

These spicy fritters pair nicely with the sweet papaya and pineapple in Festive Fruit Salsa (page 64).

1 pound Grade A conch, cleaned and tenderized
2 tablespoons corn kernels
1 garlic clove, minced
1 tablespoon chopped shallot
1/4 red bell pepper, minced
2 teaspoons minced jalapeño chile, or 1 teaspoon minced Scotch bonnet chile
2 tablespoons lime juice
2 tablespoons vegetable oil
4 egg yolks
1 1/2 cups all-purpose flour
1/4 cup yellow cornmeal
1/2 teaspoon baking powder
1 teaspoon salt
1 teaspoon freshly ground pepper
1/2 to 3/4 cup milk
4 egg whites
Vegetable oil for deep-frying

Cut the conch into small pieces and grind in a food processor or meat grinder until finely ground. Combine the conch, corn, garlic, shallot, bell pepper, chile, lime juice and 2 tablespoons oil and toss to mix. Stir in the egg yolks. Sift the flour, cornmeal, baking powder, salt and pepper into the conch mixture. Stir in enough of the milk to form a thick batter. Chill for 1 hour to allow the baking powder to activate.

Beat the egg whites in a mixing bowl until small peaks form. Fold into the batter, leaving trails of the egg whites in the batter. (This will help the fritters to puff up during frying.)

Pour oil to a depth of 1 1/2 to 2 inches in a large frying pan. Preheat the oil to 350 degrees over medium-high heat. Drop the batter in 1-inch balls in batches into the hot oil using a large tablespoon and deep-fry until golden brown, being careful that the fritters do not cling together. (If the fritters are too thick, they will not cook through, so experiment if necessary to reach the correct size.) Remove with a slotted spoon and drain on a platter covered with several layers of paper towels. Serve with tartar sauce or Festive Fruit Salsa (page 64).

Note: Most conch is now sold frozen. Do not purchase conch that has ice crystals or freezer burn. Remove any black or red meat. Conch is very tough, so even if your fish purveyor tenderized it, you may need to pound the conch with a wooden mallet on a chopping block to tenderize it more.

Makes 2 dozen

Wine Recommendations: Riesling, Gewürztraminer, White Zinfandel, or Pinot Grigio

Mussels Mariner

Serve crusty French bread with these mussels to soak up every bit of the delicious broth.

1 large shallot, finely chopped, or 2 small shallots, finely chopped
2 garlic cloves, minced
1 tablespoon olive oil
2 tablespoons chopped parsley
1 cup white wine
1 1/2 pounds mussels, well scrubbed and beards removed
2 tablespoons butter, softened
1 tablespoon all-purpose flour
1/4 cup heavy cream
2 tablespoons chopped parsley
Salt and freshly ground pepper to taste

Sauté the shallot and garlic in the olive oil in a large saucepan until the shallot is translucent and soft. Add 2 tablespoons parsley, the wine and mussels. Cover and bring to a boil, shaking the saucepan occasionally. Cook until the mussels have opened, discarding any mussels that do not open. Remove from the heat. Remove the mussels from the liquid with a slotted spoon to a serving bowl and keep warm. Boil the cooking liquid for 2 to 3 minutes or until reduced.

Mix the butter and flour in a small bowl to form a paste. Whisk 1 tablespoon of the paste at a time into the liquid until the mixture is the consistency of thick cream. Add the cream, 2 tablespoons parsley, the salt and pepper. Pour over the mussels and serve immediately.

Serves 4

Wine Recommendations: Muscadet, Chablis, Chardonnay, or Mâcon-Villages

Mussels Picante

You'll be pleased with this impressive and contemporary way to serve mussels for a crowd. When buying mussels, have the fish purveyor give the mussels a preliminary scrub; it then takes only five minutes per dozen to wash them at home.

8 dozen medium mussels (about 8¹/2 pounds)
3 cups water
2 jalapeño chiles
1¹/2 cups minced red onions (1 to 2 red onions)
¹/3 cup minced cilantro
¹/3 cup red wine vinegar
¹/3 cup lime juice
Salt and freshly ground pepper to taste

Scrub the mussels well and rinse them in cold water. Heat the water in a large heavy deep stockpot over medium heat until hot but not boiling. Add one-third of the mussels and cover with a tight-fitting lid. Bring to a boil and steam for 2 to 5 minutes or until the mussels open, discarding any that do not open. Remove the mussels and cool until they can be easily handled. Repeat the process until all of the mussels have been cooked.

Break off and discard half the shell of each mussel. Loosen the mussels from their remaining shells with a sharp knife and remove the white attachment fibers and the rubbery band that surrounds each shell edge, leaving the mussels on their shell halves.

Layer the mussels on a large platter or platters. Cover securely and chill until ready to top with the sauce. (The mussels may be chilled for 8 to 10 hours.)

Remove the seeds from the chiles using gloves. Chop the chiles finely. Combine the chiles, onion, cilantro, vinegar, lime juice, salt and pepper in a large bowl and mix well. Chill, covered, for 2 hours or longer to allow the flavors to blend. (The sauce may be chilled, tightly covered, for 8 to 10 hours.)

Remove the mussels from their shell halves, reserving the shell halves. Place the mussels in the chile sauce. Marinate, covered, in the refrigerator for 2 to 3 hours. Remove the mussels from the sauce allowing as much of the sauce as possible to cling to the mussels and return each to its reserved shell, adding extra sauce if necessary. Place on a serving platter and chill, covered, until ready to serve.

Makes 8 dozen (Serves 18 to 20 as an appetizer)

Wine Recommendations: Beaujolais, Chablis, Sancerre, Sauvignon Blanc, Riesling, or Mâcon-Villages

For easy flower arrangements, consider purchasing clear glass vases. Clear glass vases can be filled with fruit or other objects, with flowers or greenery arranged at the top of the vase. Lemons and limes work well for summer; cranberries are perfect for the holidays. Palm leaves, such as dracaena, can be layered along the inside of a glass vase for a tropical look. For a fun and unusual look, use two cylindrical glass vases equal in height but with one vase narrower than the other. Place the narrower vase inside the wider vase. Fill the area between the two vases with different colored lentils or even small pieces of glass in various colors. This also works well for supporting long leaves between the vases for a dramatic design.

Sea Scallops Home Style

It's important to use a good-quality white wine when making this easy and delicious dish.

1 1/2 pounds sea scallops, chopped into bite-size pieces
1 1/2 cups dry white wine, such as Chablis
1/2 teaspoon salt
1/4 teaspoon pepper
2 tablespoons butter
2 tablespoons finely chopped onion
1/4 cup mushrooms, finely chopped
1 tablespoon chopped parsley
1 tablespoon tomato paste
3 tablespoons fresh bread crumbs
Butter for dotting

Combine the scallops, wine, salt and pepper in a large heavy saucepan. Bring slowly to a boil and simmer gently for 3 minutes. Drain the scallops and place in a bowl. Melt 2 tablespoons butter in the saucepan. Add the onion and cook over low heat for 10 minutes. Stir in the mushrooms, parsley, tomato paste and 1 1/2 tablespoons of the bread crumbs. Bring to a boil and reduce the heat to low. Simmer for 5 minutes or until the sauce is thickened, stirring constantly. Return the scallops to the pan and coat with the sauce. Spoon into buttered shells, individual baking dishes or a large baking dish. Sprinkle with the remaining bread crumbs and dot with butter. Preheat the broiler. Broil for 1 minute or until the top is golden brown.

Serves 4 to 6

Wine Recommendation: Chablis

The Roberta Rymer Balfe Shooting Star Award was created in 1989 and 1990 under the presidency of Karyn Herterich to honor Roberta Rymer Balfe for her fifty years of service, generosity, encouragement, and ongoing creative commitment to opera education. This award is given biennially to an individual who has demonstrated a lifetime commitment to opera and made a major contribution to opera education.

Baked Avocados Filled with Creamed Lobster

*Although it seems unusual, this beautiful luncheon dish is delicious.
Serve it with wild rice combined with toasted slivered almonds.*

2 ripe avocados
1/4 cup cider vinegar
8 ounces chopped mushrooms
2 tablespoons butter
3 tablespoons all-purpose flour
3 tablespoons butter, melted
1 cup milk
1/4 teaspoon curry powder
Dash of salt
Dash of paprika
8 ounces cooked lobster meat or crab meat
2 tablespoons finely chopped green bell pepper
1 tablespoon chopped pimento
1/2 teaspoon butter
2 tablespoons bread crumbs

Cut each avocado into halves and remove the pits. Scrape out the remains of the pits from each avocado half, leaving only the ripe fruit. Place 1 tablespoon of the vinegar in each avocado half and let stand for 30 minutes.

Preheat the oven to 350 degrees. Sauté the mushrooms in 2 tablespoons butter in a skillet over medium heat until brown; drain and set aside. Stir the flour and 3 tablespoons melted butter together in a large saucepan over medium heat to form a thick paste. Add the milk gradually, stirring constantly until the mixture is creamy. Stir in the curry powder, salt and paprika. Add the mushrooms, lobster, bell pepper and pimento. Melt 1/2 teaspoon butter in a small saucepan. Add the bread crumbs and heat until softened.

Line a 10×15-inch baking pan with waxed paper. Discard the vinegar from each avocado half and fill with the lobster sauce. Place in the prepared baking pan and sprinkle each with 1/2 tablespoon of the bread crumb mixture. Bake for 15 minutes or until golden brown.

Serves 4

Wine Recommendations: Chenin Blanc, Riesling, or Pinot Grigio

Florida Lobster Tails in Saffron Sauce with Squid Ink Pasta

Fresh fish stock greatly enhances the flavor of all dishes requiring fish stock. If you prepare the saffron-flavored fish stock for this recipe, you can store what isn't used for up to three months. If squid ink pasta is too difficult to find, try whole wheat pasta. Serve with crisp bread and a green salad tossed with a light vinaigrette.

SAFFRON-FLAVORED FISH STOCK

8 cups water
8 ounces grouper or snapper, 4 fish tablets,
    or 3 (8-ounce) bottles clam juice
1/2 teaspoon thyme
3/4 teaspoon pulverized saffron

SAFFRON SAUCE

Leaves from 1 bunch Italian parsley, minced
1 cup finely chopped yellow onion
3 tablespoons olive oil
2 tablespoons garlic, minced
1/2 yellow bell pepper, minced (about 1/2 cup)
1/2 cup dry light white wine, preferably not Californian
    (to minimize the taste of oak)
Salt and freshly ground black pepper to taste

To prepare the stock, bring the water, grouper, thyme and saffron to a boil in a medium stockpot and boil for 20 minutes. Drain carefully through a sieve into a container, discarding the solids. Measure 3 cups of the stock for the pasta and reserve the remaining stock for another purpose.

To prepare the saffron sauce, reserve 3 tablespoons of the parsley for garnish. Sauté the onion in the olive oil in a large saucepan over medium heat for 2 minutes. Add the garlic and bell pepper and sauté for 2 to 3 minutes or until the bell pepper is soft. Add 3 cups stock, the wine, remaining parsley, salt and pepper. Simmer for 20 to 30 minutes or until the saffron from the stock is fully infused into the sauce. Adjust the salt and pepper to taste.

Florida Lobster Tails in Saffron Sauce with Squid Ink Pasta

(continued)

LOBSTER AND PASTA
> 4 Florida lobster tails, split
> 1/2 teaspoon salt
> 16 ounces thin black squid ink pasta, such as
>   linguini or spaghetti

ASSEMBLY AND SERVE
> 1 pound calamari bodies, cut into thin strips
> 4 red plum tomatoes, peeled, seeded and finely chopped
>   (about 1 cup), or 1 cup Pomi tomatoes

To prepare the lobster and pasta, preheat the oven to 425 degrees. Lay the lobsters meat side up in a roasting pan and bake for 15 to 20 minutes or until the lobster meat is opaque. (Do not overbake as it will continue to cook when added to the pasta.) Remove from the oven and carefully remove the lobster meat from the shell. Slice each laterally, leaving the quarter shape of the tail intact. Fill a large stockpot with water and add 1/2 teaspoon salt. Bring to a boil and then add the pasta. Cook the pasta two-third of the time recommended on the package directions.

To assemble and serve, add the calamari to the sauce and cook for 5 minutes or until almost done. (Do not overcook or the calamari will become rubbery.) Drain the pasta and add to the saffron sauce. Cook until the pasta is al dente. Add the tomatoes and cook just until warm. Spoon equal portions of the pasta into individual serving bowls with an intact sliced lobster tail on top. Sprinkle with the reserved 3 tablesspoons parsley.

Serves 4

Wine Recommendations: Chardonnay, Chenin Blanc, Riesling, Pinot Grigio, or Sancerre

Recado Rojo–Red Achiote Paste

Achiote, also known as annatto, has a rich, earthy flavor. Achiote paste is available in groceries that sell Latin American or Middle Eastern products. To make your own, use an electric spice mill or plan to spend time crushing the hard achiote seeds. Combine 1 1/2 tablespoons achiote seeds, 1/2 teaspoon cumin seeds, 1 teaspoon salt, and 2 teaspoons dried oregano. Moisten with 2 tablespoons lime juice or sour orange juice until you have formed a paste. This paste will last several months stored in an airtight container and refrigerated.

When ready to use, moisten the paste with lime or lemon juice. Achiote paste is delicious on chicken, fish, seafood, pork, and rice. It imparts a golden red color to every dish. Achiote paste is also known as Recado de Adobo Colorado.

Shrimp Manchego with Polenta

A festive Miami interpretation of shrimp and grits.

4 cups chicken broth
1 teaspoon salt
1/2 teaspoon Bijol, or .2 grams saffron
1/8 teaspoon cayenne pepper
1 cup yellow cornmeal
1/2 cup (2 ounces) shredded manchego cheese
2 tablespoons olive oil
1 garlic clove, minced
1 yellow onion, chopped
1 small red bell pepper, chopped
Pinch of cumin
1 (8-ounce) can tomato sauce
1 pound peeled deveined shrimp
1/4 cup (1 ounce) manchego cheese
Chopped parsley for garnish

Bring the broth, salt, Bijol and cayenne pepper to a boil in a saucepan. Strain and return to the saucepan, discarding any solids. Return to a boil. Stir in the cornmeal 1 tablespoon at a time until dissolved. Reduce the heat to a simmer. Cook for 20 minutes, stirring frequently. (The mixture should be slightly thickened.) Stir in 1/2 cup cheese until blended.

Heat the olive oil in a skillet. Add the garlic, onion, bell pepper and cumin and sauté until the onion is translucent. Stir in the tomato sauce and bring to a simmer. Add the shrimp and cook for 1 to 2 minutes or until the shrimp turn pink. Ladle the polenta into individual serving bowls. Ladle the shrimp mixture over the polento and sprinkle evenly with 1/4 cup cheese. Garnish with parsley.

Serves 4

Wine Recommendations: Chardonnay, Chenin Blanc, Sauvignon Blanc, White Zinfandel, or Albariño

In 1968 Young Patronesses of the Opera (YPO) created the Junior Opera Guild (JOG) to teach high school girls a love and appreciation of opera. Forty years later JOG is still going strong. JOG girls usher at the operas, help out at YPO events, and coordinate several fund-raisers each year.

Tequila Shrimp

The tequila is surprisingly subtle in this succulent dish.

1 pound peeled deveined large shrimp
2 cups finely sliced leeks
1/4 cup canola oil
2 tablespoons butter
1 cup finely sliced leeks
1/2 cup chopped shallots
1/2 cup Reposada tequila
1 cup crème fraîche or heavy cream
1 teaspoon tomato purée or lemon juice
Salt and freshly ground pepper to taste
1 tomato, chopped
1/2 cup fresh basil, chopped
1/4 cup fresh cilantro, chopped
Hot cooked rice

Cut the shrimp into 1-inch pieces. Fry 2 cups leeks in the canola oil in a skillet until crisp. Remove to paper towels to drain. Melt the butter in a heavy sauté pan or skillet. Add 1 cup leeks and the shallots and sauté until soft. Stir in the shrimp. Add the tequila and ignite with a match, averting your face from the flames. Let the flames subside. Stir in the crème fraîche, tomato purée, salt and pepper. Cook for 2 minutes over medium heat. Remove the shrimp from the pan and set aside. Stir the tomato, basil and cilantro into the sauce. Cook over low heat until the sauce is thickens slightly. Return the shrimp to the pan and cook until heated through, do not overcook. Serve over rice and top with the crisp-fried leeks.

Serves 4

Wine Recommendations: Viño Verde or Muscadet

Florida Grilled Shrimp

Please your guests by grilling these at the start of the barbecue or serve as a main course with rice and green salad, such as our Baby Greens Salad with Lime and Honey Vinaigrette (page 118).

¹/3 cup fresh lemon juice
¹/3 cup fresh orange juice
¹/3 cup chili sauce
1 garlic clove, minced
1 teaspoon dry mustard
1 tablespoon Worcestershire sauce
¹/4 cup honey
¹/4 cup vegetable oil
¹/4 teaspoon paprika
Salt and freshly ground pepper to taste
1¹/2 pounds large shrimp, peeled and deveined

Process the lemon juice, orange juice, chili sauce, garlic, dry mustard, Worcestershire sauce, honey, oil, paprika, salt and pepper in a blender or food processor until blended. Pour over the shrimp in a large bowl. Marinate in the refrigerator for 1 hour, stirring once or twice.

Preheat the grill. Drain the shrimp, reserving the marinade. Thread the shrimp onto skewers and place on a grill rack. Grill over high heat for 3 minutes on each side or until the shrimp turn pink, basting with the reserved marinade. Serve immediately.

Note: The tails may be left on or off of the shrimp according to your preference. If you use wooden skewers, soak the skewers in water for 1 hour before using.

Serves 3 or 4

Wine Recommendations: Riesling, Sauvignon Blanc, White Zinfandel, or Albariño

Throughout most of the year in Miami, you can jump in the surf and then relax on the beach with a snack and a cold drink.

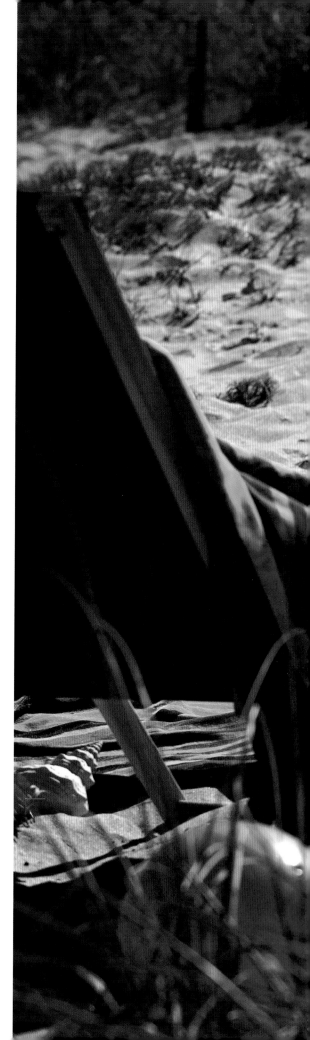

Shrimp with Rémoulade

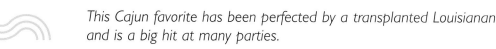

This Cajun favorite has been perfected by a transplanted Louisianan and is a big hit at many parties.

SHRIMP

1 to 2 tablespoons liquid shrimp and crab boil
3 tablespoons salt
3 pounds unpeeled shrimp

RÉMOULADE

$^1/4$ cup lemon juice
$^1/4$ cup tarragon vinegar
$^1/4$ cup coarsely ground brown mustard
$^1/4$ cup horseradish
2 teaspoons salt
$1^1/2$ teaspoons freshly ground black pepper
2 teaspoons paprika
Pinch of cayenne pepper
1 cup vegetable oil
$1^1/2$ cups finely chopped celery
$1^1/2$ cups minced green onions

To prepare the shrimp, fill a large stockpot with water and add the shrimp and crab boil and salt. Bring to a rolling boil and then add the shrimp. Boil for 2 minutes or until the shrimp turn pink. Remove the stockpot from the heat and let stand for 5 minutes. Drain the shrimp well and chill.

To prepare the sauce, combine the lemon juice, vinegar, mustard, horseradish, salt, black pepper, paprika and cayenne pepper in a bowl and mix well. Whisk in the oil, celery and green onions gradually.

To serve, peel and devein the shrimp. Arrange on a large serving platter. Pour the sauce over the shrimp just before serving. Serve with crunchy French bread.

Note: This recipe also makes a beautiful appetizer for a seated dinner served in a cocktail glass or on a salad plate over ruffled lettuce.

Serves 8

Wine Recommendations: Sancerre, Riesling, or Albariño

Plantain-Crusted Grouper with Tropical Fruit and Pepper Salsa

Homemade Plantain Chips (page 63) will improve the taste of this dish; however, commercial chips make it a very quick dish to prepare.

4 (8-ounce) grouper fillets
Salt and pepper to taste
3 cups plantain chips
1/2 cup unseasoned bread crumbs

1/4 cup shredded coconut
1/8 teaspoon nutmeg
2 tablespoons olive oil
Tropical Fruit and Pepper Salsa (page 64)

Preheat the oven to 350 degrees. Season the fillets with salt and pepper. Process the plantain chips, bread crumbs, coconut and nutmeg in a food processor until ground. Press the mixture onto the fillets. Heat the olive oil in a large ovenproof skillet over medium heat. Add the fillets and cook until golden brown on both sides. Bake for 10 to 15 minutes or until the fish is cooked through. Serve with salsa.

Serves 4

Wine Recommendations: Chardonnay, Chenin Blanc, Riesling, Sancerre, and Albariño

Pesce Parmesan

A simple and tasty way to prepare fish.

3 ripe tomatoes
1 1/2 pounds thin white fish fillets, such as
   grouper, snapper or tilapia
1/2 cup seasoned bread crumbs
1/2 cup dry white wine

3 tablespoons lemon juice
3 tablespoons butter or margarine
1/2 teaspoon garlic powder
Salt and freshly ground pepper to taste
3/4 cup (3 ounces) grated Parmesan cheese

Preheat the oven to 350 degrees. Cut the tomatoes into thin slices and place in a large baking dish. Layer the fillets over the tomatoes and sprinkle with the breads crumbs to cover lightly. Bring the wine, lemon juice and butter to a boil in a saucepan. Boil for 2 minutes and then remove from the heat. Let stand for 5 minutes to cool. Pour the sauce over the fillets and sprinkle with the garlic powder, salt and pepper. Cover with the cheese. Bake for 20 minutes or until almost cooked through. Broil for 3 minutes or until the top is light brown. Serve with the sauce.

Serves 3

Wine Recommendations: Sauvignon Blanc, White Zinfandel, Pinot Grigio, or Muscadet

Tropical Mahimahi with Papaya Couscous

The addition of couscous gives this Caribbean dish a Middle Eastern touch. Couscous should always be prepared at the last minute or it will become soggy.

$1/2$ cup olive oil
6 large garlic cloves, minced
$2/3$ cup fresh sour orange juice,
    or $1/3$ cup fresh orange juice and $1/3$ cup fresh lime juice
$1/2$ teaspoon cumin
4 fresh mahimahi fillets, skinned and boned
5 tablespoons sesame oil
1 cup chopped onion
$1/2$ cup chopped red bell pepper
$1 1/2$ to 2 teaspoons curry paste (available in Oriental markets)
1 cup chopped ripe papaya
$1 1/3$ cups chicken stock
1 cup French Moroccan couscous
$1/2$ to 1 cup chopped macadamia nuts
Salt and freshly ground pepper to taste

Combine the olive oil, garlic, orange juice and cumin in a sealable plastic bag and shake to mix. Add the fillets and turn to coat. Seal the bag and marinate in the refrigerator for 6 hours or longer.

Preheat the grill. Brush 1 tablespoon of the sesame oil on each fillet and place on a grill rack. Grill over medium heat for 10 to 12 minutes per pound. Sauté the onion and bell pepper in 1 tablespoon of the remaining sesame oil in a skillet for 5 minutes or until golden brown. Stir in the curry paste and cook for 2 minutes. Add the papaya and cook for 2 minutes, stirring constantly.

Bring the stock to a boil in a saucepan. Pour over the couscous in a large bowl and mix well. Let stand for no more than 8 minutes. Fluff with a fork and stir into the papaya mixture. Add the macadamia nuts, salt and pepper. Serve immediately.

Note: Couscous becomes too soft if allowed to sit, and the papaya will oversweeten the dish.

Serves 4

Wine Recommendations: Riesling or Sauvignon Blanc

Colorful Snapper

This is an impressive dish that takes little time to make.

1 large Vidalia onion, cut into crescent shapes
3 tablespoons olive oil
1 yellow bell pepper, thinly sliced
1 green bell pepper, thinly sliced
1 red bell pepper, thinly sliced
Salt and freshly ground pepper to taste
$^1/_2$ cup all-purpose flour
$^1/_2$ teaspoon paprika
4 snapper fillets
$^1/_4$ cup ($^1/_2$ stick) butter
2 large garlic cloves, minced
1 large bunch cilantro, chopped
2 tablespoons lime juice
$^1/_2$ cup water or white wine, such as Sauvignon Blanc
Cilantro and lemon slices for garnish

Sauté the onion in the olive oil in a large saucepan for 1 minute. Add the bell peppers and sauté for 2 to 3 minutes or until the bell peppers and onion are caramelized but still colorful. Season with salt and pepper. Remove the vegetables with a slotted spoon to a bowl and set aside. Reserve the pan drippings in the saucepan over low heat.

Place the flour and paprika in a sealable plastic bag and shake to mix. Pat dry the fillets. Place the fillets in the bag one at a time and shake to coat. Increase the heat to medium. Shake off any excess flour from the fillets and place skin side down in the reserved pan drippings. Cook for 3 minutes and turn the fillets. Cook for 5 to 10 minutes longer or until the fillets flake easily. Do not overcook. Remove the fillets to a warm platter to keep warm.

Pour off the excess oil from the saucepan, leaving any small pieces of the fillets in the saucepan. Increase the heat to medium-high. Add the butter and heat until melted. Add the garlic and sauté until golden brown. Stir in the chopped cilantro, lime juice, water, salt and pepper. Cook until the sauce is slightly reduced, stirring constantly.

Place the sautéed vegetables over the warm fish and pour the sauce over the top. Garnish with cilantro and lemon slices.

Serves 4

Wine Recommendation: Sauvignon Blanc

Grilling Seafood

It is always easiest to grill seafood that is thick and has a firm texture that won't fall apart when grilling. Delicate or thin fish may fall apart on the grill. If you have chosen a thinner fish or if your grill is not perfectly clean, use a grill basket that has been lightly sprayed with cooking oil.

If you are grilling directly on the grill, spray cooking oil on the grill before you start the fire, otherwise the oil may flame up and cause the can to explode. The grill should always be oiled well when cooking fish.

A good rule of thumb for knowing how long to panfry or grill a fish is the 1 to 10 rule. A 1-inch-thick fish will take 10 minutes to cook through. Fish thinner than 1 inch will take less time. Seafood cooks quickly, so unless otherwise indicated cook on a grill over medium heat. Test for doneness by slitting the center with a knife. Cooked fish will not be translucent. Tuna is the exception; most people prefer grilled tuna to be lightly seared with red to pink meat.

Grilled Snapper with Cilantro and Mango Vinaigrette

Snapper should be grilled in a fish basket since it is delicate and flaky.

6 tablespoons olive oil
1/4 cup chopped fresh cilantro
3/4 teaspoon cumin
3 tablespoons fresh lime juice
1 1/2 teaspoons grated lime zest
4 (5- to 6-ounce) red snapper fillets
1/2 teaspoon salt
Pepper to taste
1 large mango, cut into thick wedges
8 large red-leaf lettuce leaves
1 tablespoon chopped fresh cilantro

Whisk the olive oil, 1/4 cup cilantro, cumin, the lime juice and lime zest in a small bowl. Reserve 2 tablespoons of the vinaigrette and set the remaining vinaigrette aside. Brush all sides of the fillets and mango with the reserved vinaigrette and place in a glass dish. Marinate in the refrigerator for 1 hour. Sprinkle the fillets with the salt and pepper.

Preheat the grill. Place the fillets and mango in a fish basket and grill over medium heat for 6 minutes or until the fillets are opaque in the center and the mango is soft and beginning to brown; do not turn.

Overlap two lettuce leaves on each of four serving plates. Top with the fish and mango. Drizzle with the remaining vinaigrette. Sprinkle with 1 tablespoon cilantro.

Serves 4

Wine Recommendation: Sauvignon Blanc

Macadamia-Crusted Snapper with Avocado, Mango and Papaya Salsa

The double coating on these fillets ensures a delectable crust.

1 1/2 cups macadamia nuts
1/2 cup all-purpose flour
1/2 teaspoon salt
4 snapper fillets
6 tablespoons macadamia nut oil
2 eggs, lightly beaten
Avocado, Mango and Papaya Salsa (page 65)

Pulse the macadamia nuts in a food processor until coarsely and finely chopped, but not powdery. Spread on a piece of waxed paper 12 inches long. Mix the flour and salt together and spread on a piece of waxed paper 12 inches long.

Brush the fillets lightly with 2 tablespoons of the macadamia nut oil. Coat each fillet with the flour mixture and then the macadamia nuts. Dip into the beaten eggs and coat again with the macadamia nuts. (Each fillet should be thickly coated.)

Heat 2 tablespoons of the remaining macadamia nut oil in a large skillet. Add two of the fillets and cook until the fillets flake easily. Remove to a serving platter and lightly cover with a paper towel. Drain the skillet. Repeat with the remaining fillets and macadamia nut oil. Serve with salsa.

Serves 4

Wine Recommendations: Riesling, Pinot Grigio, Muscadet, Albariño, Chardonnay or Mâcon-Villages

The Junior Opera Guild girls make a great contribution to opera education in South Florida. These high school girls usher at operas and assist at YPO's Girl Scout Workshops. To raise funds, they participate every year in store-sponsored charity events, and they coordinate a successful garage sale and a fabulous fashion show. The JOG girls who are high school seniors model in the show, which has been sponsored since 1999 by Bloomingdale's.

Sticky Rice and Grilled Swordfish with Asian Flavors

Everyone enjoys eating Asian food! Try this delicious marinade on any fish or chicken for rave reviews from your guests.

2 cups Thai glutinous rice
4 cups water
1 cup low-sodium teriyaki sauce
1/2 cup white wine
1/4 cup low-sodium soy sauce
2 tablespoons rice wine vinegar
2 tablespoons vegetable oil
1 teaspoon sesame oil
6 garlic cloves, pressed
1 bunch scallions, chopped
1/4 cup minced peeled fresh ginger
1/4 cup packed brown sugar
1/2 teaspoon freshly ground pepper
4 (8-ounce) swordfish or tuna steaks, each 1 inch thick

Rinse the rice thoroughly. Place in a bowl and cover with the water. Soak at room temperature for 2 hours or longer. Drain and place in a steamer basket or a heatproof colander over boiling water and cook for 25 minutes or until tender. Place in a serving bowl and stir lightly with a fork.

Bring the teriyaki sauce, wine, soy sauce, vinegar, vegetable oil, sesame oil, garlic, scallions, ginger, brown sugar and pepper to a boil in a saucepan. Boil for 2 minutes or until the brown sugar is dissolved. Pour one-half of the marinade in a bowl to cool, reserving the remaining marinade in the saucepan. Place the steaks in a single layer in a nonreactive pan and cover with the cooled marinade. Marinate in the refrigerator for 30 minutes. Drain the steaks, discarding the marinade.

Preheat the grill. Place the steaks on a grill rack and grill over high heat until seared on both sides. Reduce the heat to medium and grill to the desired degree of doneness. (Do not overcook.)

Boil the reserved marinade in the saucepan until the sauce thickens, stirring frequently. Serve over the steaks and rice.

Serves 4

Wine Recommendations: Riesling or Gewürztraminer

Baked Salmon with Rich Mango Sauce

A delicious sauce for all strong-tasting fish.

6 garlic cloves, finely chopped
$^1/4$ cup finely chopped fresh ginger
$^1/3$ cup cilantro, finely chopped
1 large onion, finely chopped
1 large onion, puréed
$^1/2$ cup toasted pine nuts
1 teaspoon salt
$^1/4$ to $^1/2$ teaspoon freshly ground pepper
$1^1/2$ teaspoons cumin
$1^1/2$ teaspoons coriander
1 teaspoon cardamom
1 teaspoon freshly grated orange zest
$^1/4$ cup fresh orange juice
Juice of 2 lemons
1 (2- to 3-pound) salmon, bluefish or mackerel fillet, bones removed
3 ripe mangos, chopped
1 to 2 teaspoons honey (optional)

Preheat the oven to 350 degrees. Combine the garlic, ginger, cilantro, finely chopped onion and puréed onion in a bowl and mix well. Stir in the pine nuts, salt, pepper, cumin, coriander, cardamom, orange zest, orange juice and lemon juice. Pour into a glass baking dish or roasting pan. Place the fillet in the mixture to lightly cover. Scatter a few pieces of the mango on top of the fillet and surround with the remaining mango pieces. Drizzle the honey in rows over the fish. Bake for 10 minutes. Cover with foil and bake for 15 to 20 minutes longer or until the fillet is cooked through.

Serves 6 to 8

Wine Recommendation: Chardonnay

Caribbean Grilled Tuna Steaks with Aromatic Spice Paste

The spice paste is also fabulous on thick mahimahi fillets. Grill as you would for tuna.

Pinch of saffron
2 teaspoons water
1 to 2 jalapeño chiles, seeded and minced
2 garlic cloves, minced
1 small onion, chopped
1 tablespoon grated fresh ginger
1 teaspoon turmeric
2 tablespoons lemon juice
1/3 cup unsweetened coconut milk
1/4 cup fresh cilantro
Salt to taste
6 (4-ounce) tuna steaks, 1 1/2 inches thick

Soak the saffron in the water in a cup for 30 minutes. Process the saffron water, chiles, garlic, onion, ginger, turmeric, lemon juice, coconut milk and cilantro in a blender to form a smooth paste. Season with salt. Place the steaks in a sealable plastic bag or in a nonreactive container and spread the paste on both sides. Seal the bag and marinate in the refrigerator for 30 minutes.

Preheat the grill. Place the fish on a grill rack and grill over high heat for 3 minutes on each side or until the fish flakes easily. Serve immediately.

Note: The tuna may also be grilled 1 to 2 inches above a bed of hot coals.

Serves 6

Wine Recommendations: Riesling, Gewürztraminer, Chenin Blanc, Beaujolais, or Sauvignon Blanc

Enjoy a fun day relaxing and grilling your catch of the day on one of Miami's pristine beaches.

Pan-Fried Tuna with Spicy Roasted Tomato Sauce

Spicy Roasted Tomato Sauce, with its subtle flavor of orange, is also delicious with roasted Cornish hens. For a spicier flavor, use a more pungent chile.

SPICY ROASTED TOMATO SAUCE
> 1 tablespoon olive oil
> 4 ripe tomatoes
> 2 tablespoons olive oil
> 1/4 cup cider vinegar
> 1/2 cup water
> Salt and freshly ground pepper to taste
> 1 onion, thinly sliced
> 2 garlic cloves, minced
> 2 tablespoons tomato paste
> 1 serrano chile, seeded and chopped
> Grated zest of 1 large orange

To prepare the sauce, preheat the oven to 350 degrees. Lightly grease a baking pan with 1 tablespoon olive oil. Cut the tomatoes into halves and remove the stem ends. Place the tomatoes cut side down in the prepared baking pan. Bake for 15 minutes. Remove the skin from the tomatoes with a knife and fork. Drizzle 2 tablespoons olive oil over the tomatoes. Bake for 10 minutes. Remove from the oven and carefully remove any brown edges. Bring the vinegar, water, salt and pepper to a boil in a medium saucepan. Reduce the heat to low and add the onion, garlic, tomato paste, chile and orange zest. Simmer for 10 minutes. Combine with the roasted tomatoes in a food processor and process until smooth.

Pan-Fried Tuna with Spicy Roasted Tomato Sauce *(continued)*

TUNA

4 (4-ounce) tuna steaks, 1/4 to 1/2 inch thick
2 garlic cloves, finely chopped
2 tablespoons lemon juice
1/4 cup extra-virgin olive oil
1/4 cup dry bread crumbs
Salt and pepper to taste
1/4 cup (1/2 stick) butter
2 tablespoons chopped parsley for garnish

To prepare the tuna, sprinkle the steaks with the garlic, lemon juice and olive oil. Lightly coat with the bread crumbs, salt and pepper. Marinate at room temperature for 1 hour or in the refrigerator for up to 12 hours. (Remove the tuna from the refrigerator 15 minutes before panfrying.) Melt 2 tablespoons of the butter in a large heavy skillet over medium heat. Add the tuna and fry on both sides until golden brown, adding the remaining 2 tablespoons butter after turning so the crust will absorb the butter. Place on individual serving plates with a dollop of the sauce on the side. Garnish with the parsley.

Serves 4

Wine Recommendations: Sauvignon Blanc, Pouilly-Fumé, Riesling, or Chenin Blanc

Thanks to their successful fund-raising efforts the high school girls who are members of the Junior Opera Guild have awarded the grand prize of $15,000 to the winners of the YPO/FGO Voice Competition in 2003, 2005, and 2007.

Après Opera Dessert Party

Desserts

Attending an entertaining performance with good friends is an experience to be savored. The opera tenor's glorious aria, the ballet dancer's graceful arabesque, the conductor's perceptive interpretation of the symphony, or even the actor's hilarious pratfall, all should be reviewed and relished afterwards. What better way to continue the pleasures of the evening than a late night dessert party?

Miami has many entertainment venues, and the Performing Arts Center is the most spectacular. After leaving one of the many performances at the PAC, it seems only right that friends should gather at home and reminisce about the production. This hostess's menu reflects Miami's tropical bounty and cultural richness. It can all be prepared before the start of the evening and set out when the guests arrive.

Lit by the golden moon and tea lights, our Mediterranean courtyard is ready for guests. Intimate tables for two are dressed in burgundy crushed satin. Small tables for six are covered in cinnamon crushed satin with embroidered organza overlays. Arrangements on these tables are kept small. Bright green spider chrysanthemums, vibernum, hypericum, leucadendrum, and roses provide a lush contrast to the tablecloths.

Antique silver flatware and gold-embossed heirloom crystal and china add to the evening's elegance. The dessert table, however, is the star of the show. The desserts are displayed on cut crystal pedestals and platters on a marble-topped iron scrollwork buffet. Dramatic in color and bold in arrangement, the moss-filled topiary is embellished with Freedom roses, mango miniature calla lilies, and hypericum.

Music softly plays in the background. The hostess has chosen music from the same composer for tonight's opera— *Madama Butterfly* by Puccini. While sipping on dessert wines and cocktails made with champagne, guests leisurely recall the beautiful singing they heard this evening and make plans for enjoying the next production.

Light from small table lamps and votives gives the embroidered organza overlay cloths a shimmery glow and heightens the elegant ambience of this dessert party.

 Menu

*Fresh fruit and cheese, Coconut Cheesecake with Shortbread Crust
and Chocolate and Coconut Topping and a Champagne Kiss are
a late night feast for these guests.*

A beautiful tropical fruit platter heads the dessert buffet table. This hostess has moved a wrought-iron buffet table to the courtyard to serve her guests.

Work Plan

DAY BEFORE THE PARTY

Bake and frost Best-Ever Carrot Cake and leave at room temperature.

Prepare Pineapple Orange Sorbet and Crystallized Citrus Julienne and freeze.

Bake and assemble Amaretto Flan. When cool, remove from the mold and refrigerate until serving.

Bake Coconut Cheesecake with Shortbread Crust, but don't add Coconut and Chocolate Topping. Refrigerate until just before serving.

ON THE DAY

Prepare Chocolate Truffle Cream and keep refrigerated until served.

Bake Tres Leches Cake.

Prepare fruit for Champagne Flirtini Cocktail and Champagne Kiss Cocktail.

Remove and unmold Coconut Cheesecake and add Coconut and Chocolate topping.

JUST BEFORE SERVING

Cut Citrus Julienne for Pineapple Orange Sorbet and decorate sorbet.

Arrange Cheese board with Spanish Cheeses and display.

Cakes, cheeses, and flans should be removed from refrigerator and brought to room temperature before serving.

When requested, prepare Champagne Kiss Cocktail and Champagne Flirtini Cocktail.

Coconut Cheesecake with Shortbread Crust and Chocolate and Coconut Topping

Shortbread, chocolate and coconut with a rich creamy cheesecake——what more could you want?

1 1/2 cups all-purpose flour
3/4 cup sifted confectioners' sugar
10 tablespoons butter, softened
1/2 teaspoon vanilla extract
Pecan pieces
24 ounces cream cheese, softened
3/4 cup granulated sugar
5 eggs
1 cup coconut cream

1 cup sour cream
2 1/2 teaspoons coconut extract, or to taste
1 cup flaked coconut, lightly toasted
1/4 cup (1/2 stick) butter or margarine
6 ounces semisweet chocolate
3/4 cup confectioners' sugar, sifted
3 tablespoons water
1 teaspoon vanilla extract

Position the top oven rack in the center of the oven and position the lower rack at the lowest level. Preheat the oven to 350 degrees. Mix the flour, 3/4 cup confectioners' sugar, 10 tablespoons butter and 1/2 teaspoon vanilla together in a bowl. Press onto the bottom of a 10-inch springform pan. Sprinkle with pecans and press in gently. Bake for 15 to 18 minutes or until golden brown. Remove the pan to a wire rack to cool.

Reduce the oven temperature to 325 degrees. Beat the cream cheese and granulated sugar at medium speed in a mixing bowl until fluffy. Beat in the eggs one at a time. Add the coconut cream, sour cream and coconut extract and beat for 20 seconds.

Fill a large roasting pan three-fourths full of water and place on the lowest oven rack. The steam from the water in this pan will prevent the cheesecake from cracking in the center. Pour the cream cheese mixture into the baked crust, filling only three-fourths full. (Discard any remaining filling.) Place on the center oven rack. Pour enough hot water in the roasting pan to come halfway up the side of the springform pan. Bake for 1 1/4 hours or until the center is almost set. Remove the springform pan from the roasting pan and remove the foil. Cool on a wire rack for 2 hours. Chill for 8 hours. Loosen the cheesecake from the side of the pan and release the side. Place the cheesecake on a serving platter. Cover the top with the coconut.

Melt 1/4 cup butter and the chocolate in a saucepan over low heat, stirring constantly. Remove from the heat and stir in 3/4 cup confectioners' sugar, the water and 1 teaspoon vanilla extract. Pour into a squirt bottle and drizzle over the top and side of the cheesecake.

Note: If coconut cream is unavailable, simmer one 14-ounce can unsweetened coconut milk in a saucepan over medium heat for 10 minutes or until thickened. Let stand until cool. Measure 1 cup to use in this recipe.

Serves 12 to 14

Photograph on page 213.

Red, White and Blue Cheesecake

This gorgeous cheesecake is removed from the oven when it is almost baked, then cooled, topped with a sour cream topping, and baked again.

CHEESECAKE
- 1 1/2 cups ground shortbread cookies
- 1 cup toasted hazelnuts
- 1/4 cup sugar
- 1/4 cup (1/2 stick) unsalted butter, melted
- 1 teaspoon vanilla extract
- 1/3 cup whipping cream
- 1 teaspoon vanilla extract
- 24 ounces cream cheese, softened
- 1 cup sugar
- 4 eggs, lightly beaten
- 1/2 cup sour cream
- 2 teaspoons vanilla extract
- 3/4 cup fresh raspberries
- 3/4 cup fresh blueberries
- 1 tablespoon cornstarch
- 1 cup sour cream
- 2 tablespoons sugar
- 1 1/2 teaspoons vanilla extract

BERRY TOPPING
- 1/3 cup seedless raspberry jam
- 1/2 cup fresh raspberries
- 1/2 cup fresh blueberries

To prepare the cheesecake, preheat the oven to 350 degrees. Process the cookies, hazelnuts and 1/4 cup sugar in a food processor until finely ground. Add the butter and 1 teaspoon vanilla and mix well. Press onto the bottom and 1 1/2 to 2 inches up the side of a springform pan. Wrap the outside of the pan with foil.

Bring the cream and 1 teaspoon vanilla to a boil in a small saucepan. Remove immediately from the heat to cool. Beat the cream cheese and 1 cup sugar in a mixing bowl until fluffy. Add the eggs and beat until smooth. Add the cooled cream mixture, 1/2 cup sour cream and 2 teaspoons vanilla and blend well. Gently toss the raspberries and blueberries with the cornstarch in a large bowl. Pour one-half of the cream cheese mixture into the crust. Sprinkle with the berry mixture to cover the surface. Pour the remaining cream cheese mixture over the berries to cover. Bake for 1 hour and 10 minutes or until the cheesecake is golden brown but still moves slightly in the center when the pan is shaken. Remove from the oven and cool for 15 minutes or until the cheesecake falls. Maintain the oven temperature.

Combine 1 cup sour cream, 2 tablespoons sugar and 1 1/2 teaspoons vanilla in a bowl and mix well. Spoon over the baked layer. Return to the oven and bake for 10 minutes. Remove to a wire rack to cool. Chill, covered, until ready to serve.

To prepare the berry topping and serve, melt the jam in a small saucepan over low heat. Brush one-half of the jam over the top of the cheesecake. Arrange the berries on top. Gently brush the berries with the remaining jam. Loosen the cheesecake from the side of the pan with a sharp knife and remove the side. Serve cold.

Serves 12 to 14

Golden Caramel Flan

A classic dish passed down through the generations of a Cuban family.

1 cup sugar
1 tablespoon water
1 cup whole milk
1 cup evaporated milk
1 strip lemon peel
1 cinnamon stick
6 eggs
6 tablespoons sugar
1/4 teaspoon salt
1 teaspoon vanilla extract and/or almond extract

Preheat the oven to 300 degrees. Mix 1 cup sugar and 1 tablespoon water in a small skillet. Cook over low to medium heat until foamy and caramelized, stirring constantly. Pour into a 1 1/2-quart baking dish or flan mold.

Scald the milk and evaporated milk with the lemon peel and cinnamon stick in a medium saucepan until 180 degrees on a candy thermometer and bubbles form around the edge. Whisk the eggs, 6 tablespoons sugar, the salt and vanilla in a mixing bowl until light and foamy. Add the scalded milk gradually, whisking constantly. Gradually strain onto the top of the caramelized sugar. Place the baking dish in a large roasting pan. Add enough hot water to the roasting pan to come halfway up the side of the baking dish. Bake for 1 hour or until a knife inserted in the center comes out clean. Remove to a wire rack to cool. Loosen the flan from the side of the baking dish with a knife and invert onto a serving platter. Warm the caramel from the baking dish and serve with the flan.

Serves 12

Both the Young Patronesses of the Opera and the Junior Opera Guild support the Florida Grand Opera Young Artist and Technical Apprentice Program. FGO Young Artists serve as ambassadors for opera in the Miami community. Not only do they sing in operas, but they also perform in high schools, museums, libraries, churches, temples, and at many charity-sponsored events. FGO Young Artists receive vocal and technical training and are completely financially supported during their apprenticeship.

Cream Cheese Flan with Amaretto

1 cup sugar
1/4 cup water
5 eggs
1 (12-ounce) can evaporated milk
1 (14-ounce) can sweetened
   condensed milk

1 teaspoon vanilla extract or
   almond extract
Pinch of salt
8 ounces cream cheese, softened
1 teaspoon amaretto (optional)

Preheat the oven to 350 degrees. Melt the sugar with the water in a small saucepan over medium heat until the sugar is caramelized. Pour into a fluted mold. Process the eggs, evaporated milk, condensed milk, vanilla, salt and cream cheese in a food processor or blender until smooth. Pour over the caramelized sugar. Place in a large roasting pan. Add enough hot water to the roasting pan to come a little less than halfway up the side of the fluted mold. Bake for 1 hour or until a knife inserted in the center comes out clean. Remove from the oven to cool on a wire rack. Invert the flan onto a serving plate so the caramel will be on top. Chill until ready to serve. Drizzle with the amaretto just before serving.

Serves 12

Orange Flan

Recipe testers felt this flan has the perfect combination of flavors.

9 eggs, at room temperature
1 (14-ounce) can sweetened
   condensed milk
1 1/4 cups orange juice
1 teaspoon vanilla extract

1/2 teaspoon cream of tartar
Grated zest of 1 orange
2 cups sugar
2 tablespoons water
Twisted orange peel for garnnish

Preheat the oven to 350 degrees. Place a flan mold or small bundt pan in the oven to preheat. Fill a roasting pan with enough water to come less than halfway up the side of the flan mold and place in the oven to preheat.

Whisk the eggs in a large bowl. Add the condensed milk, orange juice, vanilla, cream of tartar and orange zest in the order listed, stirring well after each addition. Heat the sugar in a heavy saucepan over low heat until it begins to melt. Stir in 2 tablespoons water and bring to a boil. Cook over low to medium heat until caramelized, stirring constantly. Pour into the mold, rotating until the bottom and side are covered with the caramel. Pour in the egg mixture. Place the mold in the preheated water bath. Bake for 1 hour or until a wooden pick inserted in the center comes out clean. Loosen the flan from the mold by running a knife around the inner edge. Place a serving dish upside down on top of the mold and quickly invert. Dip the exterior of the mold in hot water to loosen the caramel. Pour the caramel over the flan. Garnish with orange peel.

Serves 10

Chocolate Truffle Cream

A rich, luscious dessert that is far more delicious than any chocolate mousse!

2 teaspoons instant coffee granules
2 tablespoons boiling water
2 cups whipping cream
1 cup (6 ounces) semisweet
   chocolate chips
2 eggs

2 egg whites
2 tablespoons bitter orange marmalade
1 tablespoon cognac
2 to 4 tablespoons sifted confectioners'
   sugar (optional)
Raspberries for garnish

Dissolve the coffee granules in the boiling water in a heatproof cup. Heat the cream in a saucepan until warm. Process the cream and chocolate chips at high speed in a food processor or blender until blended. Add the eggs, egg whites, orange marmalade, cognac and coffee mixture and blend at high speed for 4 minutes. Add the confectioners' sugar 1 teaspoon at a time for the desired sweetness and blend for 1 minute. Pour into a serving bowl or serving cups and chill for 3 hours or longer. Garnish with raspberries.

Note: If you are concerned about using raw eggs, use eggs pasteurized in their shells, which are sold at some specialty food stores, or use an equivalent amount of pasteurized egg substitute.

Serves 10

Cuban Natilla

Natilla is cinnamon-flavored sweet custard which originated in Spain. Cubans and Cuban Americans have modified it to make it a bit sweeter. If you prefer your custard to be less sweet, decrease the amount of sweetened condensed milk added to the recipe. Cuban Americans serve this as a side dish to cake, particularly at birthday parties.

5 egg yolks
1/2 to 1 (14-ounce) can sweetened
   condensed milk
1 cup sugar

1 tablespoon vanilla extract
4 to 6 cups milk
2 tablespoons cornstarch
3 or 4 cinnamon sticks

Process the egg yolks, condensed milk, sugar, vanilla, milk and cornstarch in a blender until smooth. Pour into a large heavy saucepan and add the cinnamon sticks. Cook over medium-low heat until thickened to the desired consistency, stirring constantly. Discard the cinnamon sticks. Serve warm or chill, covered, until ready to serve.

Serves 8

Baked Pear Pudding

This pudding can also be made with apples, apples and pears combined, or ripe mango for a softer pudding. As breakfast and brunch, sprinkle the pudding with confectioners' sugar or warm maple syrup. To serve as dessert, it is delicious with vanilla ice cream. Pure comfort food!

10 ripe pears, peeled and quartered
2 tablespoons fresh lemon juice
1/3 cup milk
2/3 cup heavy cream
2/3 cup granulated sugar
2/3 cup all-purpose flour
4 eggs
1 1/2 teaspoons vanilla extract
1/3 cup granulated sugar
2 tablespoons unsalted butter, chopped into small pieces
2 tablespoons confectioners' sugar (optional)
Warm maple syrup or ice cream (optional)

Position the oven rack one-third from the top of the oven. Preheat the oven to 350 degrees. Butter the bottom and side of a 2 1/2-quart baking dish. Arrange the pears decoratively over the bottom of the prepared baking dish. Blend the lemon juice, milk, cream, 2/3 cup granulated sugar, the flour, eggs and vanilla in a blender or food process fitted with a steel blade. Pour over the pears. Sprinkle with 1/3 cup granulated sugar and dot with the butter. Bake for 50 minutes or until the top is golden brown and the pudding is set. Sift the confectioners' sugar over the top. Serve warm with warm maple syrup or ice cream.

Serves 8 to 10

Would you like your child to learn about a particular opera, such as *Carmen*, *The Magic Flute*, or *Aida*? Our group has created Opera Funtime workbooks for twenty-three different operas. Through the use of poetry, songs, games, and artwork these books teach about the opera. Contact the Young Patronesses of the Opera at ypo-miami.org.

Wine with Dessert

Dessert wines can provide an incomparable finish to a sumptuous meal. Dessert wines are made from grapes that have reached their maximum sweetness through maturation, freezing, or other methods which concentrate the sugars. Since dessert wines vary in intensity, weight, and sweetness, it is important to understand which dessert wines complement which foods. A basic rule in pairing wines with desserts is that the wine should always be sweeter than the dessert. If not, the dessert will make the wine taste acidic.

Port, which is fortified wine primarily from Portugal, perfectly complements Stilton cheese and other salty cheeses, nuts, and chocolate and coffee desserts. Sauternes wines, which are produced mostly in Bordeaux but also in California, are extremely sweet and taste best with fruit desserts such as those made with peaches, apricots, pears, or red apples.

Roasted Pears with Pomegranate Glaze

A fantastic dessert when you want to make an impression! Bosc pears are the best because they hold their shape when cooked.

3/4 cup red wine
3/4 cup pomegranate juice
1/2 cup sugar
1 cinnamon stick
2 teaspoons grated orange zest
6 Bosc pears

Preheat the oven to 350 degrees. Heat the wine, pomegranate juice, sugar, cinnamon stick and orange zest in a medium saucepan over medium heat for 3 minutes or until the sugar dissolves.

Trim the bottoms of the pears flat so they will stand upright. Core the pears with a sharp knife, leaving a 1 1/2-inch cavity. Stand the pears upright in an 8×8-inch baking dish. Pour the sauce over the pears. Roast for 1 hour or until tender when pierced with a knife, basting every 20 minutes with the sauce. Remove the pears to a serving platter or individual serving plates. Simmer the pan juices for a few minutes to thicken to a glaze consistency, stirring frequently. Spoon over the pears. Serve a little above room temperature with rum and raisin ice cream and chocolates.

Serves 6

Pineapple Orange Sorbet with Crystallized Citrus Julienne

Crystallizing fruit rind is easy, but it is important to change the water as described to remove bitterness. The sorbet requires hours to freeze, and the crystallized orange requires hours to cook, so prepare this dish a day ahead. If you wish, substitute your favorite juice and omit the crushed pineapple for the sorbet.

1/2 cup water	2 cups commercial pineapple
1/4 cup sugar	orange juice, or 1 cup fresh
1 (14-ounce) can crushed	orange juice and 1 cup
pineapple, well drained	pineapple juice
	4 navel oranges
	1 1/2 cups sugar

Bring 1/2 cup water and 1/4 cup sugar to a boil in a saucepan. Boil until the sugar is dissolved, stirring constantly. Pulse the pineapple in a food processor for 10 seconds and drain agan. Combine the pineapple, pineapple orange juice and sugar water in a pitcher and mix well. Pour into ice cube trays or into a 9×9-inch pan. Freeze for 1 to 3 hours or until almost frozen. Pulse in a food processor until smooth. Return to the ice cube trays or pan and freeze for 1 hour. Repeat the pulsing process. Place the sorbet in a freezer container and store in the freezer.

Remove strips of the orange zest with a vegetable peeler, being careful to remove only the zest and not the white pith. Cut the zest into long thin shreds and place in a saucepan. Add enough water to cover the zest by 1 inch. Bring to a boil over high heat. Remove the pan from the heat and strain. Return the zest to the saucepan and repeat the boiling and straining process three more times. Return the zest to the saucepan. Add 1 1/2 cups sugar and enough water to cover the zest by 1 inch. Simmer over very low heat for 2 hours. Remove the pan from the heat. Cool and store the zest in the syrup in the refrigerator. When ready to use, drain for several hours on a wire rack over waxed paper. Serve plain or rolled in sifted granulated sugar.

To serve, spoon the sorbet into dessert bowls and top with the crystallized citrus julienne.

Serves 4

Photograph on page 225.

Photograph on page 225.

Wine with Dessert
(continued)

It has long been thought that foie gras should only be paired with Sauternes at the start of a meal.

Sweet Riesling and Gewürztraminer are produced from grapes that were harvested later during the harvesting season. These late-harvest wines are best paired with custard desserts, desserts made with citrus, or fresh fruit. Gewürztraminer goes particularly well with tropical fruits such as papaya and mango.

Raspberry Rosinas with Passion Fruit Coulis

A lovely and scrumptious dessert for that very special party.

1/2 cup (1 stick) butter
1/2 cup packed brown sugar
1/3 cup dark corn syrup
2 teaspoons grated ginger
1 1/2 teaspoons grated lemon zest
1 teaspoon brandy
3 drops of vanilla extract
1 cup all-purpose flour

3/4 cup frozen passion fruit
   purée, thawed
1/2 cup granulated sugar, sifted
1/2 teaspoon vanilla extract
2 cups heavy whipping cream
2 cups fresh raspberries
Confectioners' sugar
24 fresh mint leaves

Melt the butter with the brown sugar and corn syrup in a small saucepan over low heat, stirring constantly. Stir in the ginger, lemon zest, brandy and 3 drops of vanilla. Remove from the heat to cool slightly. Stir in the flour. Let stand for 40 minutes to cool completely.

Preheat the oven to 350 degrees. Line a baking sheet with baking parchment. Scoop the cooled mixture by teaspoonfuls and shape into round balls. Place three balls widely spaced in a circle on the prepared baking sheet to form each cookie. Bake for 8 to 9 minutes or until golden brown. Remove from the oven and cool for 1 to 2 minutes. Press the cookies with a large round cookie cutter to form perfect circles. Remove from the baking parchment and cool on a wire rack. (The cookies can be made ahead and stored in a sealed container.)

Cook the passion fruit purée and granulated sugar in a small saucepan over medium heat until the granulated sugar dissolves, stirring constantly. Reduce the heat to low and simmer for 6 to 8 minutes or until the coulus is reduced to about 1/2 cup, stirring constantly. Remove from the heat and let stand to cool slightly. Stir in 1/2 teaspoon vanilla. Pour into a squeeze bottle with a fine tip. (The coulis can be made up to 2 days ahead and stored in the refrigerator until needed. Remove from the refrigerator 30 minutes before serving.)

To assemble, whip the cream in a chilled mixing bowl until soft peaks form. Place in a piping bag fitted with a fine tip. For each rosina, squeeze the coulis in zigzag lines on an individual dessert plate. Place the first cookie in the center. Pipe the whipped cream into florets on the cookie, alternating with the fresh raspberries. Place a second cookie on top of the first and repeat piping the whipped cream alternating with the raspberries. Place a third cookie on top of the second and lightly dust with confectioners' sugar. Arrange three raspberries and four mint leaves on the top. Add dollops or lines of additional coulis if desired. Repeat the process five times to form the remaining rosinas.

Serves 6

Photograph at right

Best-Ever Carrot Cake

The creator of this recipe has been told by many people that her carrot cake is the best they have ever eaten. The carrots are finely chopped in a food processor, not grated, which saves preparation time.

CAKE

1 large package baby carrots
2 cups all-purpose flour
2 teaspoons baking soda
2 teaspoons cinnamon
1 teaspoon salt
4 eggs
1 1/2 cups corn oil
2 cups sugar

CREAM CHEESE AND PECAN ICING

3/4 cup (1 1/2 sticks) butter, softened
12 ounces cream cheese, softened
1 1/4 to 1 1/2 (1-pound) packages
  confectioners' sugar
1 1/2 teaspoons vanilla extract
1 1/2 cups chopped pecans or pecan
  pieces
16 pecan halves for garnish

To prepare the cake, position the oven rack in the middle of the oven. Preheat the oven to 350 degrees. Line the bottom of three 9-inch cake pans with waxed paper or baking parchment. Grease the top of the linings and side of the pans with shortening and then coat with flour. Pulse enough of the carrots (three-fourths of the carrots or about thirty-five carrots) in a food processor to measure 3 cups finely chopped but not puréed carrots, discarding any large chunks. Reserve the remaining carrots for another use.

Mix the flour, baking soda, cinnamon and salt together in a small bowl. Beat the eggs lightly in a large mixing bowl. Add the corn oil and beat at low speed until blended. Add the sugar and mix well. Add the flour mixture gradually, beating constantly at medium speed for 1 minute. Add the finely chopped carrots and beat at medium speed for 2 minutes. Pour evenly in the prepared pans. Bake on the middle oven rack with the sides not touching for 20 to 25 minutes or until wooden picks inserted in the centers come out clean. Cool in the pans for 15 minutes. Invert onto wire racks and carefully remove the waxed paper. Let stand until completely cool.

To prepare the icing, cream the butter and cream cheese in a mixing bowl until light and fluffy. Sift 1 1/4 cups confectioners' sugar into the creamed mixture and add the vanilla. Beat at low speed until blended. Add the remaining confectioners' sugar if needed for the desired sweetness and consistency. (The icing should not taste too buttery nor extremely sweet.) Continue to beat at medium speed for 2 minutes. Stir in the chopped pecans.

To assemble, spread the icing between the layers and over the top and side of the cake. Decorate the top with the pecan halves.

Serves 16 to 18

Clockwise: Pineapple Orange Sorbet with Crystallized Citrus Julienne, Champagne Flirtini, Tres Leches Cake, and Best-Ever Carrot Cake

Shortening Shortcut

Since shortening does not dissolve easily in water, an easy and clean way to measure shortening is by displacing water. To measure a cup of shortening, fill a large clear liquid measuring cup with water to the point that one additional cup would fill the cup to its top measurement. If you have a four-cup measuring cup, fill it to the three-cup mark with water. Hold the cup at eye level to make sure you have measured accurately. Now add shortening in spoonfuls to the cup and watch the water level rise. When the water reaches the top measurement, you have the one cup of shortening needed. Using the spoon, gently remove the shortening from the water, shaking it slightly to remove water drops. Add the shortening to your recipe.

Pineapple Coconut Carrot Cake

The pineapple and coconut give this cake a tropical taste.

CAKE
> 2 cups all-purpose flour
> 2 teaspoons baking powder
> 1 1/2 teaspoons baking soda
> 1 teaspoon salt
> 2 teaspoons cinnamon
> 4 eggs
> 2 cups sugar
> 1 1/2 cups vegetable oil
> 2 cups carrots, grated
> 1 (6- or 7-ounce) can crushed pineapple, well drained

COCONUT CREAM CHEESE FROSTING
> 12 ounces cream cheese, softened
> 3/4 cup (1 1/2 sticks) butter, softened
> 2 teaspoons vanilla extract
> 1 to 1 1/2 (1-pound) packages confectioners' sugar, sifted
> 1/2 cup shredded coconut
> 1 cup walnuts, chopped

To prepare the cake, preheat the oven to 325 degrees. Line the bottom of three 9-inch cake pans with waxed paper or baking parchment. Grease the top of the linings and the side of the pans with shortening and then coat with flour. Sift 2 cups flour, baking powder, baking soda, salt and cinnamon together into a medium bowl. Beat the eggs lightly in a large mixing bowl. Stir in the sugar and oil. Add the flour mixture and beat for 2 minutes. Stir in the carrots and pineapple. Spoon evenly in the prepared pans. Bake for 55 to 60 minutes or until the layers test done. Cool in the pans on wire racks for 15 minutes. Loosen the layers from the side of the pans and invert onto wire racks. Carefully remove the waxed paper. Let stand until completely cool.

To prepare the frosting, beat the cream cheese, butter and vanilla in a mixing bowl until smooth and creamy. Add enough of the confectioners' sugar gradually to make nearly of the desired sweetness and consistency. Stir in the coconut. Add the remaining confectioners' sugar if needed for the desired sweetness and consistency. Stir in the walnuts.

To assemble, spread the frosting between the layers and over the top and side of the cake.

Serves 12

Orange and Almond Flourless Chocolate Cake

The orange and chocolate with a touch of amaretto makes this small bittersweet cake a favorite.

CAKE
1/2 cup (1 stick) unsalted butter, softened
1 cup ground slivered skinless almonds
1/4 cup dried plain bread crumbs
2/3 cup sugar
3 eggs
Grated zest of 1 large orange
3/4 cup semisweet chocolate chips
1 teaspoon almond extract

AMARETTO CHOCOLATE GLAZE
2 ounces unsweetened chocolate, finely chopped
1/4 cup semisweet chocolate chips
1/4 cup (1/2 stick) unsalted butter
1/4 cup honey, or to taste
1 tablespoon amaretto

To prepare the cake, preheat the oven to 350 degrees. Line the bottom of an 8-inch cake pan with waxed paper or baking parchment. Grease the top of the lining and the side of the pan. Cream the butter in a mixing bowl until light and fluffy. Stir in the almonds, bread crumbs and sugar. Add the eggs one at a time, beating well after each addition. Stir in the orange zest, chocolate chips and almond extract. Pour into the prepared pan. Bake for 30 to 35 minutes or until a wooden pick inserted in the center comes out clean. Let cool for 10 minutes.

To prepare the glaze, melt the unsweetened chocolate, chocolate chips and butter in a saucepan, stirring constantly. Stir in 2 tablespoons of the honey and the amaretto. Add the remaining honey if needed for the desired sweetness.

To assemble, loosen the edge of the cake from the side of the pan with a knife. Invert the cake onto a cake plate and immediately cover with the warm glaze. Serve immediately or chill, covered, until ready to serve. Remove from the refrigerator 30 to 60 minutes before serving.

Serves 8

Chocolate Coffee Refresher

This delicious dessert drink serves four and is perfect for hot days. To prepare, process 1 1/2 cups cold brewed coffee, 1 1/2 cups chocolate ice cream and 1/4 cup chocolate syrup in a blender until smooth. Whip 1 cup heavy whipping cream in a chilled bowl until soft peaks form. Pour the chocolate mixture over crushed ice in serving cups and garnish with a dollop of the whipped cream.

Making Chocolate Curls and Other Shapes

Short curls are a quick and easy topping for desserts. If the chocolate is at room temperature, hold the chocolate in your hand to slightly warm it. If the chocolate remains too hard to shave easily, set the oven to the lowest setting and warm briefly. Hold the block of chocolate at an angle and shave away curls of chocolate using a sharp vegetable peeler. Work over a plate or a piece of waxed paper. To transfer, use a fork or the broad side of a round-edge knife.

When preparing larger chocolate shapes, spread melted chocolate on baking parchment laid on a baking tray or flat board. Use a large metal spatula to spread the chocolate so that the chocolate is only 1/16 inch thick. You can then stamp out circles or other shapes with a cookie cutter or knife. Before you cut each shape, dip the cookie cutter or knife into hot water and dry it before the next cut.

Warm Chocolate Lava Cakes

Be careful not to bake these too long, or you'll lose the rich, oozing chocolate lava.

1/2 cup (1 stick) butter
4 ounces Vahlrona bittersweet chocolate
2 eggs, at room temperature
2 egg yolks, at room temperature
1/4 to 1/2 cup sifted granulated sugar
2 teaspoons all-purpose flour
Confectioners' sugar for garnish

Preheat the oven to 450 degrees. Butter and flour four 4-ounce molds or ramekins twice. Tap out any excess flour. Melt 1/2 cup butter and chocolate in a double boiler over low heat, being careful that the steam does not touch the chocolate and butter. Whisk or lightly beat the eggs, egg yolks and 1/4 cup granulated sugar in a mixing bowl until combined. Stir in 2 teaspoons flour. Beat the melted chocolate mixture and stir into the egg mixture until combined. Add the remaining granulated sugar 1 teaspoon at a time until the desired sweetness is reached. (This dessert should be bittersweet.) Pour equally into the prepared molds. (The molds may be chilled for several hours before baking at this point. Bring to room temperature before baking.) Place the molds on a baking sheet and bake for 6 to 7 minutes or until the center is quite soft and the sides are set. Cool for 15 seconds and then unmold onto individual dessert plates. Garnish with confectioners' sugar.

Serves 4

Chocolate Chip Pound Cake with Chocolate Drip Icing

Decorate the top of this heavenly cake with chocolate curls.

CAKE
2 cups cake flour
1 tablespoon baking powder
1 teaspoon salt
1 1/2 cups shortening
2 cups sugar
1 teaspoon almond extract
1/2 teaspoon vanilla extract
6 eggs
3/4 cup milk
1/2 cup sour cream
2 cups (12 ounces) miniature semisweet chocolate chips

CHOCOLATE DRIP ICING
4 ounces unsweetened chocolate
1/4 cup (1/2 stick) butter
3/4 cup confectioners' sugar, sifted
Semisweet chocolate curls for garnish

To prepare the cake, preheat the oven to 325 degrees. Mix the cake flour, baking powder and salt together in a large bowl. Cream the shortening, sugar, almond extract and vanilla in a large mixing bowl until light and fluffy. Add the eggs one at a time, stirring well after each addition. Add the flour mixture and milk alternately, stirring well after each addition and beginning and ending with the flour mixture. Stir in the sour cream. Pour one-half of the batter into a greased and floured large bundt pan and sprinkle with one-half of the chocolate chips. Continue layering with one-half of the remaining batter and almost all of the remaining chocolate chips. Pour the remaining batter over the layers and sprinkle with the remaining chocolate chips. Bake for 1 hour and 5 minutes or until a wooden pick inserted near the center comes out clean. Cool in the pan for 15 minutes. Invert onto a wire rack to cool completely. (The cake may be served unfrosted.)

To prepare the icing, chop the chocolate into large chunks and place in a saucepan. Add the butter and heat until melted, stirring constantly. Sift in enough of the confectioners' sugar to thicken to a thick but pourable consistency.

To assemble, carefully place the cake on a cake platter. Pour the icing carefully over the cake, allowing it to drip down the side. Pour any remaining icing into the hollow center. Garnish with chocolate curls.

Serves 12

Photograph on page 117.

Making Chocolate Curls and Other Shapes (continued)

To make chocolate cups use paper cases, such as petit four cases, muffin cases, or truffle cases at double thickness. Paint a thin, even coating of melted chocolate inside the paper case, taking care to leave a tiny space around the rim of each case. When the first layer of chocolate is just firm, paint on a second layer. Test after the second layer, and if necessary add a third layer.

Tres Leches Cake

Tres Leches is an extremely sweet and rich dessert found in many Latin American restaurants in Miami. Tres Leches, or three milks, is a sponge cake that does not have butter or oil in the cake itself. This cake looks especially beautiful when it is decorated with fruit or edible flowers. This recipe for Tres Leches allows you to bake it three ways: in a rectangular pan and the cake is not removed and all of the cream is used to fill the cake and the sides of the cake; in a rectangular pan and after baking, the cake is inverted onto a serving platter, pricked, and some of the cream is used to fill the top and sides of the cake; and as a two-layer cake.

CAKE
- 6 egg whites
- 2 cups sugar
- 6 egg yolks, lightly beaten
- 2 cups self-rising flour
- 1 cup milk
- 2 teaspoons vanilla extract

TRES LECHES CREAM
- 2 (12-ounce) cans evaporated milk
- 2 (14-ounce) cans sweetened condensed milk
- 3 cups heavy cream
- 4 pasteurized egg yolks
- 1 tablespoon dark rum (optional)

MERINGUE
- 4 pasteurized egg whites
- 1/2 cup sugar
- 1 1/2 cups corn syrup

To prepare the cake, preheat the oven to 350 degrees. Spray a 9×13-inch cake pan or two 8×8-inch cake pans with butter spray. Beat the egg whites in a mixing bowl until soft peaks form. Add the sugar gradually, beating constantly until almost stiff peaks form. Fold in the egg yolks. Add the flour and milk alternately, beating constantly and beginning and ending with the flour. Stir in the vanilla. Spoon into the prepared pan and bake for 30 minutes or until a wooden pick comes out clean. Remove from the oven and cool in the cake pan for 10 minutes.

To prepare the cream, combine the evaporated milk, condensed milk, cream, egg yolks and rum in a mixing bowl. Beat at low speed until well blended and small bubbles appear on the surface.

To prepare the meringue, beat the egg whites at high speed in a mixing bowl until foamy. Add the sugar gradually, beating constantly. Stir in the corn syrup and beat until soft peaks form.

To assemble a 9×13-inch cake, run a knife around the edges to loosen the cake from the sides of the pan. Prick the surface of the cake with a fork. Pour the cream over the top gradually, allowing the cream to absorb into the cake for a few minutes after each addition. Continue to pour until the cream is overflowing. Chill until cool. Spread the meringue over the top of the cake with a spatula. Chill until ready to serve. (The 9×13-inch cake may be inverted onto a large cake platter, pricked with a fork and the cream poured over the top and sides gradually until absorbed. Spread the meringue over the top and sides of the cake and chill until ready to serve.)

To assemble a two-layer cake, invert one of the layers onto a cake plate and keep the remaining layer in the cake pan. Prick the bottom layer with a fork and pour one-half of the cream over the layer. Let stand for 10 minutes to absorb the cream. Place the remaining cake layer over the bottom layer. Prick the top layer with a fork and pour the remaining cream over the top until absorbed. Chill until cool. Spread the meringue over the top and sides of the cake. Chill until ready to serve.

Note: Double the meringue recipe if you are making a two-layer cake. For a lighter meringue, beat 3/4 cup heavy cream and 1 tablespoon sugar in a mixing bowl until soft peaks form. Spread a thin layer over the cake.

Serves 12

Gold Bars

Preheat the oven to 325 degrees. Combine one 2-layer package plain yellow cake mix, 2 eggs and $1/2$ cup (1 stick) margarine, melted in a bowl and mix well. Press in an ungreased 9×13-inch glass baking dish. Beat 8 ounces cream cheese, softened, 2 eggs, 1 tablespoon vanilla extract and 1 pound confectioners' sugar in a mixing bowl until smooth. Spread in the prepared dish. Bake for 50 minutes. Remove from the oven to cool. Chill, covered, for 6 hours or longer. Cut into bars. This recipe makes 2 dozen.

Brigadeiros

Miami has many relocated Brazilians who have brought the recipe for this delicious candy treat to our city. Brigadeiros are found at all Brazilian birthday parties and are a favorite of children and adults in both Brazil and America. Brigadeiros are named after Brigadeiro Eduardo Gomes, a very famous Air Force commander of the 1940s.

1 (14-ounce) can sweetened condensed milk
2 tablespoons baking cocoa
1 tablespoon butter
Sugar, sprinkles or another decorative coating

Combine the condensed milk, baking cocoa and butter in a medium saucepan. Cook for 20 minutes over low heat to 234 to 240 degrees on a candy thermometer, soft-ball stage, stirring frequently and gently. Pour onto a buttered platter and let cool to room temperature. Shape into small 1-inch balls and roll in sugar, sprinkles or another decorative coating.

Makes 1 dozen

Walnut Puffs

$21/2$ cups sugar
$1/2$ cup water
$1/2$ cup light corn syrup
2 egg whites
1 teaspoon vanilla extract
$1/2$ cup walnut pieces

Mix the sugar, water and corn syrup in a medium saucepan. Cover and bring to a boil over low heat. Uncover and cook until the mixture reaches 235 degrees on a candy thermometer, soft-ball stage. Remove immediately from the heat.

Beat the egg whites in a mixing bowl until soft glossy peaks form. Beat in one-half of the syrup mixture gradually. Return the remaining syrup mixture to the heat and cook to 250 degrees on a candy thermometer, hard-ball stage. Gradually add to the egg white mixture, beating constantly. Add the vanilla and beat until the mixture begins to lose its shine. Stir in the walnut pieces. Drop by teaspoonfuls onto waxed paper. Let stand until cool.

Makes about 2 pounds

Double Chocolate Fudgy Brownies

6 ounces unsweetened
   chocolate
1 cup (2 sticks)
   unsalted butter
6 eggs
2 1/2 cups sugar
2 teaspoons vanilla extract

1 3/4 cups all-purpose flour
1/2 teaspoon salt
1 cup (6 ounces)
   chocolate chips
1 cup chopped pecans or
   walnuts (optional)

Preheat the oven to 325 degrees. Melt the chocolate and butter in a double boiler over very low heat. Remove from the heat to cool. Beat the eggs and sugar in a mixing bowl until thick and fluffy. Stir in the vanilla. Add the flour and salt and mix until just combined. Stir in the chocolate chips and pecans. Pour into a greased and floured 11×14-inch baking pan. Bake for 25 to 30 minutes or until a wooden pick inserted in the center comes out clean. Cool in the pan on a wire rack. Cut into small squares.

Makes 2 dozen

Butterscotch Blonde Brownies with Chocolate Chunks

4 ounces semisweet chocolate
1/2 cup (1 stick) unsalted
   butter, cut into pieces
1 cup packed light
   brown sugar

1 egg, lightly beaten
1 teaspoon vanilla extract
1 cup all-purpose flour
1 teaspoon baking powder
1/2 teaspoon salt

Position the oven rack in the center of the oven and preheat the oven to 350 degrees. Coarsely chop the chocolate into pieces approximately 3/4 to 1 inch long and 1/2 to 3/4 inch wide. Melt the butter in a medium saucepan over medium heat. Add the brown sugar and cook for 1 minute or until bubbly, stirring frequently. Remove from the heat and cool for 10 minutes. Stir with a wooden spoon, scraping the mixture from the bottom of the pan. Cool for 10 minutes longer. Stir again, scraping up any mixture from the bottom of the pan. Stir in the egg and vanilla. Add the flour, baking powder and salt and stir until just combined. Stir in the chocolate. Spread in a lightly buttered and floured 8×8-inch baking pan. Bake for 25 to 30 minutes or until a wooden pick inserted in the center comes out clean. Cool before serving.

Makes 16

Photograph on page 181.

Melting Chocolate

Chocolate is easy to burn when it is heated. To melt chocolate easily, chop, or grate it first.

Use very low heat to melt chocolate in a heavy saucepan over direct heat. Stir constantly until melted. Direct heat works best when the chocolate is being melted with butter or liquid.

Low heat must also be used when melting chocolate in the top of a double boiler. Stir constantly and be sure not to let steam or water into the chocolate, which will cause the chocolate to stiffen.

To use a microwave, place the chocolate in a microwave-safe bowl. Microwave for 30 seconds and stir. Continue to microwave at 30-second intervals and stir until the chocolate is melted.

To melt chocolate in an oven, preheat the oven to 300 degrees. Place the chocolate in a baking dish. Place in the oven and turn off the oven. After 3 minutes, open the oven and stir the chocolate. Continue to warm and stir until melted.

Irresistible Cookies

1/4 cup water
1 1/2 cups Quaker 100 percent natural
  oats, honey and raisin granola mix
1 1/2 cups walnuts, coarsely chopped
1 1/2 cups golden raisins
1 cup rolled oats
1 cup (6 ounces) semisweet
  chocolate chips

2 cups all-purpose flour
1 teaspoon baking soda
1 teaspoon baking powder
1 cup granulated sugar
1 cup packed brown sugar
1 cup (2 sticks) unsalted butter, softened
2 eggs
1 teaspoon vanilla extract

Preheat the oven to 375 degrees. Heat the water in a microwave-safe bowl on High for 30 seconds. Add to the granola mix in a bowl and stir until slightly soft. Let stand to cool slightly. Mix the granola, walnuts, raisins, oats and chocolate chips in a large bowl. Sift the flour, baking soda and baking powder together. Beat the granulated sugar, brown sugar and butter in a mixing bowl until smooth and creamy. Stir in the eggs and vanilla. Add the flour mixture and mix well. Scrape into the chocolate chip mixture and mix by hand until combined. Drop by rounded teaspoonfuls 2 inches apart onto ungreased cookie sheets. (The cookies will expand while baking.) Bake for 6 to 8 minutes or until the tops are light brown, the centers are soft and the edges are set. Remove to wire racks to cool.

Makes 5 dozen

Photograph on page 37.

100 Crunchy Cookies

3 1/2 cups all-purpose flour
1 teaspoon salt
1 teaspoon baking soda
1 teaspoon cream of tartar
1 cup granulated sugar
1 cup packed brown sugar
1 cup (2 sticks) butter, softened

1 cup vegetable oil
1 egg
2 teaspoons vanilla extract
1 cup rolled oats
1 cup Rice Krispies
1 cup shredded sweetened coconut
1 cup chopped pecans or walnuts

Preheat the oven to 350 degrees. Mix the flour, salt, baking soda and cream of tartar together. Beat the granulated sugar, brown sugar and butter in a large mixing bowl until creamy. Stir in the oil. Add the egg and mix well. Add the flour mixture and mix until blended. Stir in the vanilla. Add the oats, cereal, coconut and pecans and mix well. Shape into walnut-size balls and place on ungreased cookie sheets. Flatten the balls with the tines of a fork and bake for 10 minutes. Remove from the oven and cool slightly on the cookie sheets. Remove to wire racks to cool completely.

Makes 100

Date-Filled Cookies

A family favorite perfect for giving to friends for the holidays.

1 cup (2 sticks) salted butter, softened
1 scant cup granulated sugar
1 egg
5 1/2 cups sifted all-purpose flour
2 tablespoons Grand Marnier
1 to 2 tablespoons cream or evaporated milk
2 pounds pitted dates
1/4 cup (1/2 stick) butter, softened
1 1/2 cups finely chopped walnuts
Confectioners' sugar for dusting

Cream 1 cup butter and the granulated sugar in a mixing bowl until fluffy. Add the egg and mix well. Add the flour gradually, beating well after each addition. Stir in the Grand Marnier and enough of the cream to moisten the dough. Chill for 30 minutes if the dough feels too soft.

Cut the dates into slices 1/4 inch wide. (The slices should look like small round circles.) Mix 1/4 cup butter and the dates in a bowl with greased hands. Push small pieces of the walnuts into the centers of the dates. Roll two or three pieces of the stuffed dates together so that the combined date pieces begin to form a tube shape. Place on waxed paper. Repeat with the remaining dates.

Position the oven racks so that one rack is at the bottom and one is at the top. Preheat the oven to 350 degrees. Remove one-half of the dough from the refrigerator. Shape into walnut-size balls and flatten each with the bottom of a glass into a pancake shape. Place a date-filling tube in the center of the dough and seal the edges with your fingers. Continue with the remaining dough and date-filling tubes.

Press the top of each cookie with a fork to decorate the top and place on ungreased cookie sheets. Place on the bottom oven rack and bake for 10 minutes. Remove to the top oven rack and bake for 10 minutes longer or until slightly brown on the bottom and white on the top. Cool on wire racks and dust with confectioners' sugar.

Note: To freeze, cool the cookies completely and freeze in an airtight container with waxed paper between each layer. The cookies can be reheated for a few seconds in the microwave or oven and then dusted with confectioners' sugar.

Makes 4 dozen

Photograph on page 245.

Bar Cookie Tips

When making bar cookies, pay close attention to the size of the pan called for in the recipe. Variations may affect the baking times and texture of the cookies.

Unless specifically called for, never use diet or whipped margarine or butter. The lighter density of these products will make the bar cookies watery and mushy.

With the exception of bar cookies made with a delicate shortbread crust, such as lemon squares, you can line the baking pan with heavy-duty foil to ensure easier removal later. Extend the foil several inches over the top edges of the pan to serve as handles for removal of the cookies.

Date Nut Bars

1/2 cup all-purpose flour
1/2 teaspoon baking powder
1/2 teaspoon salt
1 cup packed brown sugar
2 eggs, well beaten
1 teaspoon vanilla extract
1 cup pitted dates, chopped
1 cup pecans, chopped
1/4 cup (1/2 stick) butter
Confectioners' sugar for dusting

Preheat the oven to 325 degrees. Mix the flour, baking powder and salt together in a small bowl. Combine the brown sugar, eggs and vanilla in a large bowl and mix well. Add the flour mixture and mix well. Fold in the dates and pecans. Melt the butter in an 8x8-inch baking pan in the oven. Pour the batter into the melted butter and bake for 30 minutes. Remove from the oven to cool. Cut into bars with a knife dusted with confectioners' sugar and place on a serving platter. Dust the bars with confectioners' sugar.

Makes 16

Luscious Lemon Bars

These delicious bars get their tanginess from the lemon juice and zest. To make zesting much easier, invest in a microplane zester. Microplane zesters and graters are razor sharp and make short work of all grating. Microplane products are available on-line.

2 cups all-purpose flour
1/8 teaspoon kosher salt
1 cup (2 sticks) unsalted butter, softened
1/2 cup granulated sugar
6 extra-large eggs, at room temperature
3 cups granulated sugar
2 tablespoons lemon zest (zest from 4 to 6 lemons)
1 cup fresh lemon juice
1 cup all-purpose flour
Confectioners' sugar for dusting

Preheat the oven to 350 degrees. Mix 2 cups flour and the kosher salt together in a bowl. Cream the butter and 1/2 cup granulated sugar in a mixing bowl until light and fluffy. Add the flour mixture and mix with a pastry blender or two round-bladed knives until small crumbs form. Press in a lightly greased 9×13-inch baking pan, being careful to not allow any cracks in the dough. Bake for 15 to 20 minutes or until the crust is light golden brown. Remove to a wire rack to cool. Maintain the oven temperature.

Whisk the eggs, 3 cups granulated sugar, the lemon zest, lemon juice and 1 cup flour in a bowl. Pour evenly over the crust. Bake for 30 to 35 minutes or until the filling is set but not brown. Remove from the oven and cool to room temperature. Cut into bars and dust with confectioners' sugar. Chill until ready to serve.

Note: An alternative method is to cream the butter and sugar with the paddle attachment of an electric mixer in a mixing bowl. Add the flour mixture and mix well. Shape the dough into a ball and flatten the dough with floured hands. Press into the prepared pan.

Makes 32

Photograph on page 181.

Bar Cookie Tips *(continued)*

Bar cookies should be cooled completely before they are cut or they will be too soft to remove easily from the baking pan. It is best not to cut bar cookies until right before serving. To store bar cookies before serving, allow the cookies to cool completely and then wrap the baking pan in plastic wrap. If the baking pan is wrapped before the cookies are allowed to cool, condensation will form on the plastic wrap and drip onto the cookies.

To cut bars that are uniform and pretty, use a sharp knife to trim away the outer edges that touch the sides of the pan. Wipe your knife clean after each cut.

Versatile Key Lime Pie

This Key lime filling works well in the graham cracker crust as a pie or in the tartlet crusts used for the Lemon Tartlets (see page 243).

GRAHAM CRACKER CRUST
>   1 cup graham cracker crumbs
>   1/3 cup finely chopped pecans
>   1/4 cup (1/2 stick) butter, melted

PIE
>   2 whites
>   2 egg yolks
>   1 (14-ounce) can sweetened condensed milk
>   1/2 cup Key lime juice (juice from about 5 limes)
>   1 cup heavy whipping cream
>   1 to 3 tablespoons sugar
>   3 or 4 Key lime slices for garnish

To prepare the crust, preheat the oven to 350 degrees. Combine the graham cracker crumbs, pecans and butter in a bowl and mix well. Pat over the bottom and up the side of a pie plate and bake for 8 minutes. Cool for 10 minutes. Maintain the oven temperature.

To prepare the pie, beat the egg whites at high speed in a mixing bowl until stiff but not dry peaks form. Beat the egg yolks in a large mixing bowl and add the condensed milk. Add the lime juice gradually, beating constantly. Fold in the egg whites. Pour into the crust and bake for 8 minutes. Cool and then chill in the refrigerator. Beat the whipping cream at high speed in a mixing bowl until the cream begins to thicken. Add the sugar gradually to your preferred sweetness, beating constantly until soft peaks form. Spread over the top of the pie and garnish with the lime slices.

Serves 8

Passion Fruit

Passion fruit—the very name evokes romance! This tart, sweet, and fragrant fruit has been cultivated in South America for centuries and has successfully been grown commercially in South Florida since the 1980s. To purchase fresh purple passion fruit, choose fruit with a tough, leathery, wrinkled purple shell, which must be peeled away to enjoy the mushy, yellow pulp. The larger yellow passion fruit has a smooth, glossy shell when ripe. The pulp itself has hundreds of tiny, crunchy black seeds that many people enjoy. To remove the seeds, you must strain the pulp through two layers of cheesecloth. Passion fruit pulp is delicious with yogurt or cream and a little sugar. The pulp freezes beautifully.

Passion Fruit Pie

The addition of a chocolate layer makes this colorful pie doubly delicious.

BUTTER CRUST
  1 1/2 cups all-purpose flour
  2 tablespoons sugar
  1/2 teaspoon salt
  1/2 cup (1 stick) butter,
    cut into small pieces
  1 egg yolk
  1 to 2 tablespoons cold water

PIE
  1 envelope unflavored gelatin
  1/4 cup cold water

4 eggs, lightly beaten
1 cup sugar
3/4 cup passion fruit pulp
  or thawed frozen purée
1/4 cup Key lime juice
1/2 cup (1 stick) unsalted
  butter, cut into 8 pieces
4 ounces bittersweet or
  semisweet chocolate
Whipped cream
Chocolate curls for garnish

To prepare the crust, pulse the flour, sugar, salt and butter in a food processor until coarsely mixed. Add the egg yolk and water and process until the mixture forms a ball. Wrap in plastic wrap and chill for 30 minutes. Preheat the oven to 375 degrees. Roll the pastry into a circle. Fit into a 9- or 10-inch pie plate, trimming and fluting the edge. Prick the bottom of the pastry with a fork. Place foil over the dough and weight with dried beans or pastry weights. Bake for 10 minutes. Remove the weights and foil and bake for 10 minutes longer or until light golden brown. Let stand to cool.

To prepare the pie, sprinkle the gelatin over the water. Combine the eggs, sugar, passion fruit pulp and Key lime juice in a double boiler and mix well. Cook over hot water until thickened, stirring constantly. Remove from the heat. Add the butter one piece at a time, stirring constantly. Stir in the gelatin mixture. Place plastic wrap directly on the surface and cool to room temperature.

Break the chocolate into small pieces and place in a microwave-safe bowl. Microwave at half power for 2 minutes or until the chocolate melts. Pour into the crust, spreading to cover the bottom. Chill for 10 minutes to set the chocolate. Pour the passion fruit mixture over the chocolate layer. Chill for 2 hours or until firm. Top with whipped cream and garnish with chocolate curls.

Note: The passion fruit pulp is available in Hispanic or gourmet markets or on-line. Chocolate lovers differ significantly in their preference for semisweet or bittersweet chocolate. This recipe can handle either type.

Serves 8 to 10

Photograph on page 37.

Pumpkin Chiffon Pie

A lighter tasting alternative to the traditional pie.

Gingersnap Crust
1 1/4 cups gingersnap crumbs
3 tablespoons sugar
1/3 cup butter, melted
1/2 cup walnuts, finely chopped

Pie
2 envelopes unflavored gelatin
1/4 cup cold water
3 egg yolks
3/4 cup packed brown sugar
1 1/2 cups mashed pumpkin, or 1 (15-ounce) can pumpkin purée
1 1/2 cups milk
1/2 teaspoon salt
1/2 teaspoon nutmeg
1/2 teaspoon cinnamon
1/2 teaspoon ginger
3 egg whites
1/2 cup granulated sugar
1 1/2 cups heavy whipping cream
1 tablespoon confectioners' sugar
1/2 teaspoon vanilla extract
2 tablespoons gingersnap crumbs

To prepare the crust, preheat the oven to 350 degrees. Combine the gingersnap crumbs, sugar, butter and walnuts in a bowl and mix well. Press in the bottom and up the side of a 9-inch pie plate. Bake for 8 minutes. Remove to a wire rack to cool.

To prepare the pie, soften the gelatin in the cold water. Beat the egg yolks lightly in a mixing bowl. Add the brown sugar, pumpkin, milk, salt, nutmeg, cinnamon and ginger and mix well. Pour into a double boiler. Cook over low heat until thickened, stirring occasionally. Remove from the heat and stir in the dissolved gelatin. Chill for 30 minutes or until the mixture begins to set. Beat the egg whites and granulated sugar in a mixing bowl until soft peaks form. Fold into the pumpkin mixture. Pour into the cooled crust and chill until ready to serve. (The pie may also be frozen at this point.)

To serve, whip the whipping cream, confectioners' sugar and vanilla in a bowl until soft peaks form. Spread over the top of the pie to cover. Sprinkle with the gingersnap crumbs.

Serves 10

Blueberry and Banana Cream Cheese Pie

Since this scrumptious pie is not made from scratch, it takes about 15 minutes to prepare. Whip 2 cups heavy whipping cream in a bowl until soft peaks form. Beat 1 cup granulated sugar and 8 ounces cream cheese, softened, in a mixing bowl until light and creamy. Fold in the whipped cream. Slice 1 banana and layer the slices in the bottom of a 10-inch graham cracker piecrust. Spoon the whipped cream mixture over the bananas. Spread one 21-ounce can blueberry pie filling over the top. Chill for 3 hours or longer before serving. This recipe serves 8 to 10.

Spanish Cheeses

Spanish cheeses are often featured in tapas parties. Spain produces over one hundred varieties of cheese. Here is a sampling of the most popular in our country:

Manchego is a sheep's milk cheese with a mild, nutty, slightly briny flavor. Manchego is so popular it is sold in four stages and is labeled as such: *tierno* (soft, young); *semi curado* (half mature); *curado* (mature); or *añejo* (well matured).

Cabrales is a blue cheese made from cow's milk. It has a strong smell and a spicy flavor. Serve cabrales with a strong red or sweet dessert wine or use it in dishes as you would other blue cheeses.

Tetilla is easily recognizable by its soft, cone-like shape. Tetilla is a mild, creamy, and lightly salted cow's milk cheese and should be served with lighter wines and milder food.

Idiazabal is a hard cheese made from the milk of the long-haired Lacha sheep in the Basque country. It is sharp, acidic and slightly salty. Traditionally Idiazabal was smoked in the shepherd's night fires, but today it may or may not be smoked.

Creamy Apple Cheese Tart

Creamy and crunchy, it looks as delicious as it tastes!

CRUST
1 cup (2 sticks) butter, softened
2/3 cup sugar
1/2 teaspoon vanilla extract
2 cups all-purpose flour

TART FILLING
16 ounces cream cheese, softened
1/2 cup sugar
2 eggs
1/2 teaspoon vanilla extract
1/3 cup sugar
1/2 teaspoon cinnamon
5 cups straight-sliced Granny Smith apples
Sliced almonds (optional)

To prepare the crust, grease a 12-inch fluted tart pan with a removable bottom. Cream the butter, sugar and vanilla in a large mixing bowl until light and fluffy. Add the flour and mix well. Press in the prepared pan to make a fairly thin layer, spreading to the edge. (Any remaining dough is great for making cookies.)

To prepare the filling, beat the cream cheese and 1/2 cup sugar in a mixing bowl until smooth. Add the eggs and vanilla and mix well. Pour three-fourths of the mixture into the lined tart pan, reserving the remainder for another use. Combine 1/3 cup sugar, the cinnamon and apples in a bowl and toss to coat. Arrange the apples slightly overlapping like a deck of cards over the cream cheese mixture. Sprinkle with the almonds. Place in the oven and turn the heat to 450 degrees. (Do not preheat the oven.) Bake for 10 minutes. Reduce the heat to 400 degrees. Bake for 25 minutes longer. Loosen the tart from the side of the pan and remove the side. Serve warm, hot or at room temperature.

Serves 12 to 14

Lemon Tartlets

These pretty tartlets will delight lemon lovers.

TARTLET CRUST
>   2 cups all-purpose flour
>   2 tablespoons sugar
>   1/4 teaspoon salt
>   3/4 cup (1 1/2 sticks) unsalted butter, cut into small pieces
>   2 egg yolks
>   2 to 4 tablespoons ice water

TARTLET FILLING
>   1 cup sugar
>   5 tablespoons butter, softened
>   3 eggs
>   Juice of 4 lemons
>   3 (1/4-inch) lemon slices

To prepare the crust, mix the flour, sugar and salt in a large bowl. Cut the butter into the flour mixture with a pastry blender or two round-bladed kitchen knives until the mixture resembles coarse cornmeal. Beat the egg yolks in a small bowl. Stir in 2 tablespoons ice water. Add to the flour mixture, stirring quickly with a fork. Add the remaining ice water if needed for the mixture to stick together. Shape the mixture into a ball and chill for 1 hour. Preheat the oven to 375 degrees. Roll the dough into a large circle on a lightly floured surface. Cut into three circles 7 inches in diameter. Fit each circle into a 5-inch tartlet pan, trimming the edge. Prick the bottom with a fork to prevent the dough from rising. Bake for 12 minutes or until golden brown. Cool the crusts on a wire rack. Gently remove the crusts from the pans.

To prepare the filling, beat the sugar and butter in a mixing bowl until light and fluffy using a whisk or an electric mixer. Beat in the eggs one at a time, beating well after each addition. Stir in the lemon juice. Pour into a double boiler. Cook over simmering water over medium-low heat until thickened, stirring constantly. Remove from the heat to cool. Pour into the tartlet crusts and place one lemon slice in the center of each. Chill until ready to serve.

Makes 3 tartlets

Photograph on page 181.

Fresh Mango Tart

So lovely you will hate to cut into it, but once you eat your first bite, you'll want more!

CRUST

2 1/2 cups all-purpose flour
1 1/2 tablespoons sugar
1/2 teaspoon salt
6 tablespoons shortening
6 tablespoons unsalted butter
6 to 7 tablespoons cold water
Melted butter for brushing

TART

6 ounces cream cheese, softened
1/4 cup sifted confectioners' sugar
4 teaspoons orange juice
1 teaspoon grated orange zest
1/2 cup apricot jam
1 tablespoon Kirsch
1 teaspoon cinnamon (optional)
4 mangoes

To prepare the crust, sift the flour, sugar and salt into a medium bowl. Cut the shortening and 6 tablespoons butter into small pieces. Cut into the flour mixture using a pastry blender or two table knives until coarse crumbs form. Add 1 tablespoon water at a time, mixing with a fork. Continue to mix with a fork until the crumbs stick together. Gently press the dough into a ball and chill for 30 minutes.

Brush a 9-inch tart pan with melted butter. Roll two-thirds of the dough on a lightly floured surface into a 12-inch circle, reserving the remaining dough for another purpose. Gently wrap the circle of dough around the rolling pin and lay over the prepared tart pan. Gently lift the edge of the dough with one hand and press onto the bottom and side of the pan. Press the dough to seal any cracks. Roll the rolling pin over the top of the pan, pressing down to cut off the excess dough. Press the dough up the side of the pan to make the tart shell higher than the pan, being careful to not overlap the dough over the metal side. Chill for 30 minutes. Preheat the oven to 375 degrees. Line the shell with foil and add enough pastry weights or dried beans to evenly cover the foil. Bake until light golden brown. Remove from the oven and remove the pie weights and foil. Let stand until cool.

To prepare the tart, beat the cream cheese, confectioners' sugar and orange juice in a mixing bowl until smooth. Stir in the orange zest. Spread in the tart crust. Heat the jam and kirsch in a saucepan until the jam is melted, stirring frequently. Stir in the cinnamon. Strain the mixture. Heat again in the saucepan until melted. Cut the mangoes into slices 1/8 inch thick. Arrange in a spiral shape over the cream cheese mixture and lightly brush with the jam mixture. Chill until ready to serve.

Serves 12

Clockwise: Fresh Mango Tart and Date-Filled Cookies

Sponsors

The Young Patronesses of the Opera, Inc. wishes to thank our generous members and friends who helped sponsor *Sunny Days, Balmy Nights: Entertaining Miami Style.*

The Honorable Mercy Bach
Mrs. Robert Barusch
Mrs. Peter Bermont
Ms. Amy Block
Mrs. Richard Bohn
Mrs. Thomas Briggle
Ms. Danette Brockhouse
Dr. Connie Cabeza
Mrs. Dennis Campbell
Mrs. Lynn Chaffin
Mrs. Philip Corey
Mrs. Alfred Damus
Mrs. Carlos Deupi
Mrs. Theodore Evans
Mrs. Bennett Feldman
Mrs. José Garrigó
Ms. Ann Goodman
Mrs. K. Lawrence Gragg
Mrs. Graham Groves
Mrs. Frederick Hasty III
Ms. Elspeth Hotchkiss
Ms. Diana Ingram
Ms. Susanne Kayyali
Mrs. John Kuczwanski
Mrs. Robert Lane
Mrs. Gustavo López-Muñoz
Mrs. Oscar Mederos
Mrs. Steven Meyers
Mrs. Manny Millor
Mrs. Carl Muench

Ms. Kathleen Murphy
Mrs. Brent Nagel
Mrs. Edward Nicklaus
Mrs. Anthony O'Donnell
Mrs. Martin Pinilla
Mrs. Avelino Pinon
Ms. Diane Pistole
Mrs. Julio Pita
Mrs. Paul Plasky
Mrs. Salvador Ramirez
Mrs. William Reese
Ms. Myriam Ribenboim
Ms. Bonnie Rippingille
Mrs. Susanne Roberts
Mrs. Ricardo Román
Mrs. Edward Russell
Mrs. Terence Russell
Mrs. Barry Seidel
Mrs. Suhel Skaf
Mrs. Linda Smoak
Mrs. Raúl Suárez
Mrs. Bruce Swift
Ms. Vivian Topp
Mrs. Alvaro Varela
Mrs. William Weber
Ms. Claudine Wheeler
Mrs. Dennis Wheeler
Mrs. Malcolm Wiseheart
Mrs. Frank Young

Recipe Contributors and Testers

We wish to offer our deepest appreciation to the YPO members and members of our community who contributed their favorite recipes and spent countless hours testing and retesting the recipes featured in *Sunny Days, Balmy Nights*.

Susan Abraham
Peggy Banick
Linde Barrett
Joanna Barusch
Kerrin Bermont
Donna Blythe
Pat Bohn
Cathy Briggle
Stacy Briggle
Ramona Busot
Connie Cabeza
Dan Cabeza
Debbie Campbell
Kay Carpenter
Lisa Chaffin
Margarita Courtney
Donna Cullen
Lee Damus
Livy Deels
Bill Douberley
Valerie Douberley
Marea Edynak
Holly Evans
Garth Fairbairn
Renée Fink
Anita Friedlander

Vicky Garrigó
Judy George
Linda Goldberg
Sharon Goodwyn
Barbara Grady
Maureen Gragg
Peggy Groves
Karyn Herterich
Mary Immer
Susanne Kayyali
Isabella Kerdel
Chip Lane
Daru Lane
Laurel Lane
Nanci Lanza
Luz Norwood LeBaron
María-Rosa López-Muñoz
Nicole Lozano
Ingrid Lyall
Kathy McGilvray
Linda Meyers
Any Muench
Michael Muench
Kathleen Murphy
Ellen Nagel
Liz Parnes

Eileen Plasky
Christy Powell
Martha Quevedo
Janis Ramirez
Barbara Reese
Jenny Lou Reid
Myriam Ribenboim
Valerie Ricordi
Jane Robinson
Janice Falkanger Russell
Nicole Scagnelli
Lee Ann Schaffhausen
Sheila Schmidt
Susannah Shubin
Mellicent Singham
Lucie Spieler
Rebecca Spinale
Sheri Swanson
Melody Swift
Louise Todaro
Kathleen Weber
Ileana Porges West
Lisa Wheeler
Michèle Wiseheart
Laurel Wolfson

Members of the community and YPO members who are not committee members who loaned treasures and talents:

Henry & Margarita
   Courtney
Sissy DeMaria
Maureen Gragg
Pancho Kerdel

Brenda López-Ibañez
Ingrid Lyall
Michael McGilvray
Kevin Scott
Bruce Swift

Ana Varela
Milton & Patricia Wallace
Susan Wampler

Local Resources

The Cookbook Committee was fortunate to have the following local businesses and individuals able to provide us with the goods and services we needed to create our cookbook. We know you will enjoy using them as well.

Food and Spirits

Daily Bread Mark II
12131 South Dixie Highway
Miami, Florida 33156
Phone (305) 253-6115
Middle Eastern foods and spices

Delicias de España
4016 Southwest 57 Avenue
Miami Florida 33155
Phone (305) 669-4485
Web site
   www.deliciasdeespana.com
*Spices, food, wine, & cookware
   from Spain*

Epicure Market
1656 Alton Road
Miami Beach, Florida 33139
Phone (305) 672-1861
*Gourmet international foods
   and wine*

Fresh Choice Seafood
Phone (305) 498-8500
Web site
   www.freshhoiceseafood.com
Seafood, soups, and chowders

The Fresh Market
2640 South Bayshore Drive
Coconut Grove, Florida 33133
Phone (305) 854-7202
Web site
   www.thefreshmarket.com
Gourmet foods, wines, and spices

Gardner's Markets
8287 Southwest 124 Street
Miami, Florida 33156
Phone (305) 255-2468
7301 Southwest 57 Avenue
Miami, Florida 33143
Phone (305) 667-9533
Gourmet food and wine

Golden Rule Seafood
17505 South Dixie Highway
Miami, Florida 33157
Phone (305) 235-0661
Web site
   www.goldenruleseafood.com
Seafood and fish

Joanna's Market Place
8247 South Dixie Highway
Miami, Florida 33156
Phone (305) 661-5777
Web site
   www.joannasmarketplace.com
*Gourmet international foods
   and wine*

Joe's Stone Crab
11 Washington Avenue
Miami Beach, Florida 33139
Phone (800) 780-2722
Web site
   www.joesstonecrab.com
Seafood and sauces

Neighbors Food Market
9723 Hibiscus Street
Cutler Bay, Florida 33157
Phone (305) 235-9361
Caribbean spices and groceries

Sedano's Supermarket
16255 Southwest 88 Street
Miami, Florida 33196
Phone (305) 385-2966
Locations throughout Miami
Web site www.sedanos.com
*Cuban & other Hispanic foods
   and spices*

For the Home

Bloomingdale's
Falls Shopping Center
8778 SW 136 Street
Miami, Florida 33176
Phone (305) 252-6400
A full-line department store

Calico Corners
16810 South Dixie Highway
Miami, Florida 33157
Phone (305) 253-5400
Fine fabrics for the home

Casa Chameleon
1716 Alton Road
Miami Beach, Florida 33139
Merrick Park Shopping Center
Coral Gables, Florida
Phone (305) 534-0104
Web site
   www.casachameleon.com
*Silver, china, gifts, and home
   accessories*

Country French
7259 Southwest 57 Avenue
South Miami, Florida 33143
Phone (305) 661-0159
Furniture and home accessories

Crate and Barrel
The Falls Shopping Center
8888 SW 136th Street
Miami, Florida 33176
Phone (305) 971-9977
Web site
   www.crateandbarrel.com
*Kitchenware, home accessories,
   and furnishings*

Eclectic Elements of Miami
2227 Southwest 22 Street
Miami, Florida 33145
Phone (305) 285-0899
Contemporary furniture and
home accessories

Gift Shop at Fairchild Tropical
Botanic Gardens
10901 Old Cutler Road
Coral Gables, Florida 33156
Phone (305) 667-1651
Web site
www.fairchildgarden.org
Books, gifts, and home accessories

Home Design Store
490 Biltmore Way
Coral Gables, Florida 33134
Phone (305) 445-1421
Furniture from the Far East

House & Paper
5823 Sunset Drive
South Miami, Florida 33143
Phone (305) 661-8545
Silver, china, crystal, invitations,
& stationery

Marguax, a World Collection
5805 Sunset Drive
South Miami, Florida 33143
Phone (305) 667-6540
Linen, home accessories, and
furnishings
Full-service home decorating

Patio & Things
240 Aragon Avenue
Coral Gables, Florida 33134
Phone (305) 446-6163
Patio furniture & accessories

Preston Scott Design
with Flowers
220 Aragon Avenue
Coral Gables, Florida 33134
Phone (305) 443-0671
Gifts and home accessories
for all seasons
The finest in floral arrangements

The Rose Tree Cottage
388 Miracle Mile
Coral Gables, Florida 33134
Phone (305) 488-9688
Gifts and home accessories

Photography

Dan Forer, Inc.
6815 Southwest 81 Terrace
Miami, Florida 33143
Phone (305) 667-3646
Fax (305) 667-4733
Web site www.forer.com

Services

Diamonette Party Rentals
11091 Northwest 27 Street
Doral, Florida 33172
Phone (305) 592-1223
Full-service party rentals

Patty Forrestel Food Style
3564 Avocado Avenue
Coconut Grove, Florida 33133
Phone (305) 461-2924
E-mail patty@rsmas.miami.edu
Food styling for print media
& television

Preston Scott Design
with Flowers
220 Aragon Avenue
Coral Gables, Florida 33134
Phone (305) 443-0671
Special event design & decor

Specialty Sewing by
Maria Kokorelis
15380 Southwest 72 Avenue
Palmetto Bay, Florida 33157
Phone (305) 235-0074
Fax (305) 235-3349
Decorative pillows, tablecloths,
napkins, runners, placemats,
and table toppers

A Touch of Class
732 Northwest 76 Avenue
Miami, Florida 33126
Phone (305) 261-9162
Web site
www.atouchofclasslinen.com
Fine linen rentals

Yacht Brokerage

Allied Richard Bertram
Marine Group
1445 Southeast 16 Street
Fort Lauderdale, Florida 33316
Phone (954) 462-5527
Web site www.arbmg.com
Luxury yacht sales, service,
and rentals

Locations

Bill Baggs Cape Florida State Park
1200 South Crandon Blvd.
Key Biscayne, Florida 33149
Phone (305) 361-5811
Web site
www.floridastateparks.org/
capeflorida

The Biltmore Hotel
1200 Anastasia Avenue
Coral Gables, Florida 33134
Phone (305) 445-1926
Web site
www.biltmorehotel.com

Fairchild Tropical Botanic Garden
10901 Old Cutler Road
Coral Gables, Florida 33156
Phone (305) 667-1651
Web site
www.fairchildgarden.org

Lummus Park
Ocean Drive
South Miami Beach,
Florida 33139
Phone (305) 673-7730
Web site www.miamibeachfl.gov

Bibliography

"Annato Seed." *The Spice House.* 22 Feb. 2007
    <http://www.thespicehouse.com/spices/annato-seed>.

Cain, Ann C., comp. *Cooking Light Best Ever Test Kitchen Secrets.*
    Birmingham, Alabama: Oxmoor House, Inc., 2004. 124.

Cooper, Ann, Sandra Porier, Mildred Murphy, Mary Jo Oswald, Sandra Bobroff, and
    Amy Simonne. "South Florida Tropicals: Boniato." *University of Florida IFAS Extension.*
    July–Aug. 2004. The University of Florida IFAS Extension. 10 Mar. 2007
    <http://edis.ifas.ufl.edu/HE610>.

Duchene, Laurent, and Bridget Jones. *Le Cordon Bleu Dessert Techniques.* 1st ed.
    New York: William Morrow and Company, Inc., 1999. 203.

"History." *The Conch Republic.* 2004. Key West Services. 27 Mar. 2007
    <http://www.conchrepublic.com/history.htm>.

"Macadamia Cooking & Salad Oil." *Oils of Aloha.* 2006. 3 Oct.–Nov. 2006
    <http://oilsofaloha.com/mac.php>.

McCune, Kelly, Thomas Ingalls, and David Barich. *Grill Book.* 1st ed.
    New York: Harper & Row, 1986. 21.

Moseley, Kate. *Cocktails Galore.* 1st ed. London: MQ Publications Limited, 2006. 20.

"Papaya." *World's Healthiest Foods.* 2007. George Mateljan Foundation. 12 Apr. 2007
    <http://www.whfoods.com/genpage.php?tname=foodspice&dbid=47>.

Index

Sunny Days, Balmy Nights
Entertaining Miami Style

To order additional books, please send $35.00 per book plus
$6.50 postage and handling to:

The Young Patronesses of the Opera, Inc.
P. O. Box 347616
Coral Gables, Florida 33234
305-665-3470

Florida residents, please add $2.45 sales tax per book.

Make checks or money orders payable to The Young Patronesses of the Opera, Inc.

For credit card orders, please call for additional information.
We accept Visa and MasterCard.